D1370330

The World of
Model Airplanes

The World of Model Airplanes

William J. Winter

with the editors of *Model Aviation,*
the official magazine of the Academy of Model Aeronautics

Charles Scribner's Sons
New York

Copyright © 1983 William J. Winter

Library of Congress Cataloging in Publication Data

Winter, William John, 1912–
    The world of model airplanes.

    Bibliography: p.
    Includes index.
        1. Airplanes—Models. I. Model aviation. II. Title.
TL770.W55 1983   629.133′134   82-42649
ISBN 0-684-17877-X

This book published simultaneously
in the United States of America and in Canada—
Copyright under the Berne Convention.

1 3 5 7 9 11 13 15 17 19   F/C   20 18 16 14 12 10 8 6 4 2

Printed in the United States of America.

Photos not otherwise credited are by the author.
Historical drawings in Chapter 1 are by H. A. Thomas. Mechanical drafting is
by Herb Clukey. All other illustrations are by Hank Clark.

Opposite title page: John Warner launches a rubber-powered P-30 model at Taft, California, during the United States Free Flight Championships. (John Oldenkamp photo)

Contents

foreword

Over the past seventy-odd years, almost a thousand books have been written worldwide about building and flying model airplanes. Until 1949 it was possible to explain with reasonable simplicity what this popular hobby was all about. Since the late 1940s, however, there have been a tremendous increase in technology and an accelerated growth of aeromodeling, which have resulted in books and magazines that are highly specialized, covering small fragments of a now comprehensive and complex picture. Involved today are advanced techniques of painting and finishing, improving engine performance, profound aspects of radio control, the art and science of Indoor rubber-powered Scale models, world-class competition free-flight craft, all kinds of control-line techniques, and so on. Although an overview is an ambitious approach in one volume, this work, the nineteenth by the author, provides the wide-angle vision necessary to encompass all that is now involved.

The challenge is twofold. A comprehensive book should provide a perspective of elements of the activity, without getting lost in details. Second, there is also a need to cover the subject for the wide range of ages likely to be interested, from youngsters to 80-year-olds, with a how-to-do-it background that shows that participation by all is possible. When one considers that the number of hobbyists is equal to the number of golfers—that is to say, millions—it is obvious that no book can detail every step in every procedure. But such a book can guide, and this one does, offering a unique overview of the world of model airplanes.

Having enjoyed this hobby/sport for over fifty years, and knowing that many others had done so during the earlier Wright-to-Lindbergh era, Bill Winter conveys aeromodeling's exciting history, and its legacy. He describes the three families of models in detail, in order to provide an essential compass that directs the reader to a myriad of specialties. Every chapter, whether dealing with power plants, materials, construction, or flight techniques, relates as much as possible to the full spectrum of the modeling activity. This book also defines the avenues leading to even the most obscure aspects of the field, with effective source references—more than just places to buy products. Where does one find a club? Or the source materials that may be required for a beginner to expand interests and hone skills? What organizations exist to promote each of the numerous divisions of activity? The answers to these and other questions can be found throughout this book and in the information included in the appendices.

The author's work also leads readers to the Academy of Model Aeronautics, also known as the A.M.A., the national association for U.S. model fliers, which has thousands of members and hundreds of clubs. The A.M.A. helps those who become interested in the hobby get together for information exchange and find the most important ingredient of all—flying sites. Almost all of the models and people involved in this book are part of the A.M.A. scene, which suggests that those who are "turned on" by what they read here should also explore what the A.M.A. has to offer: a monthly magazine providing more information about activities and how-to; liability protection for peace of mind concerning legal and safety matters; an activity calendar telling what, where, and when people fly; and many other benefits.

The World of Model Airplanes proves that there is far more to modeling than most people are aware of. The comprehensive treatment is a lot to absorb, but there is something here to please every interest, and only an author of Bill Winter's experience could have put it all together for us in such an enjoyable way.

John Worth
Executive Director, Academy of
Model Aeronautics

The World of
Model Airplanes

A free-flight Oldtimer—a 1930s design—just after launching during the U.S. Free Flight Championships. (John Oldenkamp photo)

chapter one ———————————————————

The Story of
Model Aviation

Hanno Pretnner, an Austrian electrical engineer, wins thousands of dollars at Las Vegas, but he is not a gambler. A world champion flier of radio-controlled aerobatic models, he has won the Circus-Circus Tournament of Champions at Las Vegas seven times—winning prize money totaling nearly $100,000.

On summer evenings on a grassy hill in Maryland, hobbyists fly featherweight rubber-powered scale models that cruise like fireflies. In Hampton Roads, Virginia, a dozen or more youngsters, with a few supervising adult modelers, put together within an hour or two Delta Dart rubber-powered models supplied by the Academy of Model Aeronautics (A.M.A.). At a contest the same evening in the school gym, one young modeler wins with a flight of more than 30 sec.

In cities such as Dayton, Ohio, or Lake Charles, Louisiana, or Lincoln, Nebraska, or San Bernardino, California, 2,000 skilled modelers and their helpers gather at the Annual Model Airplane Championships for a week of flying all forms of models. Over sixty events accommodate everything from radio-controlled helicopters, racers, and aerobatic machines to soaring gliders and sky-probing powered free-flight planes. Jetlike models. Exotic Scale masterpieces. Gossamer-light Indoor planes. Every type of model imaginable. The meet, which attracts hundreds of thousands of spectators, has been held every year since 1923, except for the World War II years. To aeromodeling, the "Nats" is what the Indianapolis 500 is to the automotive field.

These sorts of modeling scenes are commonplace all over the world. China and Russia have the largest disciplined modeling activities in the world—vast state programs. More than 300,000 Chinese youths take part. Japan is model airplane crazy in the sporting sense. World Championships are held regularly in the categories of Indoor, Scale, Racing, Soaring, and so on; these meets, under the rules of the Féderation Aéronautique Internationale (F.A.I.), in

Al Rabe, an airline pilot, flies these beautiful scale models in control-line Precision Aerobatics; he placed second in the 1978 World Championship competition and won the Nationals for this event on three occasions. The model he is holding is a Mustang; the other is a Hawker Sea Fury. The trophy is the Walker Cup, awarded at the Nationals.

Paris, are hosted by many nations, including South Africa, England, the United States, Hungary, Russia, and Poland. Recent world champions have included young men from Israel and North Korea.

Model planes are flown in every town in America. There are several national magazines devoted to the subject. Hundreds of firms comprise an industry that produces everything from dime-store hand-launched gliders to ready-to-fly radio-controlled models that cost hundreds of dollars. The volume of the business exceeds 1/2-billion dollars yearly.

Hobby shops dot the land, there are numerous mail-order houses serving the modeler, and clubs number in the hundreds. Thousands of contests take place in towns, cities, and regions on up to the storied Nationals and the great World Championships. Hobbyists number in the millions. This is a major American pastime, a hobby/sport that attracts people of all ages, from the child with an allowance to spend to the dedicated adult, who typically spends $2,500 a year or more on radio models.

Model airplanes definitely are not toys. To the youngster who encounters his or her first simple kit at some store, yes, it is, for the moment, a toy—

but an educational toy. Those who then pursue the hobby find it an absorbing activity with ever-expanding horizons that introduce handicraft skills and a knowledge of tools, aircraft, and design. The committed hobbyist shares the elation that was the Wright brothers' after their first short flight at Kitty Hawk in 1903. It's a pursuit that appeals to young and old, offering a broad spectrum of things to do, wheels within wheels, literally hobbies within hobbies. People specialize. There are planes that slowly circle in a gym, ones that climb above parking lots and schoolyards, and others that fly up to the clouds from miniature suburban airports.

Aeromodeling is a scientific hobby, too. Models take aerial photographs and air samples for industry. Radio-controlled (RC) helicopters can duplicate every move of the real rotary-wing aircraft. RC Sailplanes, with wing spans of up to 15 ft., can soar by the hour or fly cross-country for dozens of miles. Jet-powered models perform aerobatics. Scale models may even have such remarkable features as tiny working airspeed indicators and minuscule receivers to broadcast voices from real airport control towers. Some models drop parachutists—also radio controlled—that alight on the model's own runway. Eye-in-the-sky miniature craft detect archaeological ruins from the days of ancient Rome and plot tidal flows. The piggyback Space Shuttle was flown first in model form, precisely like the real thing. Radio-controlled helicopters string pilot cables across canyons to begin bridges and power lines.

Experienced modelers fly planes equipped with retracting landing gear, wing flaps, and air brakes that duplicate every aerial maneuver known to

North Korea's World Championship-winning team in the Wakefield event, 1977: left to right, Baik Chang Son (3rd); Kim Dong Sik, individual champion, with his winning model; Kim In Sol (15th). (Ian Kaynes photo, courtesy Model Aviation)

Hundreds of millions of youngsters have flown Cox ready-to-fly plastic control-line models over the past quarter century. Shown here is a Sopwith Camel with a 0.049-cu.-in. displacement engine and recoil-spring starter.

Russian MiG jet by Byron Originals is powered by an internal 0.61-cu.-in. displacement engine turning a ducted fan at high rpm. This radio-control plane takes off, maneuvers, and flies at about 100 mph.

man. There are autogiros, ornithopters (the wings of which flap like a bird's), and even Mylar helium-filled radio-controlled blimps with small electrical motors for propulsion. Solar-powered models have also proved successful: one huge solar-powered plane, of interest to the military, was designed to climb to 70,000 feet during the day, glide all night, then resume climb after sunrise.

People from all walks of life find modeling a fascinating activity. Frank Borman, one of the astronauts who first circled the moon (now an airline executive), and Neil Armstrong, who first set foot on the moon, were model builders. So is Joe Engel, a Space Shuttle pilot. So are numerous airline pilots. There are no distinctions when modelers fly together. A nuclear scientist rubs shoulders with a bulldozer operator or stock clerk. An executive talks shop with a high school student.

World records for radio control altitude, distance, speed, and duration are astounding. The glider duration record, held by Czechoslovakia, is 32 hr., 7 min., 40 sec. Riding rising slope currents and diving down mountain canyons, RC gliders fly longer and faster than powered models. One Austrian glider flew 242.90 mph; American modelers have pushed their powered RC models to 26,929.24-ft. altitude, 267.5 miles straight-line distance, and 20-hr. 51 sec. duration. Russia holds the powered speed mark at 213.57 mph. These records are as of 1983.

Radio-controlled models are often used for scientific purposes. The Space Shuttle, for example, was flown first in model form by NASA to check the compatability of the vehicle with its scale mother ship, a Boeing 747. Luther Hux's smaller scale Shuttle duplicates the landing procedure of the real Shuttle, although his mother ship is an ordinary model that also carries a camera capable of taking excellent bird's-eye-view pictures. Two pilots and two transmitters are required. Bill Hershberger, background, pilots the mother ship, Hux the Shuttle. (Dawn Hux photo)

AEROMODELING THROUGHOUT HISTORY

Flying models have been constructed for nearly two hundred years, long before any heavier-than-air craft capable of carrying man. We know that the Montgolfier brothers achieved the first successful man-carrying machine—a hot-air balloon—in 1783, one hundred twenty years before the Wright brothers' invention. The Wrights' airplane was capable of *steered turning* flight, the real beginning of the air/space age.

In the fifteenth century Leonardo da Vinci held valid concepts of both the helicopter and ornithopter, but, as with visionaries who came after him, the missing link was always a suitable power plant. It was Sir George Cayley, born in Yorkshire, England, in 1773, who discovered the principles on which modern aeronautics is founded—with a model plane that flew.

He began with a toy helicopter with two motors consisting of feathers stuck into a cork, powered by a twisted bowstring. At the age of 26 he engraved a small silver disk with a diagram showing the forces of lift, thrust,

Leonardo da Vinci was right! Bob Meuser flies this rubber-powered ornithopter—"wing flapper" to modelers—whose basic design was first drawn by da Vinci.

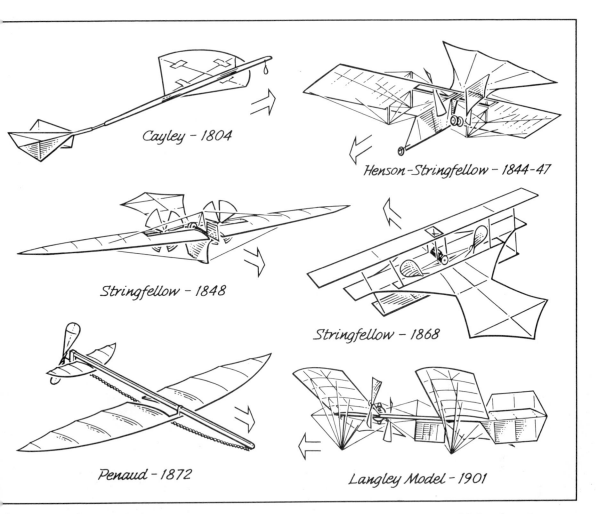

Very early model planes were scientific experiments to establish the parameters of full-scale craft. The Stringfellow models were built to prove that the Henson-Stringfellow airplane of 1844–47 would have flown had suitable power plants existed then. The Penaud model is remarkably similar to certain types of present-day flying miniatures. (Drawing by H. A. Thomas)

and drag and, on the other side of the disk, the design of an airplane with a fixed wing, dartlike tail surfaces, and two propulsive paddles. He also devised a full-size aircraft having a boatlike hull. Then he put a kite wing on a 5-ft. fuselage of wooden sticks. The leading edge of the kite was raised to a 6-degree angle of incidence (near optimum for maximum lift versus drag!). Cayley then attached a cruciform (cross) tail, using a universal joint that permit-

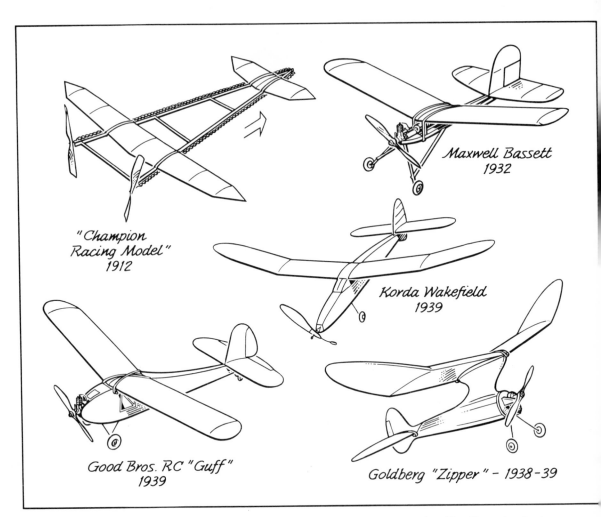

"Champion Racing Model" 1912

Maxwell Bassett 1932

Korda Wakefield 1939

Good Bros. RC "Guff" 1939

Goldberg "Zipper" – 1938-39

Created as flying models in their own right were these outstanding examples. The Champion Racing Model twin-pusher was a kit, the configuration appearing after the turn of the century and extending until the mid-1930s. In the early 1930s, the Brown-engined Bassett free flight ushered in the age of the "gas" model. The rubber-powered Korda model, timed by the author before World War II, won the international Wakefield trophy with a flight of 44 min. The Good Brothers RC won the Nationals several times and now hangs in the Smithsonian. Goldberg's Zipper outclassed all gas models for competition, and as a Comet kit was built by tens of thousands of people. (Drawing by H. A. Thomas)

ted control of climb or dive, and direction of flight. Its successful flight in 1804—it was a model, remember—is regarded as the beginning of the fixed-wing airplane. In 1809 Cayley scaled it up to carry a boy. He perceived the advantages of the curved airfoil, and that biplanes and triplanes maximized lift with minimum structural weight. When Cayley was 80, his triplane carried his coachman in an uncontrolled glide across a valley. But he could not go any further because a suitable engine had not yet been invented, and his pioneering career ended there.

In 1846, William Samuel Henson, also an Englishman, projected a remarkable design for a 150-foot monoplane with double-surfaced wings, control surfaces, and an enclosed cabin for passengers. It had a tricycle landing gear (as do modern planes), and two pusher-type six-bladed propellers driven by a steam engine within the body. Called the Aerial Steam Carriage, it was more workmanlike than many of the designs created around 1900, but, alas, it was ridiculed. A friend of Henson's, John Stringfellow, made a 20-ft. model of the machine, seeking to prove the imminence of air travel. (This model is still on exhibit at London's Science Museum.) It made only a descending glide due to the weight of its steam engine (the first successful engine designed for a model). Had a light engine been available for Henson, a half century of striving might have been saved.

In 1868, when it was exhibited in England, the Stringfellow model-plane steam engine won a £100 prize for being the lightest aircraft engine. It is now in the National Air and Space Museum in Washington, D.C. One and one-half feet tall, it developed about 1 horsepower. The engine is at right and the fired boiler at left. The valve mechanism is similar to that found in locomotive steam engines. (Smithsonian Institution Negative #76-19213)

The first person to fly a powered model was a French naval officer, Félix du Temple de la Croix, who used a clockwork engine in about 1857 and later replaced it with a tiny steam engine. By 1874 he had scaled up his successful model into a full-size machine powered by a hot-air engine. Carrying a man who exercised no control, it got off the ground briefly at Brest after gaining speed down a takeoff ramp. A Russian named I. N. Golubev made similar short hops in a steam-engine monoplane with two pusher propellers during the 1880s. Alexander Mozhaisky designed and built that machine.

In the author's collection there is a half-scale replica of the rubber-powered pusher model that Alphonse Penaud flew for more than 170 feet in 1872. A standard configuration of dihedral wing and tail, it looked like today's Stick models.

Many other men came close to success, often starting out with a working model. In 1850, the Frenchman Pierre Jullien flew a clockwork-powered airship model called Le Precurseur, which led to an airship that carried Henri Giffard from Paris to Trappes at 6 mph for a distance of 17 miles. Some credit Clément Ader of France with the first flight, in 1903, but his 150-ft. steam-powered Eole monoplane was not controllable as was the Wrights' machine. The German Karl Jatho evidently made straight hops of as much as 200 ft. with altitudes up to 12 ft., but gave up for lack of a suitable motor. In Bridge-

Between 1896 and 1902 Samuel Pierpont Langley built a series of one-quarter-scale test models preceding the ill-fated flight attempt of his Aerodrome. The best model flight covered 4,300 feet at a 100-ft. altitude over the Potomac. Fellow scientist Alexander Graham Bell took this photo of model No. 5. Although most of his models were steam-powered, Langley was the father of the gasoline-engine-powered model airplane. (Smithsonian Institution Negative #A18870)

port, Connecticut, Gustav Whitehead was "witnessed" to fly successfully before the Wrights, but the claims are not authenticated and details of the "flight" are vague. Present-day hobbyists have successfully flown models of the Penaud model and Whitehead and Mozhaisky real aircraft.

The Wrights used model test airfoils in a skillfully designed wind tunnel. Their arch rival, Samuel Pierpont Langley, built the celebrated Aerodrome, which snagged its launching device atop its houseboat launching ramp and fell into the Potomac, dunking pilot Charles Manley, who seems merely to have gone along for the ride. For some years the Smithsonian Institution claimed that Langley had been the first to fly, which so infuriated the Wright brothers that their epic machine was displayed in England and not returned to America for exhibition until after World War II. But in 1896 Langley flew the first of a series of scale models, one that spanned 14 ft. and flew 25 mph with a miniature steam engine for power.

Langley is the true father of gas-engine-model free flight, although neither he nor all but one of the modelers until now ever realized it. In his book *Gateway to Aero-Science,* Charles Hampson Grant, 86 years old as this is written and still flying models in his Vermont pasture, describes the flight of Langley's 1901 model, which was propelled by a 3-1/2-horsepower (hp) gasoline engine turning twin propellers rotating in opposite directions. Spanning 12 ft. 2 in. and weighing 55 lbs., it flew 4,300 ft. high above the Potomac, making three complete circles with faultless stability. One must sympathize with the heartbreak that was Langley's when his Aerodrome crashed, but it is important to realize that the Wright brothers' thorough engineering development of all aspects of flight, including teaching themselves to be pilots by means of gliders, is regarded by modern science as an incredible feat.

The radial engine for the full-size Aerodrome, by Manley, which is on exhibit at the National Air and Space Museum—the Smithsonian also recently completed a full-size Aerodrome restoration—still has one of the highest power-to-weight ratios of any piston aircraft engine. It developed 52 horsepower and ran on gasoline! This rather overlooked engine ranks in importance with the Wright brothers' flying machine.

After the Wrights' flight, modeling "took off" in its own right. In 1904, Ray Arden flew a gas-powered miniature plane across Van Cortlandt Park in New York City. (He invented the model "glow plug," eliminating the spark plug ignition system, in 1947.) The Illinois Model Aeroplane Club was formed in Chicago shortly after the turn of the century, as was the New York Aero Club in New York City. Contests were held before 1910. In 1909, the first major model airplane manufacturer, Wading River, did a land-office mail-order business. Wading River had absorbed the earlier White Model Aeroplane Company, as well as the Aero Accessories and Supply Company of Brooklyn, New York. In 1911, the Ideal Model Aeroplane Company became the giant of the industry, lasting until post-World War II years. In 1910–11, the American Manufacturing Corporation was advertising $2 kits for rubber-powered models of famous craft such as the Blériot English Channel crosser. Both the International Company and the American Manufacturing Company ran display advertising at that time.

Starting in 1919, Charlie Grant—later editor of the first "modern" national model magazine (there were others in the "dark ages"), *Model Airplane News,* founded in 1929—was selling yearly some $300,000 worth of his ready-to-fly models made by the Ritchie-Wertz Company of Dayton, Ohio. He founded his own model company soon after, with a moving production line and propeller-carving machinery capable of 2,000 ready-to-fly models a day. By 1929 he had joined Kingsbury Toys, where 3,000 units a day was routine. These were sophisticated products—the author flew them during the 1920s for more than 700 feet.

Charles Hampson Grant in 1980 at 85 years of age flying his 1920 Minute Man rubber-powered model, which traveled 650 feet after this hand launch. Past editor of Model Airplane News, *Grant manufactured such ready-to-fly models during the 1920s at the rate of three thousand per day. (Worth photo)*

At a secluded country model-plane flight strip, a flier launches a Cox plastic Sportavia radio-controlled model. The occasion is a beginner session with expert Don Srull (right) guiding the plane on its first test flight. (Preston photo)

There were occasional gas and even compressed-air engines before 1930, but then in 1932–33 Maxwell Bassett, using a gas engine "invented" by Bill Brown, made a shambles out of national competition. After that, the gas-powered free-flight model was king until 1946, when Jim Walker's U-Control idea revolutionized the industry. Demonstrated in the late 1930s, the U-Control model was flown in large circles under restraint by two steel control lines that ran to a handle in the operator's hand. By tilting the handle to move the elevators, the pilot could perform horizontal figure eights and wingovers, and fly inverted.

Radio-controlled models had been flown well before World War II, but the Federal Communications Commission (FCC) requirement for a "ham" license discouraged the public. When in 1947 the Academy of Model Aeronautics successfully petitioned the FCC to allow an examination-free special frequency, the aeromodeling picture was complete.

GETTING STARTED IN MODELING

How do you get started in this fascinating hobby? The sources of information are many, and include hobby shops, magazines, manufacturers, mail-

Nearly 1,000,000 of these A.M.A. Cubs have been supplied for instructing youngsters by both the Academy of Model Aeronautics and the Hobby Industry Association of America. With supervision, groups build them in an hour or two, then fly informal contests immediately afterward. (A.M.A. photo)

order catalogs, clubs, and the Academy of Model Aeronautics. The A.M.A. is a nonprofit organization with over 80,000 members. It makes the rules under which competitions are organized. The A.M.A. sponsors a youth program and selects teams to attend the World Championships. There are more than 1,600 A.M.A. clubs, some with several hundred members; they will put you in touch with a club near you. Membership in the A.M.A. includes a national magazine called *Model Aviation,* which has model plans, construction articles, news, advertising, and information about all types of models. The A.M.A. also provides a 2-million-dollar liability insurance policy for members. You can write them for more information at 1810 Samuel Morse Drive, Reston, VA 22090.

Hobby shops are listed in the Yellow Pages. Model airplane magazines, unfortunately, are not always on the newsstands, but a few do have small distribution. All are sold in hobby shops and by subscription, and you'll find mail-order houses and manufacturers—some with toll-free numbers—advertised in them. In Appendix B of this book you will also find annotated listings of reference works and publications on various aspects of aeromodeling.

If you have never built a model before, it is suggested that you begin with the simplest form of rubber-powered plane. If you can locate a local club, or find an active flying site—usually the hobby shop can steer you to these—you will find people to answer questions and learn from. Simple control-line models are also a good beginning point, especially when there are only confined areas to fly in. Many modelers prefer to start with radio-controlled craft. If you do choose radio control, the chances are overwhelming that you will require help and guidance, particularly in learning how to fly the models. Radio control clubs normally have a few members who gladly serve as advisors and flight instructors.

Until recently, modelers grew as the hobby grew, progressing happily from free flight to control line and finally to radio control, as each form of the activity became the rage. Today large numbers of people chance upon model aviation by seeing radio-controlled models being flown, and they often don't know that other kinds of modeling exist. There are so many facets to this hobby/sport that there is truly something for everyone, at almost every age—and the following chapters will tell you a great deal more about them.

_____

chapter two

The Three Families of Model Planes

A model plane is often thought of simply as a wooden glider tossed into the air by a child, or a windup "thing" with propeller and rubber-band motor, which flutters about. Actually, miniature flying machines can be surprisingly complex. To begin with, there are three distinct species: free flight, control line, and radio control.

FREE-FLIGHT MODELS

A free-flight model, like a bird, flies free of all restraint by its pilot. It is "inherently stable." The builder can preprogram its flight pattern by "trimming" so it will climb and glide in desired circles. Trimming is the adjustment of the down or sidethrust alignment of the engine (hence the propeller) and the wing and tail-surface angles. The free-flight family divides into two branches, Outdoor and Indoor; some ambivalent types are flown in both environments. Outdoor types usually are equipped with timing devices to shut off an engine (if any) after a desired number of seconds, and to operate a dethermalizing device (this is also true of gliders) to cause them to descend steeply to earth before they fly out of sight.

Gliders

There are two common types of gliders, hand launched and towline. Flown for competition or just fun, little hand-launched (HL) gliders are made from sheet balsa with a stick body, or they may be skillfully crafted for high performance with an airfoil cross-section wing (see page 182). For competition, sophisticated HL gliders remain aloft for a minute or more indoors and can

Alain Landeau performs a typical javelin hand launch of an F.A.I.-class free-flight model during the 1981 World Championships. The 0.15-cu.-in. displacement engine is turning about 25,000 rpm. (Cynthia Sabransky photo from John Oldenkamp)

Gary Stevens with a gaggle of Indoor hand-launched gliders (HLG) at a recent Nationals. Times for these planes approach 1 1/2 min. Stevens once held a teen-age Outdoor HLG record.

The parts of an aircraft.

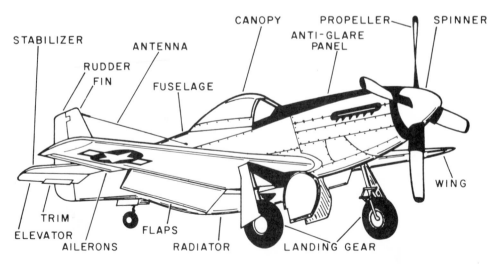

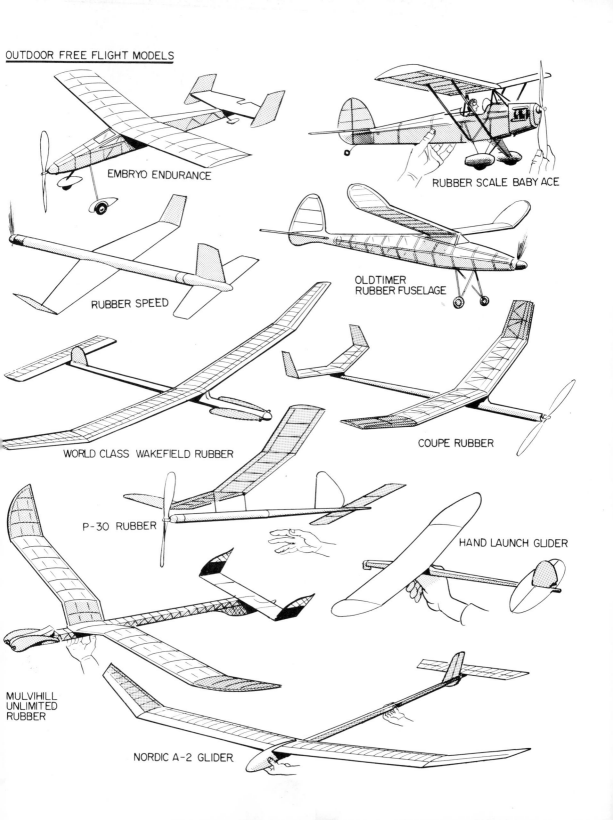

OUTDOOR FREE FLIGHT MODELS

EMBRYO ENDURANCE

RUBBER SCALE BABY ACE

RUBBER SPEED

OLDTIMER
RUBBER FUSELAGE

WORLD CLASS WAKEFIELD RUBBER

COUPE RUBBER

P-30 RUBBER

HAND LAUNCH GLIDER

MULVIHILL
UNLIMITED
RUBBER

NORDIC A-2 GLIDER

soar for many minutes outdoors, even disappearing overhead in rising "thermals" (vortexlike columns of heated air).

Towline gliders are larger and more lightly built, and are covered with special tissue paper similar to that used in tea bags, or plastic film. Using a monofilament towline (fishline), these gliders are towed aloft like a kite, a small piece of cloth or a tiny chute dragging the line free from a hook on the bottom of the fuselage at the apogee of the launch, after which the plane soars free—about 150 ft. high when released. Normally flown only in competition, such craft are towed by running sometimes hundreds of feet, and can have complicated towline release hooks to permit towing the model in a circle and "zoom launching"—an extra 50 ft. or so gained by a final tug at the moment of release. (This is discussed in more detail in Chapter 8.)

Towline gliders are called Nordics, and they come in two competition sizes, A-1, the smaller, and A-2. Respective wing spans are about 4 and 6 ft. In competition, both are permitted a limited-length towline.

An alternate launching method for towline gliders is the hi-start. With this

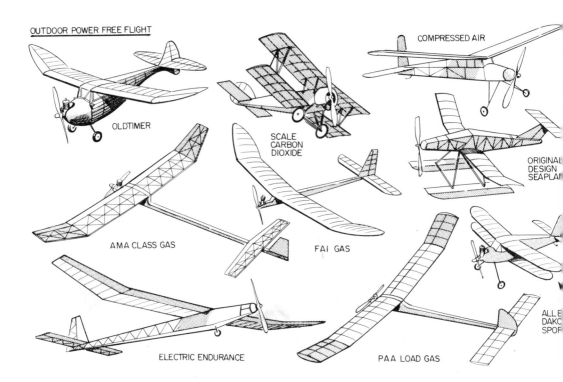

OUTDOOR POWER FREE FLIGHT

COMPRESSED AIR

OLDTIMER

SCALE
CARBON
DIOXIDE

ORIGINAL
DESIGN
SEAPLAI

AMA CLASS GAS

FAI GAS

ELECTRIC ENDURANCE

PAA LOAD GAS

ALLE
DAKO
SPOF

Ten-year-old Marnie Meuser (at 1977 Nationals) won first place in Easy-B, Paper Stick, F.A.I. Stick, A.M.A. Stick, and Pennyplane classes, setting three National records. She built the Pennyplane shown herself—it holds nine Indoor records in various classes. (Meuser photo)

technique, up to one-tenth of the towline is a rubber loop or length of surgical tubing; the rubber end is tied to a stake driven into the ground. The flier walks the plane away from the stake until the line is stretched to the maximum. After release, the model ascends almost vertically, then gradually arches overhead, at which point the towline slides off the hook on the plane. The craft then soars freely on the air currents.

Powered Models

Planes with gas engines and rubber power are the most common in this category, but electric power is coming on strong. A carbon dioxide engine may also be used for fun with small models, especially tiny Scale planes. In addition, there are slow-burning rockets (Jetex) and compressed-air engines, but these are seldom seen.

RUBBER POWER Rubber-powered models vary from tiny rise-off-ground (R.O.G.) planes through Stick and Fuselage types, and even up to Scale. The R.O.G. resembles the hand-launched glider—it may be sheet balsa or lightly built up from balsa strips and tissue—but it is fitted with a propeller and a stiff-wire landing gear with tiny wheels. Propellers are carved from balsa, bent from thin plywood for ultra duration, or are ready-to-use molded plastic. Simple R.O.G.'s are found at retail outlets, as are hand-launched gliders. Many hobby shops have rubber-model centers.

Stick models are nowadays reserved almost exclusively for competition. Resembling built-up (open-framework) R.O.G.'s, they can be far larger (as long

Gossamer-light microfilm-covered Indoor Stick models have remained aloft as long as 45 min. in amphitheaters and other flying locations. Few people can handle the wood for this plane, which may be as thin as 1/32 or even 1/64 in. (A.M.A. photo)

Launching this Lublin rubber-powered Scale craft is master builder/flier Bill Noonan. Though it is powered by rubber, the model requires a large unobstructed area for its 2-min.-plus flights. (Noonan photo)

as 4 ft.), have no landing gear, and are hand launched. The fuselage for an Outdoor sport machine is merely a sturdy strip of balsa, but competition machines have built-up boxlike fuselages, or a tubular fuselage formed by wrapping water-soaked sheet balsa around a tube or dowel, and heat-drying it in an oven. The large Outdoor competition Stick model is termed Unlimited, and is powered by a "rope" of rubber strands, with a huge, carved balsa propeller, the blades of which fold back after power is expended, for improved gliding. An Indoor Stick model for competition uses a balsa "motor stick" or tube for a fuselage. It is somewhat smaller than the Outdoor type and is so lightly constructed its weight is measured in grams or thousandths of an ounce.

The rubber-powered fuselage model with a cabinlike body is mostly a fun machine, built from balsa strips and/or sheet balsa, with covering similar to that used on towline gliders. As a rule, it varies in size from 1 to 2 ft., though some competition designs are double this size. Simple kits for such models are a big step up from HL gliders and R.O.G.'s. Lightweight versions are flown

Joachim Loffler of East Germany and his World Championship Wakefield rubber-powered model. The propeller blades fold back when power is expended in order to improve the glide. The white object at the tail is a slow-burning fuse that releases a spring-loaded stabilizer to a 45-degree negative angle to produce steep descent after the flight limit is reached, in order to prevent loss and to come quickly to "scratch" for the next round of flights.

indoors, either for fun or in competition; ultralight designs are flown by a handful of experts. The Indoor models are extremely fragile, built from very thin, soft balsa and covered with transparent microfilm, which is made by pouring a few drops of special fluid on the surface of a pan of water, then using a wire loop to lift it free as a sheet.

Models for some classes of Indoor competition are covered with superfine tissue, condenser paper, or other special materials.

Rubber-powered Scale models vary from the tiny Peanut class (13 in.-span, or 9 in.-length measured from behind the propeller) up to huge Jumbo Scales whose wing spans range from 30 in. to as much as 5 ft. Typical outdoor rubber Scale designs span about 20 to 24 in., weigh only 1 to 1-1/2 oz., and have an endurance of as much as 90 sec. without benefit of thermal currents, in which they can fly for many minutes.

Worlds apart from Sport modeling, the competition Wakefield rubber-powered Fuselage model (originally sponsored by England's Lord Wakefield, who put up the prestigious Wakefield Cup in the early 1930s to encourage international competition) is an elite type flown at special contests and World Championships. Combined wing and horizontal tail areas are limited to between 263.5 and 294.5 sq. in. The minimum weight of the airframe is 6.7 oz., with an additional 1.41 oz. for rubber.

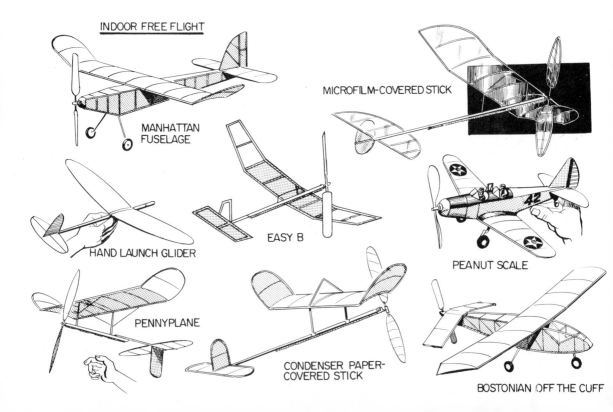

INDOOR FREE FLIGHT

MICROFILM-COVERED STICK

MANHATTAN FUSELAGE

HAND LAUNCH GLIDER

EASY B

PEANUT SCALE

PENNYPLANE

CONDENSER PAPER-COVERED STICK

BOSTONIAN OFF THE CUFF

To promote informal competition, individuals and clubs have created numerous classifications for rubber-powered models (some for Indoor, some Outdoor) that have modest followings. These classifications have such names as Manhattan, Bostonian, Pennyplane, Easy-B, P-30, No-Cal, Coupe, Oldtimer, and Antique. Also, there are "freak" forms, such as helicopters, ornithopters (flapping wings), and autogiros. There is a book on Indoor models alone, and another just on Peanuts (see Appendix B). The Academy of Model Aeronautics has a supply and service department that handles such books. Columnists in the A.M.A.'s official magazine, *Model Aviation,* cover these "folklore" types.

GAS POWER   Small Sport models, usually with 0.02- to 0.049-cu.-in. displacement engines, are infrequently seen, but competition types, including classes for various size engines, are very popular at the Nationals and many special contests. The climb rate and altitude attained by competition designs after hand launching are so incredible that cutoff devices necessarily stop the engines after a mere 7 to 12 sec.—to prevent the models from going straight up out of sight! The glide is so efficient that a dethermalizer is required to bring down such models after an allotted time, 2 to 5 min., depending upon the size of the field that flights are made from. Getting the

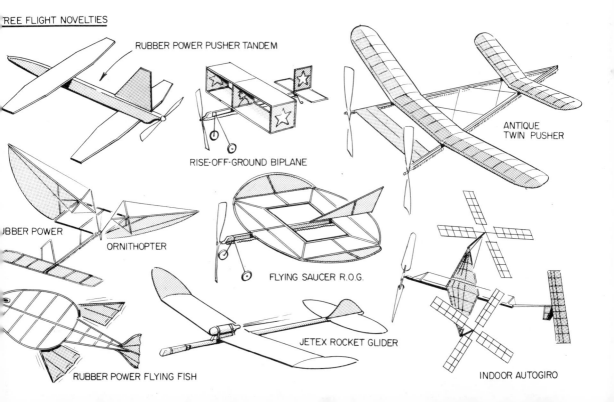

FREE FLIGHT NOVELTIES

RUBBER POWER PUSHER TANDEM

RISE-OFF-GROUND BIPLANE

ANTIQUE TWIN PUSHER

RUBBER POWER

ORNITHOPTER

FLYING SAUCER R.O.G.

RUBBER POWER FLYING FISH

JETEX ROCKET GLIDER

INDOOR AUTOGIRO

Huge Class D gas-powered free-flight models at a contest in Taft, California—note the wide-open spaces needed for these high-flying aircraft. Elaborate decorations testify to the builders' skill. Powered by 0.40- to 0.60-cu.-in. displacement engines turning over 20,000 rpm, such ships live on the razor's edge, but experts seldom crash them. (Meuser photo)

competition model back for the "next round" often involves strenuous chasing. Sometimes motorbikes are used for retrieval.

Official classes for A.M.A. free flights are: Class 1/2A—models with 0.000- to 0.050-cu.-in. displacement engines; A—0.051 to 0.200 cu. in.; B—0.201 to 0.300 cu. in.; C—0.301 to 0.400 cu. in.; D—0.401 to 0.650 cu. in. (such planes may span 6 ft. or more). When equipped with floats for seaplane take-offs, engine runs are 2 to 3 sec. longer in competition.

• Oldtimers and Antiques: The Society of Antique Modelers (S.A.M. models included in the A.M.A. rules book) has sparked an activity that attracts thousands of sport fliers as well as competitors. Oldtimers are models whose designs appeared before December 31, 1942; Antiques those before December 31, 1938 (see page 45 for S.A.M. radio-controlled models). In free-flight competition there are five classifications: Antique; Oldtimer

Pylon; Oldtimer Cabin; Oldtimer Rubber Power (both Cabin and Stick); and Vintage Special Events. Antiques are limited to ignition-type engines (as in the old days), have 6-ft. minimum wing span, and are permitted a fuel allotment, or a 30-sec. engine run—in which case no size limitation exists. Oldtimer Cabin and Pylon models must weigh a minimum of 8 oz. per square foot of wing area, as in the early days. There are three engine-displacement classes, A, B, and C, each of which varies according to whether the engine is ignition or has been converted to glow-fuel operation. Old Timer engine runs are 20 sec. when models are hand launched; 25 sec. when taken off the ground.

Antiques are allowed a 30-sec. engine turn or fuel allotment of 1/8 oz. per lb. of model weight. Rubber-powered models have no limit on the amount of rubber used but must use the same prop design as on the original model.

• Payload and Cargo: Originally sponsored by Pan American Airways just after World War II, these rather scientific events are still flown at some contests. Payload models have a maximum span of 36 in. and a maximum engine displacement of 0.025 cu. in. A 1-oz blocklike simulated pilot of specified dimensions is carried. The Cargo model is limited to a 48-in. span and has the same engine requirement as the Payload, but carries as much weight as can be lifted, the goal being to fly a minimum of 40 sec.

ELECTRIC POWER More commonplace than free-flight gas models for sport flying, but less so in competition, these almost silent fliers compete under A.M.A. rules that limit motor runs to 25 sec. and flights to a maximum of 3 min. However, aficionados of electric power organize all-electric meets open to a startling variety of designs flown in a number of unusual events. Motor sizes 02 up to 40 correspond in power to gas engines of the same numerical displacement. (Electric motor sizes do not use decimal points, since such motors have no displacement; the numerical cubic inch displacement of the corresponding gas engine is expressed with a decimal point before the number.)

CONTROL-LINE MODELS

A control-line (CL) model is flown captive in circles around its pilot by means of restraining control lines that also impart up-and-down elevator movement when the operator tilts a control handle. The public is more aware of the plastic ready-to-fly CL models by Cox or Testor's, which have been sold by the millions for some thirty years. Powered by 0.049-cu.-in. engines,

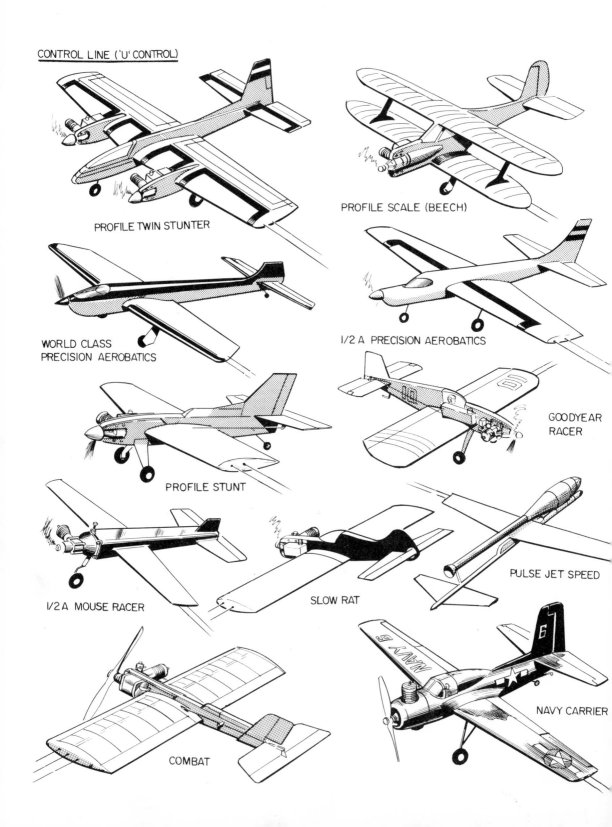

CONTROL LINE ('U' CONTROL)

PROFILE TWIN STUNTER

PROFILE SCALE (BEECH)

WORLD CLASS
PRECISION AEROBATICS

1/2 A PRECISION AEROBATICS

PROFILE STUNT

GOODYEAR
RACER

1/2 A MOUSE RACER

SLOW RAT

PULSE JET SPEED

COMBAT

NAVY CARRIER

they are quite small, usually scaled to resemble famous racers or fighters, and are guided by Dacron lines tied to the control handle and to the bellcrank inside the plane, which transforms the pull of one line or the other, as the handle is tilted, into a linear motion by a pushrod that actuates the elevators. (Flight procedures are discussed in Chapter 9.)

Most control-line designs are flown for fun, most enjoyably for stunting. CL is an ideal way to safely fly a scale model that could take months to build. The typical aerobatic Sport design has a thick balsa-wood fuselage profile, with a built-up, open-frame wing with spars and ribs and sheet-balsa tail surfaces. Except for those used with some 0.049 powered models (called 1/2A), the control lines are of steel, either a single strand or a braided cable. Normally, two lines are used, but special bellcranks permit the use of a trigger-actuated third line (at the handle) to vary the engine throttle setting, depress wing flaps, deploy landing hooks on Navy Carrier-type planes, etc. Some Speed-type models use only one line, with a special control mechanism, to reduce the air drag of two or more lines.

Control-line Speed models take off from releasable "dollies." Note the tuned pipe almost as long as the fuselage, and the tiny elevator on the inner side of the stabilizer. (Tuned pipes serve as mufflers and augment the thrust.) Such craft are flown only by experts in competition. (A.M.A. photo)

Performing an intricate sequence in a Control Line Aero-batics event, ex-world champion Bob Gieseke makes con-secutive, inverted-flight laps with his Top Flite Nobler. The plane is about 70 ft. away from him. (Laird Jackson photo)

There is an amazing variety of competition craft, including Speed, Combat, Aerobatics, Team Racing, and Navy Carrier. The line lengths (and specific thickness of wire diameter) vary with the purpose, size, and power of the designs, from, say, 15 to 70 ft.

Speed

Rarely flown for sport, these machines are highly specialized and piloted by dedicated experts. They fall into four size classes: 1/2A, A, B, and D, with engine displacements varying from 0.049 to 0.65 cu. in. The larger versions have surpassed speeds of 200 mph. Safety precautions are elaborate, including pull-testing of lines before flight (common in CL events). The flier's control hand rests in a special pylon at the center of the flying circle. Also, there is a pulse-jet event, using a power plant similar to that of the German buzz bombs of World War II—the noise is incredible. These, too, surpass 200 mph. Piston engines are hopped-up, metal fuselage pans are used, and fuels are doctored to yield rpm figures above 20,000. Although several relatively simple variations exist to encourage the less expert, in truth all Speed models are difficult.

Aerobatic

While any design that can loop, fly inverted, and do other simple stunts is aerobatic, the competition Aerobatic machine is flown by specialists who perform an elaborate "pattern" of maneuvers or figures in the sky. During the 1950s, the "stunt" model was kingpin, but competition always evolves machines beyond the sport category. The typical stunter today spans 4 ft. or so and is powered by an engine averaging about 0.46 cu. in., with a total weight of 50-odd oz. To see a good machine go through its paces is an unbelievable experience.

Combat

Almost exclusively competitive (not flown for fun), the Combat model is a short-coupled machine (it is "stumpy"), having a lightly built-up or shaped Styrofoam wing, sheet-balsa tail, and a short Profile fuselage—sometimes with a boom or booms to support the tail. In competition, engine sizes are the 0.15, mostly for F.A.I. or international rules, and the 0.35 for major A.M.A. events. These high-powered machines fly in both the Fast and Slow classes and travel faster than 100 mph while doing tight maneuvers—perhaps five loops per second! Two planes are flown simultaneously, each plane trailing

Combat flier Gary Frost's pitman launches his Fast A.M.A. Combat control-line model to "dog fight" a rival. The covering is transparent Fascal. (Charlie Johnson photo)

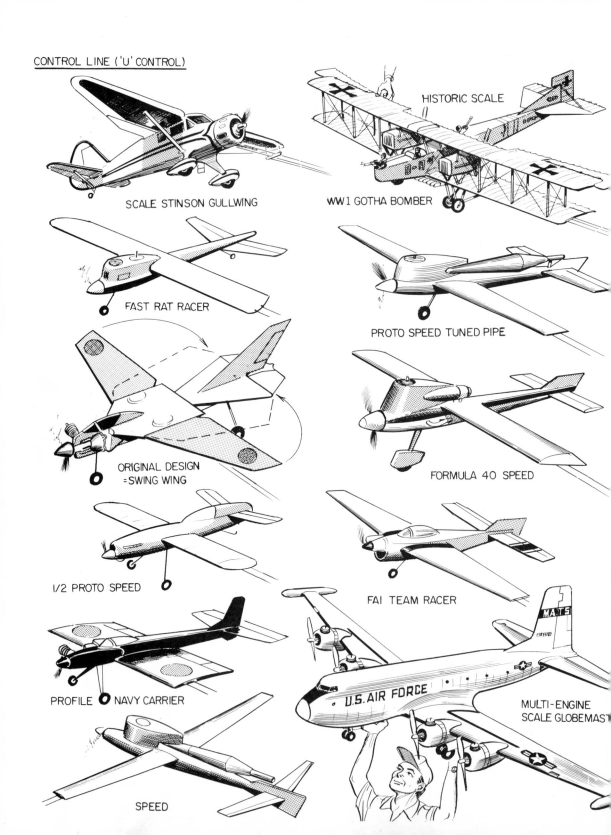

CONTROL LINE ('U' CONTROL)

SCALE STINSON GULLWING

HISTORIC SCALE

WW1 GOTHA BOMBER

FAST RAT RACER

PROTO SPEED TUNED PIPE

ORIGINAL DESIGN
= SWING WING

FORMULA 40 SPEED

1/2 PROTO SPEED

FAI TEAM RACER

PROFILE NAVY CARRIER

U.S. AIR FORCE

MULTI-ENGINE
SCALE GLOBEMAST

SPEED

a paper streamer. The object is to achieve cuts on the opponent's streamer, or to cut off the streamer—which is considered a "kill." The maximum model weight is 4 lb., and the maximum line length (multistrand steel) is 59-1/2 to 60-1/2 ft. Active fliers smash so many planes during strenuous maneuvering close to the ground that hobbyists have perfected mass-production methods for fast building or repairing. A machine is built in jigs and may be finished in an evening.

Slow Combat does not imply a beginner type. Intended to encourage activity, Slow limits wing area to a minimum of 300 sq. in.; requires a Profile fuselage with a cockpit canopy; forbids fuel pumps and pressure systems, common on both Speed and Fast Combat models; and has certain other limitations—but it is faster than 100 mph!

Navy Carrier

Originally sponsored by the Navy in 1948, this event is still flown in competition and requires planes loosely based on naval designs of any period. A simulated carrier deck, shaped like an arc to suit the flying circle, is used for both takeoffs and landings. To touch the ground off the deck is the equivalent of a forced landing on the water. Machines are timed for low- and high-speed runs and are equipped with extendable carrier hooks to snag arresting lines stretched across the deck and held by small sandbags. A three-line control system provides the means of varying throttle settings and speeds, and wing flaps facilitate the slowest possible flight and smooth deck landings. The maximum wing span of these planes is 44 in. and maximum weight 4 lbs.

Class I Carrier jobs are permitted a maximum engine displacement of 0.4028 cu. in.; Class II models are allowed 0.4029 to 0.65 cu. in., or pulse jet. The Profile class is limited to 300 sq. in. of wing area, with front-air-intake engines not larger than 0.360. Profile is simpler and more fun, and is often flown by young boys and girls skilled enough to give the adults a difficult time. Classes I and II are the Scale classes; in Profile, scale outline is encouraged.

Racing

Racing planes are flown in a number of distinct competition events. There may be two to four planes in the air simultaneously, so the antics of the fliers in the center of the circle are something to behold as they try to keep lines from becoming entangled as their planes pass each other. The races are thrilling to watch because pit stops are required, since the fuel-tank capacity is limited. A good pitman will catch a landing model, refuel it, restart the engine, and release it for takeoff in a matter of seconds—just as they do in Indianapolis. Races are run in qualifying heats to determine Feature Race machines.

RAT RACING Generally resembling a Speed-type craft, the Fast Rat racer may or may not have a Profile-type fuselage. Its 0.4028 cu. in. maximum displacement engine may even be neatly cowled in for streamlining, and a landing gear is required, usually only one-wheel. The Qualifying Races are 70 laps long (with one mandatory pit stop), the Feature Races 140 laps (with three mandatory pit stops). Usually, only two fliers at a time compete. There are no restrictions on wing area.

SLOW RAT RACING A Profile-type fuselage is required for these races; pressure fuel-feed systems and tuned exhaust pipes are not permitted. The planes must have a minimum wing area of 300 sq. in., minimum wing thickness of 1 in., and a fixed landing gear. Engines are limited to 0.36 cu. in. The qualifying heats are 70 laps, and Feature Races are 140 laps.

SCALE RACING These planes must be based upon a real Goodyear-type racer, but have Profile fuselages with uncowled engines—engines without an

During a control-line Team or Rat race, pilots at the center of the flying circle perform an incredible ballet as one plane passes another. Avoiding each other's flying lines requires the utmost skill. Shown here (left to right) are Stu Willoughby, "Doc" Jackson, and John Ballard. Their three pitmen manage pitstops in a matter of seconds. (Laird Jackson photo)

Team Racing at the 1980 World Championship: J. E. Albritton, the pilot (left), and Walt Perkins, the pitman. Note the Racer is a "flying wing," without tail surfaces. The gear on the pitman's "hot arm" is for refueling, restarting for a turnaround taking only seconds. (A.M.A. photo)

exterior shaped shell to streamline them. (After World War II, Goodyear encouraged the popularity of full-size plane racing by establishing rules for smaller, less powerful planes. Model Scale Racing emulates the appearance of the full-scale Goodyear types.) Scale is 1-1/2 in. to the foot. The paint scheme is Scale-like (which means it resembles closely that of a particular real aircraft, but it is not required to be precisely to scale), and racing numbers are carried. Either two or three fliers compete simultaneously in 70-lap heats, with 140-lap finals. Engines are limited to 0.1525-cu.-in. displacement. Control lines measure 59-1/2 to 60-1/2 ft.

TEAM RACING Once flown under A.M.A. rules, as well as international F.A.I. rules, this event now is purely International, culminating in a World Championship. The big differences in Team Racing are that Scale machines are not required and a minimum of one pit stop is specified. With limited fuel permitted, the economical diesel engine is a virtual necessity. (Diesels run on a mixture of kerosene, ether, and oil, whereas gas engines use nitromethane, methanol, and oil.) In all Racing and Speed events, engines are highly specialized for rpm and economy, and are not generally advertised in the popular market. Many are handcrafted by machinists. Three machines are flown simultaneously with Elimination Races and Semi-Finals run over 100 laps (6.214 miles), and Finals over 200 laps (12.43 miles). Control-line lengths are approximately 52 feet. Fuel-tank capacity is limited to 0.4271 cu. in.

A Supplemental Competition event exists for both Mouse Racing and 1/2A Scale Racing. For both types, the maximum cubic-inch displacement of the engine is 0.0504. There is no configuration limitation on Mouse Racers, except that they take off and have a fixed landing gear. The 1/2A Scale Racer is a Profile-fuselage version of a real Goodyear racing plane with a minimum scale of 1 in. to the foot (one-twelfth scale).

Mouse Racing appeals to young beginners interested in achieving contest skills—it usually involves a father/son or father/daughter team. Because. women often enter competitions of all kinds, mothers do sometimes get involved in Mouse Racing.

RADIO-CONTROLLED MODELS

The variety of types, sizes and forms of activity in this modeling category are seemingly endless. Designs range from roughly 20 in. to 9 ft. or more in span, engines from tiny 0.02s as big as a forefinger joint to 6-lb. chain-saw derivatives that can swing propellers 2 ft. or more in diameter. Some radio-controlled (RC) planes perform all the maneuvers that full-scale aircraft do. The models include jets, helicopters, sailplanes, multiengine Scale ships, and other forms of aircraft.

Each channel of control provided by a transmitter moves one airborne servo (such as to the rudder) proportionately in either of two directions. Control systems consist of simple rudder-only types; those with rudder and elevator; and those with rudder, elevator, and ailerons—and they can have such additional features as retractable landing gear, wing flaps, air brakes, lift spoilers, parachute or bomb drops, smoke trails, and cameras. Generally, the throttle is controllable. Planes with a two-wheel landing gear (which usually have steerable tail wheels) are "tail-draggers," and those with three-wheel gear (and a steerable nose wheel) are "trike" models. (Radio control systems and flight techniques are dealt with in Chapters 10 and 11.)

Sport Models

A sport model is any aircraft that is not specifically designed for competitions such as Pattern and Pylon Racing, or for some type of record attempt, such as Speed, Altitude, or Endurance. Hundreds are advertised, with Falcons, Kadets, Ugly Stiks, Eaglets, Air Scouts, and Q-Tees some of the popular models. The most popular have about a 4-1/2-ft. wing span and are powered by engines of 0.15- to 0.40-cu.-in. displacement. Such machines may have either a low-shoulder or high-wing Cabin-type configuration, and are operated by three- to seven-channel radio systems. Most people favor the four-channel craft with rudder, elevators, ailerons, and throttle, though many models are designed to fly without ailerons. The smallest (about 2 ft.) powered craft may have nothing but a rudder; intermediate varieties may have just a rudder and elevator, and usually a throttle.

Gliders

For sport and competition, gliders—or sailplanes—generally fall into two classes, Standard and Unlimited (the former limited to a 6-ft. wing span, the latter sometimes as large as 12 to 15 ft.). Now becoming popular is the "two-meter" glider, which has a two-meter wing span to suit F.A.I. rules. Whereas power models take off, gliders are tow-launched by hand, by an electric winch, or by the hi-start method described on pages 20–21. Most are flown with two command channels for rudder and elevator. Others using three or four channels have more controls, such as wing-lift spoilers to increase the rate of "sink," making it possible to descend rapidly and land accurately, and perhaps wing flaps and/or air brakes to increase drag for related purposes. Many advanced fliers favor ailerons in addition to rudder and elevators.

Radio-controlled sailplane being released to attain high altitude for Soaring. It is towed aloft by an electric winch winding in a monofilament line of 700 ft. or longer. At altitude, the drag of the tiny parachute where the line attaches to the tow hook pulls the line free. Some flights last for hours, with the planes reaching the clouds. (A.M.A. photo)

RADIO-CONTROLLED MODELS

MOUNTAINEER SLOPE SOARER

BYRON ORIGINAL'S MUSTANG

GL H 1/2 POWERED
PYLON RACER

PRATHER LITTLE TONY
PYLON RACER

ACE PRIMARY TRAINER

HERB SMITH 2-METER SAILPLANE

TAIL FIRST PUSHER

ELECTRIC ASTRO FLIGHT
MONTEREY GLIDER

SNAPSHOT 1
CAMERA PLANE

MIDWEST DUCTED FAN

ART BY HANK CLARK

TAILLESS GLIDER

BANNER TOWER

FLYING FLATIRON

FOCKE WULF AUTOGIRO

SIG KAVALIER AILERON TRAINER

GOLDBERG EAGLET TRAINER

DRAKE AMPHIBIAN

HOWARD DGA -15 (G-S PRODUCTS)

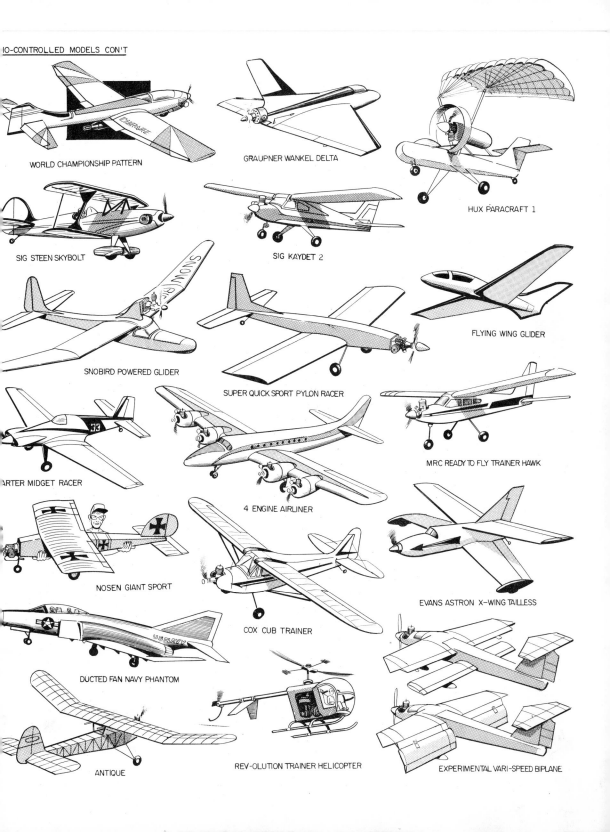

WORLD CHAMPIONSHIP PATTERN

GRAUPNER WANKEL DELTA

HUX PARACRAFT 1

SIG STEEN SKYBOLT

SIG KAYDET 2

SNOBIRD POWERED GLIDER

SUPER QUICK SPORT PYLON RACER

FLYING WING GLIDER

ARTER MIDGET RACER

4 ENGINE AIRLINER

MRC READY TO FLY TRAINER HAWK

NOSEN GIANT SPORT

COX CUB TRAINER

EVANS ASTRON X-WING TAILLESS

DUCTED FAN NAVY PHANTOM

ANTIQUE

REV-OLUTION TRAINER HELICOPTER

EXPERIMENTAL VARI-SPEED BIPLANE

Scale

These realistic craft, used for both sport and competition, range from tiny to gigantic. For small flying sites, the sport-only Schoolyard Scale is powered by 0.02- to 0.15-cu.-in. engines, spanning from 2 to 4-1/2 ft. For larger fields, 5- to 6-ft spans are common. Giant Scale planes are usually one-fifth, one-quarter, or even one-third scale to real life. Multiengine creations appear, such as a B-25 twin-engine bomber or a B-17 Flying Fortress four-engine spectacular. On rare occasions, multiengine machines are built that are so big and heavy (up to eight engines and 150 lbs.) that it may require two operators, each with a transmitter, to separately handle flight and engine controls. Only extremely experienced hobbyists should attempt such projects, which otherwise can be very dangerous.

Scale divides into two classifications: Precision, or A.M.A. Scale, and Sport Scale. Precision, or A.M.A. types (almost exclusively competition), attempt to duplicate every feature of a real aircraft, down to the last rivet. Sport Scale planes, which are judged from a distance of 15 ft., are remarkably lifelike but do not have the intricate details that could not be observed from the judging circle. They are quite popular at everyday flying sites. Gliders are also built for either Precision or Sport Scale. For competition, Glider Scale is a provisional, not an official, event.

Scale types are judged on a point system for accuracy, appearance, and flight schedule. The rules specify that a single-engine model weigh not more than 15 lbs. and a multiengine model not more than 25 lbs. (The huge, exotic models previously mentioned are individual or group efforts not eligible for competition.) Competition gliders are limited to a maximum wing area of 2,325 sq. in. and a maximum weight of 11.023 lbs.

Giant RC Scale is a provisional event when flown in competition. Many such models are built for pleasure only, and at nationwide fly-ins are demonstrated without competition. For competition, power is limited to engine(s) of not less than 1.25-cu.-in. displacement, and a maximum of 3.67 cu. in. If models are multiengine, total displacement is limited to 4.4 cu. in. If they have 4-stroke engines, displacements are permitted to be 20 percent greater than those just given. The scale is 2-7/8 in. to the foot, or larger. The minimum weight of these planes is 15 lbs. for a single-engine and 20 lbs. for a multiengine model; the maximum weight is 40 lbs. in competition.

The reader may wonder about the mention of sizes and weights that exceed these rules. Rules do not deter hobbyists from creating superlarge planes that we loosely call "monsters." These are individual or group efforts, and monster models are carefully flown only at special fly-ins or demonstrations. The rule that limits the weight of such planes to 55 lbs. is related only to the limits of what A.M.A. insurance will cover. Beyond that figure, the thrilling projects sometimes seen in magazines are the insurance responsibility of their owners.

Helicopters

These models, intended for both competition and sport, are powered primarily by engines of 0.40- to 0.60-cu.-in. displacement. Recently, some smaller models have appeared on the scene, one popular machine being powered by a 0.25-cu.-in. engine. There are Japanese and English models that are powered by electric motors—others undoubtedly will appear in the future.

Model helicopters require a considerable degree of piloting skill and involve prolonged training, in various stages of complexity, before the pilot is really proficient.

In some helicopters, engine throttle variation is used to set the speed of the rotor (propeller- or wing-like blades), thereby enabling the model to climb or descend. This type of chopper has no collective pitch control for the main rotor and is referred to as a "fixed pitch" helicopter.

A tail rotor, spinning in a vertical plane, is provided with variable blade pitch ("collective pitch") control—the ability to vary the rotor blade's angle of attack to the air—and is used to keep the machine from spinning around

A Scale Jetranger radio-controlled helicopter flies a tight circle around the photographer. Like full-sized helicopters, such models are quite difficult to fly. (Mass photo)

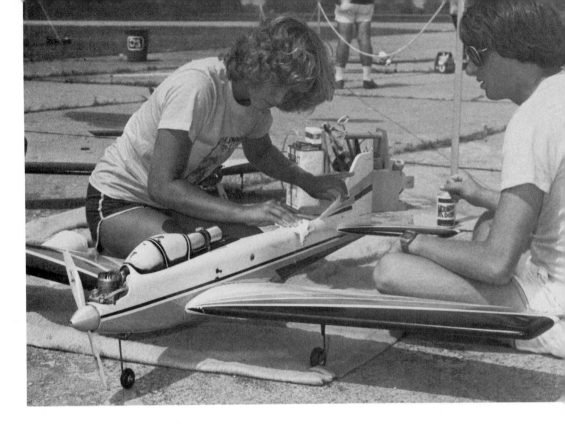

After a flight at the 1980 National Contest, a pilot and helper wipe away exhaust residue on their Precision Aerobatic Pattern-type RC machine. The tuned exhaust pipe, for maximum power, projects to the rear of the "pilot" canopy. (A.M.A. photo)

helplessly. It is the copter's "rudder," and is controlled by one radio channel.

The helicopter is commanded to move forward or backward, or to the left or right, by tilting the main rotor in the appropriate direction. This is called "cyclic control," and is accomplished by two RC channel-actuated servos, acting through a complicated set of levers, pushrods, and sliding plates.

More complex helicopters operate just like full-scale machines: they use collective pitch control of the main rotor blades to cause the model to climb or descend. Here, the throttle is either trimmed by radio to maintain a desired rpm, or it may be coordinated with the collective pitch movement by means of mechanical linkages. The collective pitch is controlled by the pilot via one RC channel. (In some of the more advanced RC systems, this control interconnection is made by means of special trim adjustments in the RC transmitter, thereby significantly reducing the mechanical complexity of the model.)

In some model helicopters, even the tail rotor pitch is coupled to the collective pitch in the main rotor.

Expert pilots can perform astonishing maneuvers with their model RC helicopters—loops, rolls, even inverted flight! These choppers are seldom scratchbuilt. Most are made from kits, increasing numbers and varieties of which now appear on the market. Most models are either true Scale models, or else they *look* quite Scale-like, even though they are original designs.

Pattern and Sport Aerobatics

King of the competitive hill is the Pattern model: about 5 to 6 ft. in wing span, weighing from 7 to 12 lbs., powered by an up to 0.61-cu.-in. displacement engine, and usually fitted with a trike retractable landing gear, which is operated mechanically by servo or pneumatic action. Wing flaps and air brakes appear in "ultimate" machines. Fuel systems feature pressure from either a muffler tap or a crankcase tap, and fuel pumps are common. Sometimes, transmitter mixer controls allow simultaneous deflection of ailerons as flaps, but retain the ability to fly the ailerons. Transmitters have rate switches to vary the limits on control-surface movement for special maneuvers, and there are such extras as electronic coupling of two controls, and even a "roll button." Better transmitters also provide "exponential" control, which gives progressively more response as a control stick is deflected, with less control movement near neutral. Conspicuous tuned pipes serve as mufflers and thrust augmentors to boost engine rpm. These models approach speeds of 100 mph. Judging in competition is based mostly on a complex, standardized sequence of maneuvers.

Sport Aerobatic models must resemble full-scale aircraft, either monoplanes or biplanes. They are judged for Scale appearance, and must be flown according to a continuous flow of maneuvers called Free Style or individual maneuvers judged one at a time. Sport Aerobatic models are of greater variety than Pattern types, with different sizes, weights, and engine power.

Pylon Racers

Races using these models have as many as four ships flying simultaneously around pylons on a racetrack-shaped course. Competitors for the Feature Race are selected through a series of elimination heats.

• Formula I: Exclusively for competition, these swift craft have a maximum engine displacement of 0.4030 cu. in., and must be replicas of full-size 190-cu.-in. Formula I racing planes. The minimum wing area for the models is 450 sq. in., the weight between 5 and 6-1/2 pounds, and speeds far in excess of 100 mph.

• Sport Pylon: Supplemental rather than official, this event is easier to fly than Formula I and is quite popular at the club level. There are three

Sport classes: Class I, A.M.A. Sport; Class II, Formula 500; and Class III, Formula 500, limited to side exhaust engines. Class I permits engines of from 0.07 to 0.90 cu. in. displacement, and wing area limitations matching eight engine sizes, of from 200 sq. in. to 800 sq. in. Both Classes II and III require a maximum cu. in. engine displacement of 0.40, and a minimum wing area of 500 sq. in. (These figures are based on the 1982–83 Rule Book; changes may occur in later rule books, as the limitations are going through a bit of a shake-down period.)

• Quarter-Midget: Exclusively for competition, these smaller racers are much like Formula I, but limited to a maximum displacement of 0.1524 cu. in. with a minimum wing area of 300 sq. in. The allowable weight is 20 to 32 oz. The models are replicas of real racing planes.

• 1/2A Pylon: This event is provisional rather than official in major meets, and is popular at the club level. The maximum engine displacement for these models is 0.0519, the weight 20 to 32 oz., the minimum wing area 200 sq. in. Hand launching rather than taking off is employed.

Helpers restrain RC Pylon models for a "race horse start" when the flag is dropped. Special "ear muffs" protect hearing from the whine of 20,000-plus rpm engines. Pilots control their planes around pylons on a triangular course. (A.M.A. photo)

Antiques and Oldtimers

Based on free-flight models prior to 1943, these lovely, slow-flying machines can be built smaller or larger as well as to the same scale as the original, with engines normally varying from a tiny 0.02 up to 0.40-cu.-in. displacement. Even "monster" sizes sometimes appear. Radio systems for these models depend on the size of the plane, and vary from rudder only through elevator, rudder, and throttle. While these planes are widely flown for sport, there also is competition under the S.A.M. rules (mentioned on pages 26–27). For either Antiques or Oldtimers, S.A.M. rules also provide for "Texaco Event"-type RC ships, the great endurance machines of the mid-1930s.

Since S.A.M. competition roughly duplicates the flying of ancient free-flight types—but with "RC assist"— variety has narrowed in competition to the most effective types of bygone days: the Comet Zipper, Cleveland Playboy, and so forth.

Less climb-efficient, more realistic classics are quite popular for merely "tooling around"—for just-fun fliers. These graceful historic types (plans and kits are offered by small manufacturers and plan service operators) provide a "new" kind of radio-controlled flying. Such planes climb slowly to great heights and then soar like big gliders. Because the pilot has time to seek out areas of high "lift" due to thermals, flights achieve an hour or more duration. The effect is hypnotic! The designs come from old magazines published since 1929, or from kits held by collectors. Among many dozens of famous classics are such favorites as the Grant-Kovel KG, Henry Struck's New Ruler, Berkeley's Buccaneer, the Comet Sailplane, and the Buzzard Bombshell—dream ships loved by thousands of long-time modelers.

chapter three ───────────

Materials

"Materials" is a dull word, suggesting bits of wood, glue, paper, and wire. But when blended together to create a flying model, materials spring to life. Some model planes are truly art forms.

All the materials described in this chapter are not used in all types of models. It is only with complex types, such as radio-controlled aircraft, that one becomes involved with resins and epoxies, molded fiberglass shells, Styrofoam wing cores, and so on. Most simple Sport planes require only basic materials, such as balsa wood, Japanese tissue, and model airplane cement.

Today, virtually every model is built from sophisticated kits that have excellent drawings, instruction booklets, die-cut parts, accessory packages of metal fittings, and sundry shaped, formed, or prebent parts. Even many experts build from kits. Scratchbuilding appeals to independent souls who have the expertise to work from plans alone or to create and fine-tune designs for ultimate performance.

Consider this: the superlight Indoor model (a novelty in the public eye) weighs a few ten-thousandths of an ounce, whereas gigantic radio-controlled models for outdoor sites weigh as much as 150 lbs. While the latter should be put from your mind for practical reasons, the criterion in all cases is maximum strength-to-weight ratio. Some models weigh thousands of times as much as others, yet may be more susceptible to damage or poor performance than those that weigh much less. Fortunately, the kit manufacturer does this thinking for us. However, kits almost never contain "liquids," that is, glues and dopes. Some don't include covering materials. Others require additional items or an accessory package—all things that can be purchased separately at the hobby shop. High-quality kits list on their labels the "extras" you must buy.

Peanut-sized rubber-powered models by Sterling show the possibilities of all sheet-balsa construction and colored tissues. The propellers are molded plastic.

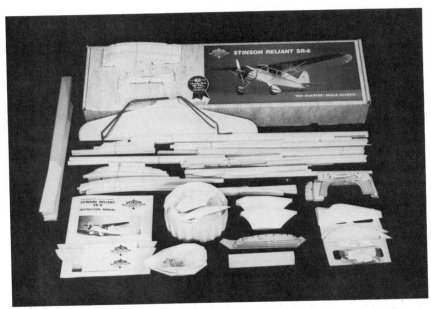

Materials in a prefabricated kit, a Stinson SR-b for radio control. The kit includes balsa and spruce strips banded together, cutout plywood parts, intricate shapes molded from plastic, prebent wire parts, finished wing ribs, and the usual small parts envelopes.

Balsa wood comes in many more sizes than the representative selection shown here. The 1/4 × 3 × 36-in. piece on the scale weighs less than 2 oz.

WOODS

Balsa Wood

Virtually all balsa comes from South American trees, which grow as much as 6 ft. a year. Balsa is extremely light, easy to cut, sand, and glue. It comes in many strip and sheet sizes. Balsa also has an extremely high strength-to-weight ratio. Its weight varies from 4 to 20 lbs. a cubic foot; the lightest wood is used for Indoor models, the heavier for spars, longerons, wing trailing edges, etc., on Outdoor models. Depending on the way the wood is sawed from the log, the grain varies and the three basic cuts differ in stiffness and cross-grained bendability. Specific plane parts require specific balsa cuts. (See Chapter 5.)

Spruce and Pine

Spruce, once universally employed for full-size aircraft construction and still common in home-built airplanes, is frequently used in modeling. It has a high strength-to-weight ratio, but is heavier than balsa. Tough and "springy," it is used for longerons and spars on big models, mostly "monster" RC Scale planes, that fly fast or are heavily loaded (these parts are shown in the drawing on page 89). Aircraft-grade spruce is normally Sitka or Engelman because ordinary lumberyard spruce is rather brittle. Clear white pine can be substituted for spruce where stress is not extreme, but balsa is too weak.

Other Common Woods

Rock maple is used for engine-mounting bearers, or for supports to which plywood or aluminum motor-mounting plates are attached. Bass is noted for its even grain texture, and it is nice for carving. Mahogany is also available at hobby shops, but is generally used for marine modeling.

Plywood

Plywood comes in many thicknesses, ranging from 1/64 to 1/4 in., in hobby shops. Greater thicknesses are found in lumberyards and hardware establishments that stock lumber. Plywood is made from cross-grained laminations or plies glued together. Always ask for aircraft grade, which is far superior to more porous low-cost plywood. If you do not have a hobby shop or aircraft supply source, ask for Finnish Ply. Normally, a 1/16-in. thickness has three plies, those of 3/32, 1/8, 3/16, and 1/4 in. five to seven plies. Sig markets Lite-Ply, which is less strong and dense, but desirable for bulkheads (formers), platforms, etc., because aircraft plywood may be weight overkill in such locations. Aircraft plywood is a must in high-stress areas—fire walls (bulkheads on which engines are mounted), landing gear foundations on big models, wing spar joiners—and for fuselage-side doublers (1/32 to 1/16 in.) on large control-line and radio-controlled models.

Veneers

Mahogany veneer of 1/64-in. thickness is used to sheet the surfaces of a Styrofoam wing core on high-performance CL or RC craft; the 1/32-in. thickness is often used to simulate veneer on the sides of fuselages of some classic-era Scale craft. Skinning of foam-core wings usually is done with 1/16-in. balsa sheet, sometimes with 1/64-in. plywood. Veneer can be soaked in hot water and shaped around forms for D-shaped wing leading edges. (These techniques are discussed in Chapter 5.)

GLUES

Model Cements

Most simple models are put together with model airplane cement, a transparent, thick liquid that ordinarily comes in a tube. Drying time varies; some harden overnight, others in a few minutes. Common brands are available at hobby shops; retail outlets, drug and hardware stores, etc., stock similar

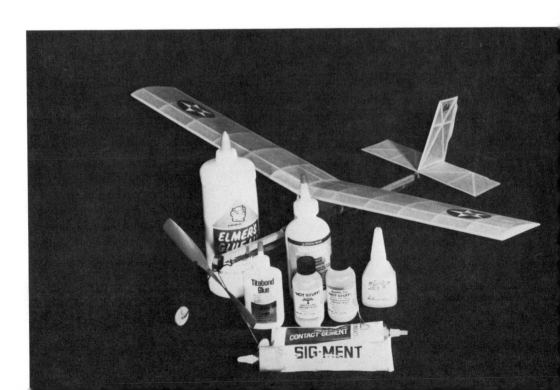

cements manufactured by firms such as LePage and DuPont (Duco). Amber-colored Ambroid is an old favorite in both hobby shops and hardware stores.

"Instant" Glue

These extremely thin glues (cyanoacrylates) generally are used on joints already in place and penetrate the wood by capillary action. Most come in small plastic bottles with a thin plastic feed tube, which is positioned by the purchaser. One drop of these glues adheres a small joint so strongly that the wood will be ripped apart before failing. There are two types: one that sets instantly and one that gives you a few seconds to move pieces around. The slower type fills slightly imperfect joints, while the other requires precision fits. "Instant" glues available in hobby shops include Zap, Superjet, and Hot Stuff. They are more expensive, but they save enormous amounts of time and considerable weight, which is important in small, fragile frames. They are extremely dangerous to the eyes and must not be accessible to children. The manufacturer's directions should be carefully followed. (See page 160 for more about important safety measures.)

Other Glues

Where aircraft weight is not at a premium, the common white glues, such as Elmer's, are extremely strong and dry hard and transparent overnight. They are best for butt joints, crosspieces to longerons, and so forth, especially for spruce and hardwoods where some model cements are deficient. These water-base glues are fairly thin and have good wood penetration where a tight joint could squeeze out some other cements. White glues should not be used when long joints or seams must be sanded. The glue is so hard that adjacent balsa is torn away by sanding. Other similar, but different-colored aliphatic glues (brown, yellow, etc.) are somewhat less resistant to sanding. These include Franklin's Titebond and Sig Yellow glues. All these glues, most of which are intended for cabinet-making work, are found almost anywhere, including hobby shops. (Sig's cements and glues are formulated only for model-building purposes.)

When used to make large-area joints—as between two pieces of plywood—these glues are handled in the same way as furniture glues, with the joint held tight overnight by C-clamps or a vise. They are not used to laminate large balsa areas, or attach thin plywood doublers to sheet-balsa fuselage sides. (The moisture content in this case deforms the balsa wood.) Aliphatic

Grouped around a kit-built Sig R.O.G. are basic glues. The three larger plastic bottles, left, are water-based glues: Elmer's, Titebond, Sig. The twin bottles, middle, are Instant Bond and Gap-Filling Instant Bond by Hot Stuff; right, Goldberg's Superjet Instant Glue. In the foreground are Elmer's contact cement and Sig-Ment. The model is covered with Japanese tissue. Instant glues are cyanoacrylates, to be used with caution per the manufacturer's instructions. Model airplane cements such as Sig-Ment are recommended for younger hobbyists. (Preston photo)

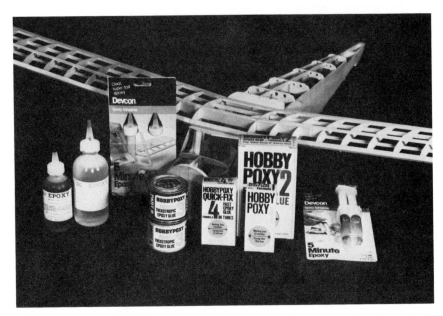

Epoxy glues harden by chemical reaction when two parts are mixed, and can take 5, 10, 30, 45 min. Devcon 5-min. glue (right) is packaged in a plastic pump that ejects both parts equally when the plunger is depressed. (Preston photo)

glues can be used on Styrofoam, a material that is dissolved by many other glues and dopes. Model cements are preferred to aliphatic types on small models because they are lighter when dry—the solvents evaporate.

Contact Cements

These cements work the same as the rubber cement used to join sheets of paper. They usually are applied with a coarse brush to both surfaces to be laminated, allowed to dry to the touch, and then the surfaces are pressed together. They are excellent for laminating balsa sheets or applying plywood doublers to balsa fuselage sides, but are not good for joints in tension, such as crosspieces. Contact cements also are useful for attaching patterns to large pieces of sheet balsa or plywood when parts such as big wing ribs or bulkheads are to be cut out. If one coat is applied and the pattern pressed down before drying, it is easily removed when the work is done.

Contact cements are not all the same. Some dissolve Styrofoam. Although those found in hobby shops do not have these injurious characteristics, when in doubt, test a material sample first.

Epoxy

Used for high-stress joints and in places where fuel would dissolve model airplane cements, epoxy comes in two containers (called Part A and Part B)—

one the resin, the other the hardener. When mixed, usually in equal quantities (but otherwise according to directions), a chemical reaction takes place to set the glue. The time required to set the epoxy is stated on the container. After setting, the joint cures rockhard in a time period depending on the particular mixture (from, say, an hour to overnight). Setting and curing depend on room temperature, and can be speeded up by warming under a lamp (but don't overheat the piece). Rubberlike gloves, found in hardware stores, protect the skin if large quantities of epoxy are used. It is advisable to avoid contact of any chemical liquid or glue with the skin. Epoxy is heavy, and thus is used on larger models.

Dopes and Thinners

Dope is used to attach tissue, silk, nylon, polyester cloth, and other coverings to a framework. It is diluted 50-50 with a compatible thinner and is brushed over the dry frame surface, usually two or more times. If colored dope is used over the clear dope after covering, two or three coats are

Liquids include dopes, paints, and thinners for brushing and spraying. Two-part epoxy paints are represented by Hobbypoxy (left) and K&B (right). These are for super finishes by experienced modelers. Sig's butyrate dopes and thinners (center) are representative of easy-to-use materials popular with modelers in general, as is Pactra's AeroGloss. Pactra's Formula-U dopes and thinners are polyurethane, and will take on film-type coverings. Sig's Plastinamel is used on formed plastic parts. (Preston photo)

brushed on. However, spraying with an airbrush gives a more consistent fin-ish, requires fewer color coats, and saves weight. There are no hard-and-fast rules for thinning dopes. Good builders as a rule prefer to thin all dopes by 50 percent. Spray doping requires that the dope be so thinned. Average modelers simply brush on dope full strength as it comes from the bottle or can.

Once, nitrate-type dopes were used exclusively; today, butyrate dope is most common. Nitrate is still used by discriminating builders for light frames because, once taut, it does not continue to shrink over a period of months, thus making a model less prone to warping. Nitrate does not pull free of inter-sections between flying surfaces to form bubblelike fillets. Butyrate is more fire-resistant than nitrate. The two kinds are not compatible.

Model dopes are much thinner than full-strength dopes bought at an air-port, which usually must be thinned. (Builders of large models sometimes buy dope by the gallon at airports.) Modeling dopes contain a "plasticizer" that reduces the tendency to shrink overtight on light structures. Two or three drops of castor oil per ounce of dope will serve as a plasticizer if you use airport-bought dopes. Sig low-shrink dopes are a safeguard against warps; all Sig colored dopes are low shrink. (See also Chapter 7, Covering and Painting.)

In humid conditions, dope may blush—turn white in spots—although blush inhibitors are contained in model dopes. (White spots can be removed by brushing thinner over them.)

Dopes—and modeling finishes in general—should be used only in well-ven-tilated places. Inhalation can be harmful. (The use of respirators and other safety measures is discussed on page 160.)

MISCELLANEOUS PARTS AND MATERIALS

Music Wire

This tough steel material, also called piano wire, comes in many diameters, from less than 1/32 in. on up to 1/4 in. Principal among its many applica-tions are rubber-model propeller shafts and hooks, and landing gear in gen-eral. Available in 3-ft. lengths, music wire is found in tubelike racks at the hobby shop.

Special Liquids, Fillers, and Sealers

These products are used to fill wood grain before painting, to improve adhesion of iron-on coverings to wood surfaces, and for overcoating to seal

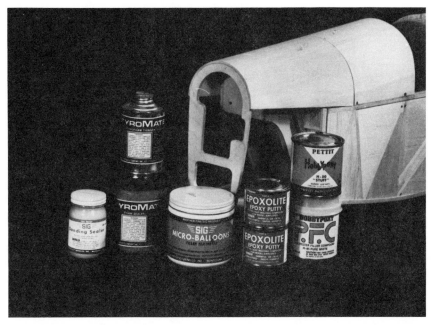

A few of the special-purpose products for sealing and filling surfaces before covering and painting, and for molding fillets, etc. (Preston photo)

To facilitate covering with iron-on films, sealing seams, priming wood surfaces, Coverite has many special liquids. Also included here are Sig's Core-Bond and Goldberg's Blue Goo, contact cements for attaching sheet balsa or thin plywood skins over foam wing cores. (Preston photo)

If you wonder how steel wire landing gears are formed, this ram-and-jig table will intrigue you. The scratchbuilder must bend his or her own wire, which is tough when one gets involved with the thicker sizes. (Sig photo)

Lightweight foam wing cores are quickly cut by a hot wire sliding over templates attached to the end of Styrofoam blocks. Some hobbyists have the equipment to do this themselves. The wire is heated to the proper voltage by a model-railroad-type transformer. (Sig photo)

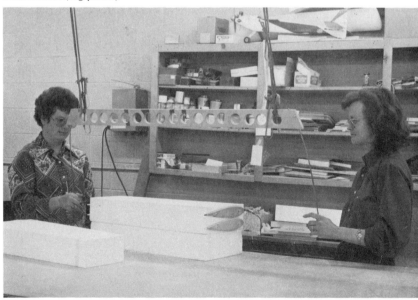

seams and protect finishes. Ranging from talcum powder mixed with thinner and clear dope to epoxy-base brush-on liquids and auto body filler pastes, these materials are detailed in Chapter 7.

Molding Materials

For molding, filleting, and so on in advanced modeling, unique materials are available. Microballoons, for example, are minuscule hollow glass beads, seemingly weightless, which when mixed with dope or epoxy form light-weight sculptured shapes, such as wing fillets (a curving of the joint between two parts). Because the microballoons are hollow, the hardened material molded from them sands easily. Epoxolite is a two-part epoxy mixture, each part already blended with microballoons. It forms rocklike sculptured shapes of moderate weight and adheres to metal, plastic, or wood. The beauty of Epoxolite is that it is readily molded with a moistened finger. Microballoons may be mixed with slow-curing epoxy or model cement to form fillets. Plastic Wood is useful but comes out rough-finished and requires difficult sanding. Very large fillets should be cut to shape from stiff paper, or thin plywood or veneer, to save weight; but intricate curvatures with plywood or veneer normally require finishing off with Epoxolite or other suitable material.

Sheet Metal

Brass and aluminum come in foot-long lengths in a variety of convenient thicknesses. Parts are cut out with scissors or metal snips, or sawed to an outline, as with a Dremel jigsaw. Metal is typically used for screw-on plates to retain landing-gear struts and for wing-strut fittings.

Metal Tubing and Shapes

Aluminum and brass tubing come in the same lengths as music wire in various diameters, generally up to 3/8 in. You'll find tubing displayed in the same way as music wire in hobby shops. Also, there is streamlined crosssec-tion aluminum tubing in many sizes (for wing struts), and an extensive variety of structural cross sections in metal or plastic. These shapes are a shorter length and are found in their own display racks. Tubing is graduated in sizes for telescopic fits, especially useful in brass, which can be readily soldered. All such materials are special-purpose, mostly required by scratchbuilders.

Hardware and Special Parts

A number of manufacturers have special display racks holding J-bolts, wheel axles, wheel collars, nylon bolts, washers, fuel-line tubing, every conceivable size and type of nut and bolt, and so on. It is hard to say where the

Clothlike materials include heat-shrinkable polyester, nylon silk, silk-rayon, fiberglass cloth, Japanese tissue, and SilkSpan paper. (Preston photo)

line can be drawn between materials and minor accessories. Goldberg, Du-Bro, Sig, and Perfect offer extensive lines of accessory items, and there are many other brands as well, many specializing in ingenious convenience devices.

COVERING MATERIALS

Japanese Tissue

Much lighter and stronger than common tissues, this material usually comes in folded sheets in white and various colors and is ideal for all forms of rubber-powered and other small models. It is adhered to open framework with clear dope, then watershrunk by misting with a spray, or by swabbing lightly with wet cotton, allowed to dry, then given two to three coats of clear dope to close the pores and maintain tautness. Appropriate colors of tissue are finished with clear dope only. Experienced modelers may dye white tissue for non-Scale rubber and gas-engine-powered free-flight types: the tissue is placed in a shallow pan containing a mixture of water and a dye such as Rit. Clear-doped tissue can also be painted with colored dope, thinned 50-50.

SilkSpan

Somewhat heavier and tougher than Japanese tissue, this material is the same as that found in tea bags. It is applied like tissue and is generally used on larger gas-powered free flights, big rubber-powered models, and smaller RC craft. More open-pored than tissue, it requires more dope. It, too, can be dyed.

Silk

Modeling silk is lightweight with a closer weave than the common silk found in scarves. Far stronger than any paper, it is lighter but not as strong as clothlike nylon or polyester. It sometimes is preferred for large-size craft and helps give an authentic appearance. Normally silk comes in natural white, but sometimes it is available in colors. It stretches around compound curves such as those for nose blocks and wing tips, without wrinkling. At one time silk was *the* material when tissue would not suffice; now synthetic materials (see below) are most often used.

Nylon, Silron, Polyester, and Other Synthetics

Available at hobby shops in several thicknesses and weights, these synthetic woven cloths are applied to the framework in the same way as tissue and silk. They are very puncture resistant; hence they are preferred to silk on larger planes.

Iron-On and Heat-Shrink Covering

By far the most popular material for RC Sport models, from the smallest to all but superlarge, iron-ons are preferred because of easier application and light weight. Most resemble plastic, but some have clothlike textures and look like fabric. They are applied to framework edges by pressing with a small, temperature-adjustable, hobby-type iron, then shrunk tight by rubbing lightly with the iron or by using a modeling heat gun—much like a hair dryer. Wrinkles disappear and the finish is drum tight.

   • Top Flite's MonoKote: First on the market some twenty-five years ago, this product comes in rolls in many colors, including metallics. No dope or painting is required. Color schemes and decorations are achieved by combinations of colors, one ironed on over the other, and by means of Trim-Sheet strips that allow pattern-cutting of numerals, letters, and intricate design

Believe it or not, there is no paint on this Top Flite Headmaster 40. It is covered and decorated with FabriKote lightweight iron-on textured film. Top Flite, Pactra, Coverite, and other manufacturers produce a variety of high- and low-temperature films and heat-shrinkable weaves in all colors of the rainbow.

details (see below). EconoKote is an economical grade that takes a lower iron temperature. High-temperature film, such as MonoKote, cannot be used directly on Styrofoam components, which melt. Both grades have a transparent peel-off backing on the adhesive side, which is not sticky to the touch.

Top Flite also markets Trim-Sheet, a film that comes in a great variety of colors, with a peel-off backing on which stencil outlines are printed for numerals and letters. After cutting around the desired stencils with an X-Acto No. 11 blade, you can peel off the resulting characters. Or you may cut any desired trim shape—such as long arrows or broad stripes—before removing the backing. Trim-Sheet is generally known as "Trim Film" among modelers.

• Coverite: This firm produces three types of high-temperature covering materials that have a fabriclike texture to simulate real aircraft. All three types come in rolls.

Super Coverite is dyed with various colors, and is excellent over difficult compound curves. Coverite Permagloss is impregnated with four coats of its color, in a wide variety of choices ideal for those who would avoid the work and weight of painting for superior, Scale-like finishes. Coverite Silkspun is a superlight colored material popular with RC Scale builders.

Coverite materials (there are still others!) accept a variety of finishes, airplane dope, acrylics, and epoxy paints. Coverite also offers pressure-sensitive, die-cut, colored vinyl graphics trim sheets in letters, numerals, and stars.

• Coverite Micafilm: This superlight film is extremely strong, and has a somewhat clothlike appearance. It has a smooth and a rough side, and is applied with either side down—it has no peel-off backing. The rough side feels slightly gritty but resembles real aircraft covering. Either side may be painted, but the rough side looks more realistic when painted. The structure must first be painted with a temperature-sensitive adhesive, such as Coverite's Balsarite.

• Solarfilm: Pactra's plastic film in various colors is intended for low-temperature application; thus it may be applied over ready-to-use Styrofoam wings and bodies without melting the foam.

• Top Flite's FabriKote: This material is especially useful for large models requiring more covering strength than MonoKote, and for added realism. A clothlike material that comes in various colors, it accepts compound curves without wrinkles, and can be painted with typical hobby dopes and finishes. (FabriKote does not have to be painted. But although it is available in a number of popular colors, other colors or combinations of colors may be required, notably when you are duplicating particular aircraft when building Scale.) Though it has a clothlike texture, it may be applied without reference to grain direction. Tissues, silk, nylon, and many other covering materials have a grain, and must be placed lengthwise or spanwise on the surfaces they are to cover.

Crossover Materials

We have coined the term "crossover" because these are materials that can be doped to framework (or attached with thinned white glue) at the surface edges, heatshrunk, then doped and painted if desired. They are often made of polyester. People who build large planes may purchase lightweight drapery linings to save money. Modeling versions have various trade names, such as Sig's Koverall. Koverall works best when it is wet first, then adhered to the edges of the framework with dope. It pulls tighter when dried. It shrinks drum-tight when heated with a modeling iron or heat gun. Such materials are relatively heavy but immensely strong, and are used where weight relative to the size of the model is not significant.

Glass Cloth

Fiberglass cloth comes in several thicknesses. It is used over localized areas where reinforcement and sealing against fuel leaks are essential. Application is with epoxy or (over large areas) epoxy thinned to a brushing consistency with a butyrate or epoxy thinner. Heavy grades reinforce the center section joint of a big wing; the thinnest grade can be laid over sheet-wood

Wood surfaces of big models are finished with epoxies and/or fiberglass cloth applied with polyester glass resin. The catalyst for the Hobbypoxy Quick-Prep resin is inside the container's top; for Sig's resin, in the small bottle to the right. These materials are for advanced adult hobbyists. (Preston photo)

surfaces with thinned epoxy for brushing—notably on big-scale models. It sands well, and when filled takes a smooth painted finish.

Various weights of fiberglass cloth are laid up over patterns or molds with epoxy resins, to mold enclosures such as cowlings for the engine and "wheel pants" on larger scratchbuilt and scale-like models. High-performance Pattern-type, Racing, and some Scale models commonly have "glass" fuselages molded to streamlined contours. Normally, such items are supplied finished in plane kits or can be ordered custom-made from special suppliers.

Acrylic Enamel and Epoxy-Type Colored Paints

All such paints are frequently used by advanced modelers for shiny, hard finishes with a minimum number of coats, when weight saving is not vital. These materials have good covering qualities. An airbrush is recommended. Hobbypoxy and K&B Super Poxy are two popular brands; Hobbypoxy has a wide line of special products for general building usage.

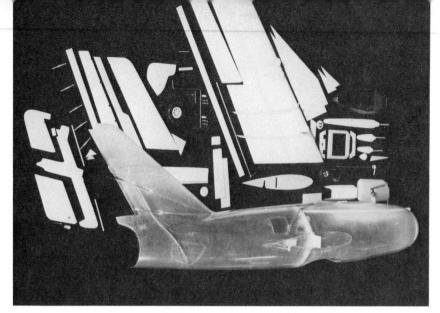

Byron Originals' ducted fan-jet Russian MiG for expert radio control hobbyists displays the fiberglass molded fuselage complete with fin and internal bracing.

Top Flite, Coverite, Goldberg, Royal, and others make decorative tapes, numbers, letters, stars, and decals. (Preston photo)

A well-organized work area. The bench top is composition board; small tools and parts storage boxes are convenient, with paints and dopes in the background, upper right. There is a flexible spotlight for detailed work. Not shown in this photo to the right is another long bench for assembling large models and, where the camera stands, a design and drafting area with overhead adjustable light-box projector for scaling plans to different sizes. (Preston photo)

chapter four _____

Tools

The majority of model planes can be built with a handful of simple tools that fit in a shoe box. There are a number of glamorous tools on the market for the "modeler who has everything." So before you buy, consider these basic factors.

Probably nine out of ten planes are built from kits that supply prebent wire, die-cut wood parts, molded pieces of plastic, and parts that a scratchbuilder would have to laboriously fabricate. Some people need little more than sandpaper and pins, but others use bench saws, belt sanders, powered jigsaws, lathes, and other machines. Tools should be matched to the desired activity. As you progress, various intermediate tools may be acquired.

All hobbyists specialize. Model-plane building really is a collection of hobbies. When considering tools to buy, one can fish from a rowboat or a cabin cruiser, so to speak.

Some companies specialize in hobbycraft tools. X-Acto's small hand tools are widely available, individually or in special chests for families of tools, on up to a large one with a complete line of small tools. If you need more robust tools for heavier work, shop the hardware stores and hardware departments in Sears, Roebuck, Montgomery Ward, and other chain department stores. For motorized tools, Dremel specializes in the model airplane field with economical, robust tools, but if you want heavy-duty, costly machine tools, try the alternate sources mentioned. Lathes are not discussed here, since relatively few aeromodelers need them. Sturdy precision machines may cost many hundreds of dollars and the essential add-on devices for them are also costly.

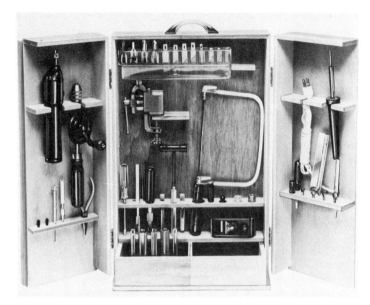

This deluxe tool chest by X-Acto contains most tools possibly needed by the typical hobbyist, from the hand-held motor tool at left to the soldering iron at right. At the top are various gouge and knife blades made to fit universal handles.

ESSENTIAL TOOLS

Pins

This ubiquitous tool holds framework pieces to be glued together. Pins should be steel, not brass, which bends easily. The common dressmaker's pin is ideal, but banker's pins or pins with ball heads are easier to use when a hammer is not needed to push them home.

Hammers

You need a lightweight tack hammer or ball peen hammer for forcing pins into the workboard for holding assemblies. A lightweight hammer is also useful for bending materials such as thin-gauge sheet metal in a vise.

Pliers

Modelers most often use the versatile needlenose type of pliers. A round-nose pliers is needed for making smooth bends in music wire. The diagonal or "dike" pliers is best for cutting soft wire. Pliers found at the hobby shop are for light work. Using undersized pliers distorts the jaws and ruins the tool. For example, tough music wire damages cutting pliers if they are too small. It is desirable, therefore, to keep a large-size backup set of pliers for some tasks. A large electrician's pliers is best for cutting thicker wire. (See also p. 81.)

Files

It is generally true that bargain-basement tools are no bargain at all; this is especially true of files. You can find excellent files and other small tools at a hobby shop—notably brands such as K&S and X-Acto. Remember, though, that typical hobby shop files, while good, are for light work only. You may need only a small flat file to start, but you will eventually find various types and sizes desirable, such as round files and triangular files. The former is good for rounding corners, enlarging holes, deburring the ends of metal tubing; the latter for notching music wire to be cut while held in a vise, and other special purposes. The rattail file is round, with a mildly tapering cross section—it's handy for enlarging holes. You may wish to acquire file sets, with graduated sizes to cover fine to coarse work.

Rasps

These are nothing but very coarse-toothed "files" intended for wood work, and are a convenience more than a necessity. They are found in hardware stores.

Saws

Most handy is the razor or Zona saw, which has a very sharp, fine-toothed, replaceable blade that inserts into a wooden handle. It is ideal for cutting crosspieces that are too big for accurate cutting with razor blades or knives; it also cuts metal tubing and thin sheet metal. You can buy this saw in hobby shops. For deeper cuts in larger wooden pieces, the common coping saw is a good one to have. Reverse the direction of the coping-saw blade so that it cuts when you pull downward; the teeth catch with a pushing motion. The replaceable blade is adjustable for tension. A cheap coping saw requires force to compress it for blade replacement. On a better saw, threaded fittings permit easy replacement and slanting of the blade, which is helpful when the width of the material jams against the handle, as when you are cutting out holes in large plywood bulkheads. The better coping saw has a thread adjustable handle, similar to a hacksaw. A hacksaw is convenient for cutting metal held in a vise, especially music wire.

Knives

Most balsa is cut with a single-edged razor blade or balsa knife. The most popular knife sets are distributed by X-Acto, although a number of high-quality brands exist. The X-Acto knife is a thin, penlike metal cylinder with a knurled handle section for gripping; there is a slot and threaded chucklike arrangement to hold the blade tightly. All sorts of blade shapes are available,

Illustrating the use of a balsa knife is internationally famous scale modeler Don Srull (his work area is shown on page 64). Note at the left a Zona saw; at the right, a soft brush to keep the surface clear of scraps and sawdust. (Preston photo)

MODELER'S TOOLS

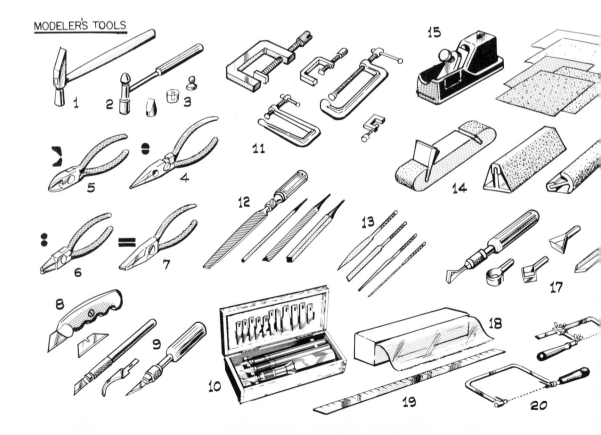

(1) small, lightweight hammer; (2) X-Acto hammer; (3) interchangeable heads for X-Acto hammer; (4) needle-nosed pliers; (5) cutting pliers; (6) round-nosed pliers; (7) Duck-bill pliers; (8) Stanley knife; (9) X-Acto knives; (10) X-Acto knife chest with interchangeable blades; (11) assorted C-clamps; (12) basic files; (13) miniature files; (14) commercial sanding tools; (15) small block plane; (16) assorted sandpapers; (17) X-Acto handle with interchangeable gouges and chisel; (18) wax paper or Saran Wrap; (19) steel straightedge/ruler; (20) coping saw; (21) jeweler's saw; (22) assorted screwdrivers, including a Phillips head; (23) jeweler's screwdrivers; (24) scissors; (25) sheet metal snips; (26) miter box and razor saw; (27) adjustable bench vise; (28) hand-held vise; (29) Dremel Moto-Tool; (30) hand drill; (31) bits, 1/16 to 1/8 in.; (32) interchangeable grinding and cutting bit for motor tools; (33) small soldering iron, resin-core solder, and paste—interchangeable elements; (34) Allen wrenches; (35) small wrenches; (36) clamps; (37) masking tape; (38) spirit levels; (39) Top Flite film-covering iron; (40) Top Flite gun for heat-shrink covering; (41) airbrush—compressor not shown; (42) draftsman's scale; (43) protractor, triangle, T-square; (44) tweezers.

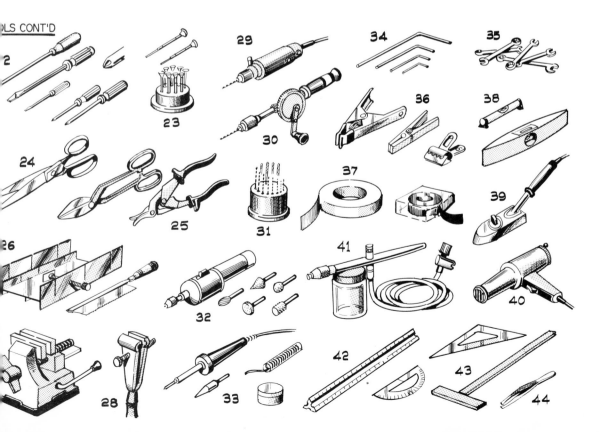

TOOLS CONT'D

but the No. 11 blade is the most widely used by artists and hobbyists. (Always keep a spare pack of No. 11s!)

For heavy-duty cutting, many modelers use the Stanley knife, though there are other brands (available at the hardware store). It has a sturdy, long blade that is inserted and replaced by means of a lock screw in the side of the two-piece handle (which splits lengthwise). The common penknife is good for carving. Replacement blades for all hobby knives are sold in display racks.

Wood Planes

Most of the modeler's work that needs this kind of tool is done with ultra-small wood planes that take shallow cuts. The miniature block plane is universal, but variations are found at the hobby shop. Some special planes use a razor blade instead of the conventional thicker cutting blade.

Sanding Blocks

Modelers are forever sanding things. Merely rubbing sandpaper back and forth is not such a good idea; it's better to use sanding blocks, boards, and sticks. A simple block sander is made by wrapping a properly sized piece of sandpaper around a block of wood, and thumbtacking the edges in place on top of the block. Sanding boards can be made in several convenient sizes by adhering the paper to one side of a piece of 3/32- or 1/8-in.-thick plywood with contact cement. In the same way, sandpaper is applied to short pieces of various diameter wooden dowels. Cheap sanding tools are found in hobby shops and in paint and hardware stores. Worn sandpaper can be easily replaced, since precut paper is packaged to fit them.

Sandpaper

The abrasive surface is usually composed of sand particles, but more expensive grit types last many times longer. The coarseness of all these papers or cloths is numerically designated, but we suggest you examine the sandpaper rack at a hardware store, to learn firsthand which papers appear to suit your specific needs. Two kinds of paper are sufficient: common sandpaper and wet-and-dry, which can be used wet for finishing filled or painted surfaces. The grades can be thought of as coarse, medium, fine, and super-fine. Your choice will depend on the size and delicacy of the wood used in a particular model. A coarse paper for hogging out a rough-shaped nose block on a big model would tear up more delicate material on a small airplane. Fine paper appropriate to thin strips in a small model might be good only for final finishing of some large framework.

Wet-and-dry paper is black. Modelers generally use the finer grades, wet in water, for smoothing coats of sealers used on wood (to close pores), or on filler coats of doped covering, and on successive coats of colored dopes and paints when super finishes are desired.

Drills

Lightweight jobs require the smallest of hand drills. If heavy work is done, a larger, more robust hand drill should be obtained from a hardware store. The leverage on the larger crank handle is essential. For small models, you may need to drill holes from 1/16- up to 1/8-in. diameter. Modelers who tackle monster projects need capacities up to 1/4-in. diameter, possibly 3/8, and should probably get a big drill press.

The serious hobbyist invariably ends up with a drill press. These vary from the Dremel drill press (an inexpensive stand and table that clamps a hand-held Dremel Moto Tool in place), which is found in hobby shops, up to crafts-

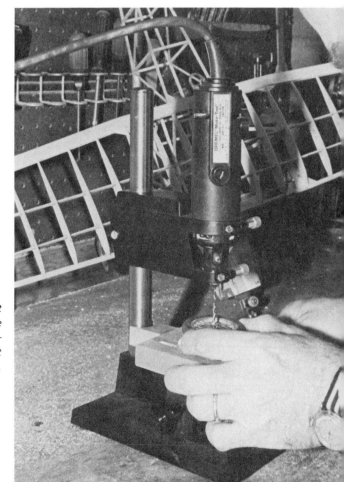

e Dremel drill press consists of an adjustable base that mps Dremel's hand motor tool in place. The table ves up to meet the drill (which makes holes a maxi-m of 1/8 in. in diameter). This tool is suitable for light bby work; heavy-duty drill presses are more costly. eston photo)

man and industrial-size motor-driven drill presses that may cost well over $100. A drill press assures ease and accuracy. It is almost impossible to bore an accurately aligned hole with a hand drill in large, thick pieces of material, especially metal.

Drill Bits

There are wood- and metal-cutting drill bits, but the metal-cutting ones cover virtually all our needs. Bits may be purchased singly or as sets. The drill bit-set normally covers diameters from 1/16 to 1/4 in., and is packaged in a handy metal container with shelflike racks that have holes corresponding to the bit sizes. Sometimes—infrequently—a metric drill is required because of the gradual conversion to the metric system—many imported engines, for example, use metric-size machine screws, bolts, etc. We'd suggest obtaining an inexpensive drill-bit set to begin with, then rounding out the collection with larger individual bits as necessary. Any drill bit that is dull, or that is bent so that it wobbles, will make oversize holes, and should be replaced.

Chisels and Gouges

These tools are convenient for hollowing out pieces, such as wing tips and nose blocks. The typical carpenter's chisels (available in many widths and sizes) have a wedge-shaped cutting edge—rather like a wood plane—and a wooden handle. A special nonmetal hammer or mallet is used to tap them without damaging the handle; these hammers are found in hardware stores. Hobby or craftsman chisels and gouges are most useful, however. They are about the size of a small screwdriver, with wooden handles. Four or five with assorted shaped cutting edges come as sets, usually in a small wooden box.

X-Acto has inexpensive sets with cutting blades shaped for the modeler's specific purposes. The blades fit into a wooden knife handle, somewhat like the familiar X-Acto knife but larger. The advantage is that blades are replaceable. Nonreplaceable blade chisels and gouges must be occasionally sharpened on a whetstone, since only the keenest blades cut balsa smoothly.

Clamps

The metal C-clamp is often needed to hold pieces together while glueing; for example, plywood laminations. These clamps come in a wide range of sizes, but one whose jaws open from 1 to 2 in. will fulfill most of your needs. Larger sizes can be added as necessary. Plastic modeling clamps (some are shaped like a measuring gauge with jaws compressed by rubber bands), found at the hobby shop, are adequate for lighter work.

Vises

You will find a vise a great convenience in holding metal pieces to be drilled, or sheet metal or wire that is to be bent when pliers won't do the job. A small vise satisfies most builders, but there are times when large, heavy-duty jaws come in handy. A vise can be quite large. You need to consider whether the vise attachment opens wide enough to grip the thickness of your bench surface. If you intend to bend music wire 3/32 in. or larger, the vise should be fairly substantial, and in this case one that attaches to the bench by means of bolts is preferred because it will not twist on the bench when considerable force is applied. A 4-in. jaw satisfies most requirements. Check the vise at the store for smoothness and precision of operation. A cheap vise with wobbling jaws is a nuisance.

PANA-VISE This trade name covers a variety of ingenious vises that cleverly position the work. The head rotates 360 degrees and tilts 180 degrees from vertical to horizontal. Pana-Vise offers interchangeable heads, bases, and accessories for every conceivable function. Investigate these products at better hobby shops.

Pana-Vise produces an extensive line of adjustable tilt vises and material holders. Here, the builder drills a mounting bolt hole for the nose hatch of the RC glider in the background.

Electric and Hand Drills

For light work and thin materials, the hand drill is sufficient. For larger, deeper holes where speed and power are required, the electric drill is a good investment in any tool collection. Hardware store drills last for years. There are even cordless types with rechargeable batteries that are not tied to an outlet.

Taps

Sometimes one must drill and tap a hole to accept a machine screw or bolt. This occurs most often with metal (generally aluminum) mounts; the support arms usually have no holes for the mounting bolts. Taps come in sets of various sizes, the same as drill bits, but they are made to cut threads in predrilled holes in wood, metal, or plastic. Holes are drilled slightly under-sized, then the tap is screwed in to cut the threads. If the material is wood, the tap is screwed continuously without requiring special skill. For metal, the tap is turned in a bit a short distance, then backed off, then screwed in some more, and so on until the hole is threaded. Ask someone to explain how this is done.

Tap sizes usually indicate the required hole size. There are tap guides and charts—Sears and other department stores are good sources—to match hole and tap. The tap is turned by a tap wrench, a T-shaped handle equipped with a chuck to accept different sized taps. There are metric tap sets as well.

Precision small tools by HS include screwdrivers, left; nutdrivers, center; files, right; and, top, various jeweler's screwdrivers, tiny open end wrenches, etc. (Preston photo)

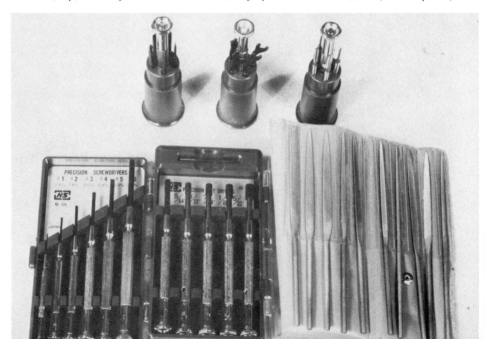

Screwdrivers

In addition to the familiar slot-head screw, many modeling items have Allen heads (a round-headed screw with an interior socket having six sides) or Phillips heads (a cross-shaped slot). Therefore, along with an assortment of at least three standard screwdrivers, you will need corresponding Phillips screwdrivers (check hardware stores for the larger sizes), and Allen wrenches (at hobby shops and hardware stores).

JEWELER'S SCREWDRIVERS For tiny screws, found on RC servos and other parts, a set of jeweler's screwdrivers is nice to have. A set normally includes five screwdrivers; the blades vary from small to very tiny. The flat head of the screwdriver can be held with downward pressure of a finger, while the barrel of the tool is turned with the other fingers.

Wrenches

A set of small, open-end flat wrenches may come in handy. As noted before, Allen wrenches are a virtual necessity; you will need several sizes, from the tiniest possible up to perhaps 1/8 in. (The largest hobby size most commonly used is for 6-32 machine screws.) The Allen wrench is L-shaped, with one long arm. "Old-fashioned" hardware stores may have T-handled Allen wrenches, extra long for reaching into difficult places. Allen wrenches also come in sets, the same as drill bits and taps, and work like a screwdriver. Miscellaneous Allen-head machine screws (a "classy" strong bolt with fine threads) are sold at hobby shops, usually under the Du-Bro name; each envelope of four similar screws (there are many sizes available, including 2-56, 3-48, 4-40, 6-32) comes with the proper size Allen wrench. (Larger sizes are at hardware stores.) Wheel collars and other small modeling parts have tiny socket-head screws that require ultrathin Allen wrenches, which are packaged with them.

Soldering Irons

The common pencil-tip electric soldering iron satisfies almost all the modeler's needs. Various tips screw in like flashlight bulbs. Acid-core solder is never used by modelers due to corrosiveness, especially on electrical connections; instead, resin-core solder is available in convenient spools, as is resin soldering paste in small cans. If you do much soldering, consider getting an iron holder, which protects the operator and work surface from burns. A special sponge and holder are used for frequent wiping of the iron's tip, to reduce oxidation and prevent contamination. Good joints cannot be made with tips that are dirty.

Pistol-grip irons with on/off triggers (and sometimes a built-in light) are

Soldering a wire-wrapped landing-gear joint with a trigger-gun iron. The music-wire struts are held in the nylon-faced jaw of a Pana-Vise, which has an adjustable ball socket. The pencil-tip soldering iron (foreground) is for fine electrical work. Both irons are made by K&S Engineering. (Preston photo)

generally hardware store items, although K&S pistol-grip irons are found in better hobby shops. Very fine electrical work (such as receptacles) requires a pencil-tip iron. A trigger iron should not be used close to servo motors because its magnetic field can damage the motor's magnet.

Brushes

Brushes are used to apply clear dope to a framework to be covered with tissue, silk, nylon, or polyester. They are also used for painting and for applying fillers and finishers, epoxy, and so on. Naturally, the size and type of a brush's hair or bristles vary to suit these different materials. An epoxy brush, for example, has very stiff bristles and is disposable. Craft, paint, and art-supply stores may have brushes not found in smaller hobby shops. Depending on the size of the model and the nature of the task, brush quality and expense vary greatly. Cheap brushes for dope and paints are prone to shed bristles, thus marring the work.

Grumbacher's brushes are popular with knowing hobbyists. Their quality is excellent; prices are higher than the run-of-the-mill "cheapies." Found in better hobby shops, art stores, and in modeling catalogs, the common types are Ox Hair Single Stroke, Camel Hair Flat Glaze, Red Sable Spotting-Pointed, Red Sable Spotting and Detail, Red Sable Flat Shader, Camel Hair Round Translucent, Fine Selected Camel Hair, Fine Camel Hair, Goat Hair, and several types of extra-quality camel hair. In general, the brushes range from pointed tips up to 1/8 and 1/2 in. Cost rises rapidly with width due to the amount of hair. A 1-in. brush may cost more than double a 1/2-in. brush in high-quality types.

CONVENIENCE TOOLS

Pin-Vise

About the size of a jeweler's screwdriver, this item has a simple chuck end to grip a straight pin or a drill bit up to 1/16 in. It is used for making holes to be drilled to bigger sizes, making small holes in thin wood, or starting holes for screws.

Miter Box

Found at hobby shops, these small sawing guides assure accurate perpendicular cuts at 90 or 45 degrees when used with the razor or Zona saw.

An airbrush and spray gun by Miller (note the pistol grip on the spray gun), with airhose, left, and air compressor, right. Airbrushes are for delicate work, spray guns for larger areas requiring greater capacity as well as volume of spray. They are made by many manufacturers and at a wide range of prices. (Preston photo)

Awl

Similar to an ice pick, the awl is good for making starting holes for drilling so that the bit does not "skate." It makes holes in sheet balsa that can be reamed out with rattail files.

Spray Guns and Airbrushes

Modelers incorrectly consider all spraying equipment to be airbrushes. We also use spray guns, which are larger and typified by a pistol grip. The airbrush, for delicate work, is not practical for the overall painting of any but the smallest model, whereas the spray gun is used for covering large areas. Prices and quality of these tools vary widely. When comparing prices, consider that you will need a source of compressed air or "propellant." The following list of equipment and brands is representative, and by no means complete. Those that we describe provide guidelines to assist you in making selections. The prices are current as of spring 1983. Incidentally, a professional artist's airbrush is too fine for model airplanes, except for static-display plastic Scale models.

The Badger Basic Spray Gun Kit includes a No. 250 Paint Spray Air Brush, 5 feet of vinyl air hose, a 3/4-oz. jar of paint, an air regulator, and an extra 3/4-oz. paint jar. It is priced at $13. Propel pressure cans, in 11-oz. and 17-oz. sizes, are purchased separately. Badger's deluxe kit includes 6 feet of hose, both Hobby and Touch-Up airbrushes, a Propel can, and three 3/4-oz. paint jars. Badger's Mini Spray Kit, at $16.50, includes the gun with attached 8-ft. hose, a 4-oz. paint container, an air regulator, and an 11-oz. Propel can. For a few extra dollars you can get an air regulator that attaches to the Propel, eliminating the on/off valve and adjusting pressure from 10 to 50 pounds per square inch (psi). Badger's deluxe airbrushes are also good buys.

Intermatic's Hobby-Gun Outfit, priced at $69.95, includes a small air compressor, which is something you may need when painting large models.

A really good air compressor is costly. Binks has one that retails for $106 and weighs 9 lbs., including a 1/8-hp electric motor delivering a pressure of 18 psi. Binks also has the Wren Air Brush ($36.75) with three nozzle choices. The Binks Air Brush Kit comes with an electric-motor-driven compressor and costs $152.30.

Inexpensive airbrushes are made by MRC (Humbrol), X-Acto, Intermatic, and others. If you go for broke, Sears and other such outlets have compact, industrial-size equipment with compressors that can handle big jobs—or even a house!

Both Miller and Paasche have extensive lines of quality airbrushes and related equipment. For occasional use and portability, Paasche's 2P Travelers Kit with self-contained aerosol pressure tanks is especially handy. If you want a robust, compact compressor, the Miller Model 2000 is hard to beat. Miller's AB-100 brush kit, for shading, and the Model 14-G spray gun, for detailed work, merit consideration.

MISCELLANEOUS SMALL TOOLS

Wire Benders

Bending music wire of a diameter greater than 1/16 in. is difficult using pliers. The Higley bender has a solid metal base that clamps in a vise, with two upright steel pins protruding. Medium-size wire placed between the pins is easily bent around the the desired radius. K&S Engineering has a similar wire bender. The Mr. Muscle Wire Bender, by Dave Brown Products, can bend coils—as for shock-absorbing nose struts—in wire up to 5/32 in. diameter. Rhom Air has a bender on the same principle as Higley's, for use with wire up to 5/32 in. There are also heavy-duty benders that bolt to a bench, with a long lever arm for working wire up to 3/16 in.; for these, shop around and try nonhobby sources. K&S makes one for music wire up to 1/4 in., and its base must be held in a *very* secure, bench-mounted vise.

Tubing Benders and Cutters

K&S Engineering has tools for both these purposes. The Bender Kit handles tubing with a diameter of 1/16 up to 3/16 in. The tubing cutter handles diameters up to 5/8 in.

The Higley (also K&S) wire bender clamps in a vise, has a grooved head for the wire, and a steel pin around which the wire is formed. Heavy music wire cannot be accurately bent with pliers. (Preston photo)

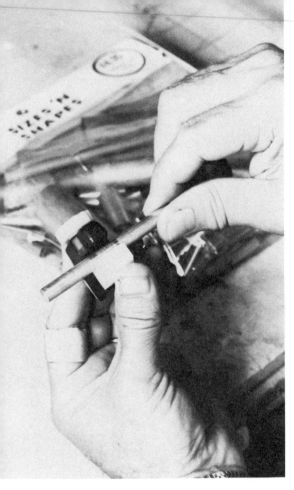

The K&S tubing cutter. The clamp screws tightly against the tubing, and when the tool is rotated around the tubing, a sharp cutting wheel severs the piece. Cutting tubing with ordinary hand tools is tedious. (Preston photo)

Z-Bend Pliers

Z-bends, for pushrod ends, are almost impossible to make with standard pliers. To accommodate this need, Custom Model Products offers a special Z-Bend pliers. Harry Higley makes a Zee-Bender (which is not a pliers) for RC servo pushrod ends.

MOTOR-DRIVEN BENCH TOOLS

Quality lathes, drill presses, and so on, can be very expensive. Fortunately, Dremel offers economically priced motor tools that are very popular with general hobbyists. Kits are available in a number of sizes and varieties; these

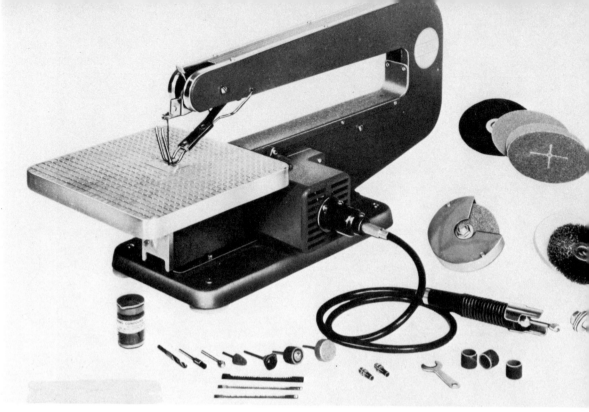

Dremel's Moto-Shop is a versatile tool for the serious hobbyist. The basic unit is a motor-driven jigsaw with tilt table and a side outlet for sanding and buffing wheels. It also has a side feed for a hand tool that takes drills, routers, grinding heads, etc. (foreground). (Fred Marks photo)

are hand-held tools (a distant cousin to a dentist's tool) with a high-speed, self-contained electric motor. The top of the line is Model 381, with fingertip speed control up to 25,000 rpm. Thirty-four accessories, for carving, grinding, polishing, sanding, drilling, engraving, and deburring wood, plastics, metals, and other handicraft materials, fit its chuck. Even 1/4-in. music wire is quickly cut with the appropriate cutting wheel. A highly regarded, versatile tool, it can mount on Dremel's economical No. 210 drill press for drilling holes up to 1/8 in. in wood or metal. The No. 229 router attachment enables you to cut slots, dadoes, rabbets, and chamfers, using high-speed router bits and cutters.

Dremel Moto-Shop

A most worthwhile addition to the modeler's workbench, this tool is worth its weight in gold as a scroll or jigsaw; it also has a side outlet for disk sanding or buffing wheels, and for flexible-shaft tools such as those found in Dremel's Model 573 Accessory Kit. The table adjusts up and down and tilts to 45 degrees for bevel cutting. It has the clearance for work up to 15 in. long. (Saw blades can be set at three positions.) Its longest dimension is 23 in. and it weighs about 12-1/2 lbs. It rests on vibration-absorbing corner pads and takes over one hundred attachments and accessories.

Dremel 580 Four-Inch Tilt Arbor Table Saw

Weighing less than 10 lbs., with its largest dimension 13 inches, this handy tool accurately cuts lengths of lumber and rips strips of balsa, spruce, maple, and other woods, and has a 2.2-ampere (A) motor that turns 9,800 rpm. Its work table is 10 × 12 in., and its motor and blade tilt 45 degrees for bevel cuts. It also offers a dust chute that can be attached to a bag or vacuum cleaner. While not strictly comparable to expensive, heavy-duty equipment that is not intended primarily for hobby use, this table saw is far from a toy. All useful table-saw features are engineered into it.

Dremel Disk Belt Sander

This tool, driven by a 2.2-A motor, has a 6 × 3 in. table and a 1 × 30 in. endless sanding belt. An additional tilt table on one side provides for accurate

Dremel's belt sander accelerates heavier work on large models. The side table for the sanding wheel is tilt adjustable and also handles such duties as dressing edges of sheet-metal parts. (Preston photo)

Tilt-table disk sander is useful for making accurate beveled edges, dressing crosspiece ends, and making small objects; it sands wood, metal, and plastic. (Preston photo)

sanding and grinding with a 5-in. disk. It weighs 15 lbs. and is 15 in. high. It can be bolt-mounted to the bench. It sands, shapes, cleans, sharpens, and polishes wood, metal, plastics, and other materials, and is most useful for rough-sanding nose blocks, plywood edges and shapes, and dressing edges. If you build ultralarge RC models, this tool greatly reduces work time.

Jarmac Tilt Table Disk Sander

This 4-in. disk sander is excellent for precision work on small parts, and can be used on wood, metal, and plastic. A 4 × 5 in. table tilts 45 degrees.

Covering Irons

Although temperature-adjustable household irons can be used for applying and shrinking iron-on covering materials, a much smaller iron intended for hobby use is preferred, particularly on small models. Top Flite Models, for example, produces a heat-sealing tool; thermostatically controlled for temperatures up to 450 degrees, it has a Teflon shoe and is held by a wooden handle rather like a trowel. Edson Enterprises' heat-sealing tool has a square handle containing the temperature control, with the iron proper being interchangeable with a temperature-controllable soldering iron.

Heat Gun

For shrinking iron-on films already applied, heat guns made by companies such as Top Flite tighten heat-shrink coverings. These guns, which resemble hair dryers, avoid direct contact with the material, so scratches are eliminated. They can also be used to oven-dry parts dust-free, and to set resins, glues, and paints. They put out a stream of air at a much higher temperature than a hair dryer does.

FOR FURTHER INFORMATION

In addition to the tools described, there are hundreds of items ranging from feeler gauges to propeller balancers. Many are advertised in model airplane magazines. For a complete rundown we suggest these representative catalogs.

• *Tower Hobbies R/C Catalogue:* Published by Tower Hobbies, P.O. Box 778, Champaign, IL 61820, this is a 400-odd-page illustrated listing, with extensive tool coverage. (Note that other mail-order houses advertising in magazines have catalogs as well.)

• *Model Builder's Wishbook:* This 125-page catalog, published by Sig Manufacturing Co., Inc., Montezuma, IA 50171, includes a broad spectrum of kits, tools, accessories, and materials, as well as numerous other brand lines.

• *Ace R/C Inc.:* Like the Sig *Wishbook,* but devoted exclusively to radio control, this catalog covers a multitude of accessories, materials, and electronic equipment by both Ace and virtually every other manufacturer. Order it from this address: P.O. Box 511, Higginsville, MO 64037.

Artist Bill Noonan, a master craftsman who builds nothing but classic rubber-powered Scale subjects of his own design, works on a Messerschmitt M20b, a German airliner of the 1920s. (Noonan photo)

chapter five _____

Construction

In the construction of all aircraft, full-scale or model, the strength-to-weight ratio is a primary consideration. Depending on a real plane's design purpose, this ratio varies greatly. An overweight machine has inferior performance.

Engineers of full-scale aircraft calculate the stresses imposed on a machine and design structures accordingly. Model designers cannot precisely predetermine such things, but acquire a rule-of-thumb expertise that enables them to select materials and their sizes that result in a framework that is sufficiently strong without being overweight.

Model kit makers select materials and parts for special-purpose designs. But it is what we do with glues and paints, and how well we follow plans and directions, that determines results. Scratchbuilders, especially those who design their own craft, have a more difficult task. A plan alone specifies materials, but an original design requires knowledge of what materials and sizes to use. The scratchbuilder must be a very experienced modeler.

We have no yardstick that tells us, for example, that a 3-ft. model should always weigh 10 oz. Just as real planes vary tremendously in weight according to design purpose, even when they are the same size, so do models vary in weight, hence the type of construction, for the kind of flying desired. A full-scale light plane is weighed in hundreds of pounds, but a jet fighter is weighed in tons. So it is that a rubber-powered Scale model weighs only an ounce or two, while a radio-controlled model of the same dimensions may weigh 2 lbs. Even so, the strength-to-weight ratio of a rubber-powered model weighed in grams often is greater than that of a 25-lb. monster RC ship with a chain-saw-type engine!

The structural "density" of different types of models is variable. Just as a real plane may be a light framework of steel tubing and wood with fabric covering or a massive assembly of metal, a model may be built from thin balsa strips glued together or fabricated from denser materials with virtually no framework, its components being shell-like rather like those of a super-sonic fighter. Whenever maximum flight duration is the goal, the lightest construction is required. This is obvious in free-flight models. The minimum gross weight in relation to the wing area (called wing loading, and measured in ounces carried per square foot of area) is our yardstick. We come to know acceptable wing loadings for the types of models we favor. For example, an RC Schoolyard Scale model is ideal at 4 to perhaps 8 oz. per square foot of wing area, but becomes too fast and difficult to fly in small spaces at about a 10-oz. loading. A monster RC Scale model flies at relatively the same visual speeds at loadings well beyond 30 oz. a square foot. (This is due to scale effect, a phenomenon related to plane size: A tiny model flits about at unreal-istically high speeds; larger models fly more smoothly and realistically because their wings are hitting a greater number of air molecules.) Most modelers who build kits usually know only the acceptable gross weight of the aircraft. For example, a 5-1/2-ft. RC Pattern ship with a 0.60-size engine weighs from 7 to 9 lbs. or more. The heavier it is, the faster it must fly through maneuvers. In the same way, Indoor modelers know what their models *must* weigh—and think in terms of gross weights of a few ten-thou-sandths of an ounce. They use precision scales to weigh models and their components, and work with balsa that weighs as little as 4 lbs. a cubic foot— whereas load-carrying parts (like spars) in other types of models should weigh several times as much.

The point of all this is that careful construction is essential to achieving maximum strength with minimum weight. A beginner's model may weigh twice as much as that built by the more experienced hobbyist. Weight, like excess fat, is a deadly enemy.

FUSELAGES

A small rubber-powered aircraft is the traditional design that most people think of when they say "model plane." The fuselage (body) in the lightest form is a box consisting of four longerons (main pieces) and crosspieces.

The side frames are constructed flat, one at a time, on the workboard, with waxed paper beneath to prevent glue sticking to the plans. The longerons are pinned in place (pins against the sides of the wood, not through it) over the plans. Individual crosspieces are cut to length, fitted snugly in place, then glued.

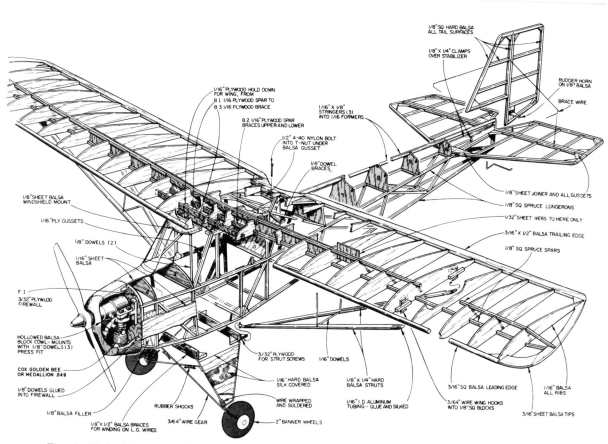

The glorified rubber-powered model type construction in this Taylor E-2 Cub is typical of Schoolyard Scale radio-controlled models. A two-channel "mini" radio system operates the rudder and elevators of this craft with a Cox 0.049 engine. (Drawing by Hank Clark, courtesy Model Aviation)

The difficult part is joining the two completed sides to make the box. Generally, the top and bottom crosspieces at the front and rear of the cabin area are installed first, checking with a draftsman's triangle for accuracy. The top and bottom crosspieces are held in place by pressing small pins through the sides of the longerons until the glue dries. The partially assembled frame is placed over the top view of the plan as work proceeds to see that crosspieces coincide with the drawings, and that there is no departure from the centerline.

Since it is extremely difficult to hold two side frames while inserting the top and bottom crosspieces, builders improvise jigs to hold the elements in place, and to preserve accurate alignment. Temporary rectangles of sheet balsa are cut to the desired inside width of the fuselage (this is the same dimension as the crosspiece length). The sheet balsa is pinned, not glued, between the side pieces of the body at two fuselage "stations." After the crosspieces are fitted and glued in place, the sheet-balsa jig pieces are removed by extracting the pins that held them.

The tail joint (rudder or sternpost) of the body must be exactly on the centerline. If one side is curved more than the other when viewed from the top, the plane will never fly properly. Its fin and rudder will be inclined to the flight path, which causes the plane to turn, perhaps violently.

Variations on the Open Frame

The fuselage is not necessarily square or rectangular in cross section, especially in scale models. Formers and stringers may be added to a basic "box" to achieve the necessary cross sections. A former, usually made of sheet

A simple method for joining fuselage sides at the cabin area. Temporary sheet-balsa pieces jig and align sides, while crosspieces are glued in place.

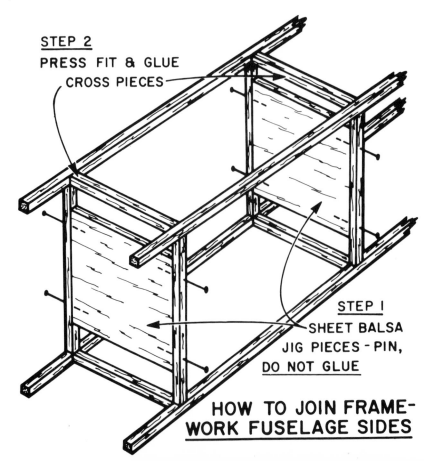

STEP 2
PRESS FIT & GLUE
   CROSS PIECES

STEP I
SHEET BALSA
JIG PIECES - PIN,
DO NOT GLUE

HOW TO JOIN FRAME-
WORK FUSELAGE SIDES

This tiny French Farman-like model is intended for the Bostonian, a sport event for clubs that fly Indoor planes with a note of realism. The model has one loop of 1/8-in. rubber and weighs only 17 gm. (Noonan photo)

balsa but sometimes plywood in a high-stress area, is cut to the desired cross-sectional shape of the fuselage at each station. Thin pieces of balsa or spruce, called stringers (the wood used is determined by the plane's size), are fitted and glued into notches in the outer edges of the formers, and extend lengthwise from nose to tail. Frequently only the top or bottom of the fuselage (sometimes both) requires contouring. In this case, the formers are not complete cross-sectional shapes, but only smaller portions of the cross section, and are glued to the crosspieces of a basic fuselage within. For example, the portion of the top of the fuselage from the cockpit to the tail may require a shaped cross section; then, of course, the stringers are shorter in length to match that portion of the body. Some Scale models have dozens of full-length stringers, others may require only a few. In brief, stringers provide external contours, while formers support the stringers. A simple square or rectangular cross-sectional fuselage may also employ formers instead of crosspieces, because construction is easier.

The better mousetrap, Don Srull's Dornier push-pull fighter fuselage for rubber power, assembled as a one-piece shell. The top and bottommost longerons are first laid down on the plan with vertical holder pieces glued to them with Ambroid. Holders are glued to a board held in a vise during assembly, and afterward are removed by softening glue joints with thinner.

Often, there is no basic "box." A series of cross-sectional sheet-balsa formers are located by attaching one stringer on either side, and another to both top and bottom. Other stringers are added one at a time at opposite points on the frame so that warping does not result.

This type of assembly is common, but relatively difficult. It is much better to construct two half-shells that are then joined together along the fuselage centerline. One half-shell is begun by fastening down the top and bottommost stringers ("crutch" pieces), then glueing each half former (bulkhead) upright onto these stringer pieces. Additional stringers are then added, bending and glueing them into notches of the previously cut (or die-cut) formers.

When the half-shell is completed, it is lifted from the bench, and the half bulkheads and stringers of the other side are added to it. The first half-shell may bow slightly as all the bent stringers seek to regain their original shape. Therefore, soak all stringers in warm water before locating them. Some builders prefer to spot-glue in place a few temporary diagonals to prevent distortion; these are removed once the full shell is together.

Sheet-Balsa Construction

This versatile wood has many applications, ranging from all-wood small models to fuselages and tail surfaces for medium-size craft and wing skinning on big machines.

Kits usually include either die-cut pieces or printed sheet-balsa sides to be cut out on the lines. Sometimes only blank sheets are provided on which the builder must trace or reproduce the side profile of the body to be cut out.

Lines are drawn on the sides with a square to indicate bulkhead positions. On large models, it may be necessary to butt-join along their length two or more pieces to make each side. Because balsa is not always precisely straight, the edges to be butt-joined often must be trued up. A metal straight-edge or ruler is used to mark an accurate edge, which is then trimmed with a balsa knife.

If you buy balsa from the hobby shop rack, sight along any sheet or strip piece selected for straightness. Be sure its hardness is appropriate for the intended use. Fuselage side pieces should be straight-grained, of a medium-soft to medium density with resistance to bending along the grain.

Sheet-balsa sides are matched for hardness, because if one side is stiffer than the other (if it is, it will feel heavier), it becomes difficult to join the sides at the rear with an identical bend. The result is a fuselage that meanders off the top view centerline. If you encounter this problem during construction, thin the stiffer side with a sanding board.

If a sheet is to be bent (wrapped)—as for the rounded-off top of some fuse-lages (called the turtle deck)—it must be capable of bending along the grain to avoid splitting during installation. Soak it in hot water for 15 min. before bending.

Assembling an Eaglet RC fuselage from a kit. All four sides are die-cut to shape with tabs that fit into holes in the sides. Rubber bands hold parts together during gluing.

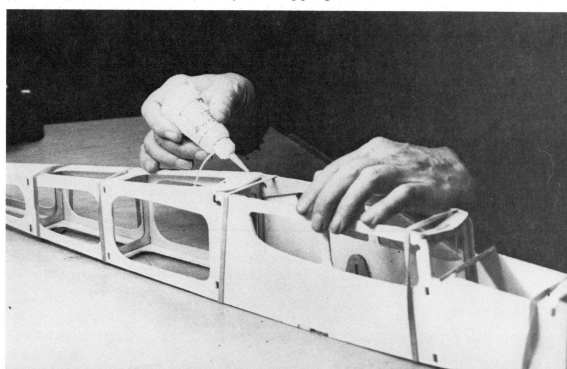

Sheet-balsa fuselage sides are normally joined together with bulkheads, which come die-cut in most kits. Bulkheads usually have large die-cut lightening holes. Directions for all but the smallest craft will call for reinforcing strips glued cross grain at the top and bottom of such bulkheads.

The trick in assembling the sheet-sided fuselage is first to attach the sides to the bulkheads located at the front and rear of the cabin area. Place cement on one edge of one bulkhead where it will meet the side, then pierce the side with two or more pins to hold it firmly to the glue joint. Quickly repeat the process for the rear cabin bulkhead. Place cement on the opposite edges of both bulkheads and attach the other fuselage side with pins. Before the glue sets you must align the frame. If the fuselage has a flat top or bottom in the cabin area, rest the body flat on the bench, then sight downward on the frame to ensure that the bulkheads are at right angles to both sides and parallel to each other. If they are out of line, gently push one side backward or forward until the bulkheads line up—before joining at the tailpost. Place the body on top of the plan, so distortions are immediately evident. If the bulkheads are square or rectangular, that is, flat sided, the body necessarily will be true when viewed from the front.

However, some models may use crosspieces in lieu of bulkheads, or a combination of bulkheads and crosspieces, the latter usually found between the rear of the cabin and the stern. When installing crosspieces, sight as before, but in addition check with a draftsman's triangle resting on the bench and against the fuselage side at each crosspiece station. Before the glue dries after each set of crosspieces is installed, force the partially assembled frame into true alignment to agree with the triangle.

Once the cabin area is locked in place, the sides are drawn together at the very rear, glued, and pinned. (Pins are removed when the job is done.) Bulkheads and/or crosspieces are then inserted from the rear of the cabin area to the tail. If the sides must be pulled in to fit a narrower nose, use light rubber bands wrapped around the front, just strong enough to pull the sides in to make a tight fit with the nosepiece, which is glued and pinned as was done with the bulkheads. Don't overdo it with the rubber bands or you could collapse the nose. Rubber-band-loaded modeler's plastic clamps are also good for this purpose, but use only enough rubber tension on the clamps to draw in the sides without cracking them.

On larger models, the initial procedure is a bit different. RC designs frequently use plywood bulkheads in the cabin area. One side is pinned to the bench, then the front cabin bulkhead glued in place and checked with a triangle to ensure that it is at right angles to the side. The rear cabin bulkhead is attached in the same way and, after both glued joints have set, the opposite

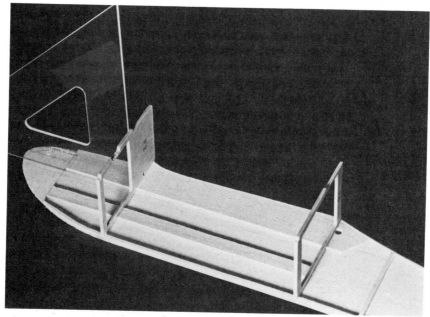

Alignment is vitally important. Locating the first two bulkheads in a radio control fuselage, a triangle is used to check trueness. This photo also shows a doubler in place. (Randolph photo)

side is placed on top of the bulkhead sides projecting up from the bench. If the sides are parallel forward to the nose, the plywood fire wall is glued in place in the same manner as the bulkheads.

This form of construction is most widely used on popular RC designs such as the Sig Kadet, but also is seen on competition free-flight and control-line stunt models and Scale machines. Since more strength is needed for RC, additional steps are required. First, the fuselage side sheets are prepared as before. However, here you must contend with doublers and other bracing structure not found on little craft. A "doubler" is an extra thickness of material, laminated, usually with contact cement, to the inner faces of both fuselage sides. Don't make two left-hand, or two right-hand, sides! The doubler may be sheet balsa with its grain crosswise, or at an angle to the side proper. Or it may be (and usually is) thin plywood (1/32 to 1/16 in.) that extends rearward beyond the front cabin bulkhead, perhaps as far as the rear cabin bulkhead. If this plywood is not die-cut (often it is not), it must be marked and accurately traced to the outline of the fuselage side. Most such craft also have balsa-strip rails glued to the top of the sides, on the inside, and extending between the front and rear cabin bulkheads. This provides a firm seat for the wing and minimizes structural damage in a crash.

The procedure is to pin the sides flat to the workboard, then glue in place the doublers and all vertical pieces, rails, and corner strips, if any. Doublers are attached first with contact cement. A corner piece is a triangular cross-sectioned strip, or smaller square strip, which, when the top and bottom sheeting are added, will reinforce the lengthwise corner joints and permit rounding off those corners with sandpaper until the corner strip shows through. Assembling the sides is done as previously described, after the corner pieces are installed. The top and bottom of sheet-balsa fuselages almost always consist of short crosswise lengths of sheet, glued and pinned to the sides, with each length butt-joined and glued to its neighbor. After the glue is

Typical Profile fuselage control-line model (the Ringmaster), showing laminations of plywood on both sides of the nose and a wing cutout. The wedge tank is held in place by aluminum-sheet straps and screws.

dried, the projecting sheet balsa is trimmed neatly with a single-edged razor blade or balsa knife.

It is imperative that any fuselage be properly sanded. Do not hold loose pieces of sandpaper (fingers cause grooves). Don't sand continuously in a straight line with the sanding board; sand with a circular motion. To round off corners, use narrow strips of sandpaper held in two hands, as when shining shoes. The surface must be free of glue bumps, conspicuous edges where pieces have been joined, and so on; otherwise finishing and covering will be unsightly.

The Profile Fuselage

Profile models are most commonly control-line planes, though they are sometimes small free flights. The most typical CL models are Sport stunters and trainers. The Profile also is found in certain CL competition Racers and the Profile Navy Carrier. The Profile fuselage is usually die-cut or sawed to outline in a kit, but otherwise would have to be duplicated from the plan. It varies in thickness from 1/8 to 3/8, and sometimes 1/2 in., depending on the size and power of the machine.

A little CL Profile model typically is cut from 3/16-in.-thick balsa sheet. A 1/16- to 1/8- or even 1/4-in.-thick plywood fire wall (bulkhead), to which the engine attaches, is glued to the front of the profile "slab" and is supported by triangular blocks glued to both sides of the slab behind the fire wall. Sometimes these blocks are rounded off to a shape. The plywood fire wall may be round, oval, square, etc., and the blocks shaped accordingly. The wing and tail, almost always made of sheet balsa, are glued directly to the fuselage, as plans specify. The fuselage/wing joint is reinforced with corner blocks glued to both surfaces and rounded off—or given a concave shape to simulate a fillet. Without this bracing, the wing would quickly tear off, or the fuselage split. On bigger models of this type, the tail surfaces also require corner supports at the fuselage joint.

On all but the tiniest CL Profile-type designs, the wing/fuselage joint requires reinforcement. Plywood doublers from 1/16 to 3/32 in. thick are used. These doublers, one on each side of the slab fuselage, extend back to at least one-third to one-half of the wing chord (the wing width). Doublers exactly match the profile outline and generally slope diagonally toward the rear, from roughly the leading-edge position on the slab top, to the wing top on typical low-wing designs. The rear edge of the doubler may be perpendicular to the wing. Doublers have a notch cut out to fit over the front of the wing, top and bottom.

The doublers are glued to the profile slab with an aliphatic glue or 30-min.

epoxy, and the entire "sandwich" is pressed together with C-clamps. Excess glue should be wiped off. Since the doublers are applied to the sides of the slab, hardwood motor-mount beams are inserted between them at the time the doublers are glued in place. Usually both the slab and the doublers that come in kits are die-cut to leave sufficient space to seat a side-mounted engine. Viewed from the side there is a U-shaped opening at the nose. Holes are marked and drilled through the bonded doublers and slab for the engine mounting bolts, which engage blind nuts on the far side.

Miscellaneous Fuselage Construction

Kits for the experienced hobbyist, and models made by gifted scratchbuild-ers, display great ingenuity. Beautifully contoured fuselages achieve stream-lining and ultrarealism in many ways. For example, the simple shell-type fuse-lage described may be "planked." Planking consists of a large number of flat balsa strips laid one at a time, as one would place planks on a boat hull. As these planks converge toward the tail or nose, they are pretapered, and their edges sloped, to provide tight fits that result in what is called a monocoque fuselage—one in which the outer skin carries the major part of the structural stresses.

Once, patient craftsmen made fiberglass-shell fuselages for big radio-con-trolled models by "laying up" laminates of thin fiberglass cloth over (or inside of) specially prepared molds of wood, plaster of Paris, etc. Two half-shells would be mated along the centerline, at the top and bottom. Today, RC Pat-tern model kits and deluxe Scale kits costing as much as several hundred dollars frequently include finished fiberglass half-shells, or a completed fuse-lage shell with key structural members, such as motor mounts and servo rails, already epoxied in place.

Just as there are always exceptions that prove the rule, there are numer-ous exotic procedures for making a fuselage, especially in Indoor Stick and some forms of Outdoor free-flight and RC gliders. Typical is the tubular fuse-lage, or boom, which connects an abbreviated fuselage with the tail surfaces. Usually a long plank of thin, pliable sheet balsa (perhaps only 1/64 in. thick for some Indoor models) is soaked in hot water or ammonia, then wrapped around a dowel or rod, held in position by a bandagelike masking-tape wrap-ping, and placed in an oven until dry. After the form is withdrawn, the length-wise seam is trimmed and glued. Even arrow shafts have been used for tail booms, usually on Soaring gliders. However, modelers are unlikely to run into such building problems unless they become interested in competition; only in Indoor is the rolled fuselage tube commonplace.

WINGS

Because of the wide range of strength-to-weight ratios required in different kinds of models, construction of wings involves a fascinating array of materials and methods. While individual designers of kits and magazine projects blend a modest number of basics in so many ways that there is no such thing as a standard wing for any type of machine, we can generalize the types of wings as solid and open framework. The former category includes the sheet-balsa wing of a child's small rise-off-ground (R.O.G.) and hand-launched glider; the thicker, airfoil wing of the competition hand-launched glider, or control-line trainer, Racing, and Speed models; and even the custom-cut foam wing of an RC trainer, or the foam-core wood-skinned wings of some control-line stunt machines and many Scale, Sport, and Pattern-type RC ships. Open-framework wings, which consist of spars and edges with suitably spaced wing ribs, are described below.

The following descriptions relate to construction used in the overwhelming majority of models, the basic proven methods. Photographs detail the construction of some of the more "off-beat" designs that the beginner and sport flier do not normally encounter.

Open-Framework Wings

With the exception of small and novelty craft, the built-up framed wing is universal in powered free-flight, towline, and RC Soaring gliders (possibly skinned with sheet balsa); in rubber-powered craft, such as Wakefield and Scale; in many control-line machines, such as Stunt and Scale; and in the majority of RC ships, including Sport and Scale. The framed wing may be delicate and light when used in free flight, or robust and relatively heavy for other forms of aircraft. For example, the gossamer-light Indoor model wing has no spars, or spanwise strips; a single piece of extremely thin and light balsa is usually bent to form the wing outline, and therefore the leading and trailing edges are the sole load-carrying members (often a bracing system of hairlike tungsten wire is employed). Wings for bigger and faster Outdoor craft may have a sturdy single spar, two spars, or a considerable number of multispars.

Whatever the design, two factors are important. First, balsa must be carefully selected for trueness, straight grain, type of grain, and appropriate weight, hence strength. Spars and edges are hard, stiff wood to provide strength. Quarter-grain balsa, distinguished by its speckled appearance, resists bending parallel to the grain direction, whereas other cuts are more or

Open frameworks are assembled over waxed paper on the working surface. Here, the author locates a wing rib on a Goldberg Eaglet RC model. The opposite wing panel and stabilizer are pinned down at left.

less pliable along the grain. For wing sheeting one would select the most pliable balsa because it must be easily bent. The second factor is that pieces should never be force-fitted, because warping of the frame results.

The open-framework wing is built flat on the bench. Wings that have dihedral, that tilt upward in a shallow vee, are built in two or more panels, each panel finally joined to its neighbor(s) at a stipulated angle. To assemble, waxed paper is placed over the plans, the bottom wing spar(s) pinned in place (unless plans specify otherwise), followed by the leading- and trailing-edge pieces, then the wing ribs. Finally, top spars (if any) and wing-tip pieces are added. (The sequence varies with different designs.) Unless the kit provides shaped edges, the edges must be shaped with a razor blade, razor plane, and/or sandpaper after the panel is completed, but before dihedral is incorporated. Dihedral is incorporated by blocking up the wing panels to the proper angle and facing the spar joints (like splints) with thin plywood. The butt ends of the spars and edges to be joined are slanted with a sanding board to fit.

Many rubber- and gas-powered free-flight models use multispar construction, with numbers of thin spanwise strips on both the top and bottom of the ribs. On the long, narrow wings typical of competition Wakefield and Unlimited-size rubber-powered models, or Soaring gliders, the main load-carrying spars consist of hard balsa or thinner spruce strips, one on top of the wing and one directly beneath. The spaces between the ribs are filled by thin sheet-balsa webs (grain vertical) glued against the rear faces of the spars, or between them.

The portion aft of the main spar sometimes has ribs that run at an angle from the spars to the trailing edge. Or diagonal strips are located between ribs aft of the main spar. This prevents warping and flutter in flight. The portion of the wing forward of the spar is often covered with thin sheet balsa (1/16 to 3/32 in.), running spanwise and overlapping the single main spar and the leading edge (which afterward is rounded off or shaped). If the forward area cover is sheeted on the bottom as well, a "D-tube" results, the strongest open-frame wing possible, particularly when spar webs are used.

Any wing panels to be joined at the center for dihedral are blocked up to the proper angle with the root parallel to a straight-edged workboard. The sanding board slides along the edge of the work surface, automatically sloping all spar and edge ends to mate with the opposite panel.

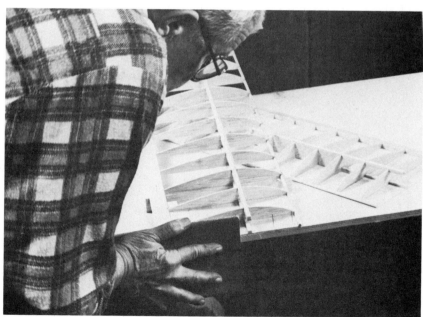

To incorporate dihedral, one wing panel is pinned down to the work surface, the opposite panel blocked up to the proper angle, and all centerline joints glued. Note the plywood "joiner," which reinforces the main spar joint.

Typical construction of a competition gas-engined free-flight model. Diagonal ribs in the wing and stabilizer minimize warping and protect against flutter of the lightweight structure. The wings have polyhedral, achieved by making four panels.

Wing sheeting is always difficult. Here the thin sheet balsa, glued to spar, ribs, and leading edge, is held by banker's pins. (Ron Moulton photo)

Masking tape and clothespins hold leading-edge sheeting in place until the glue dries. (Courtesy *Flying Models*)

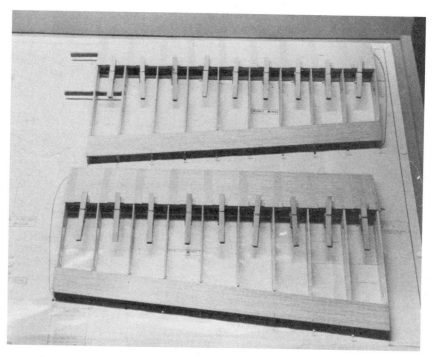

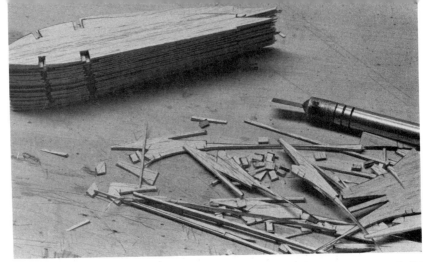

Scratchbuilders outline wing ribs with a template, cut them out with a balsa knife, then stack them together with pins before sanding to an identical outline. (Randolph photo)

Very often, thin ribs are reinforced top and bottom with thin cap strips, glued to the ribs.

Occasionally, it is necessary to cut your own ribs (when they are not already die-cut) from printed or even unmarked sheet balsa. If the balsa is not printed, make a rib pattern (template) from thin cardboard or plywood and trace the outlines of the required number of ribs. After cutting them out, stack the ribs together, pinned through both sides of the stack so that all the ribs can be simultaneously smoothed with a sanding board to an identical contour. Trial pieces of spar material are fitted in the spar notches for trueing up.

Control-Line Wings

Whereas a free-flight model requires light wing loadings, the control-liner has a more rugged airframe and compact configuration, and there is no emphasis on gliding ability. Considering the generally smaller sizes of the planes, engine displacement and power are far greater than in free flight. Not only is framing more substantial, but different kinds of flying (Speed, Aerobatics, etc.) result in many construction methods.

The open-frame wing of a CL model usually has one of three basic spar arrangements. First, thick, shaped leading and trailing edges may serve as spars; notches for the ribs are precut in kits. Second, a single spar is sometimes added, running through precut holes in the ribs—it is in the middle of the wing when viewed from the front and does not contact the covering. You can see this method used in the Sterling Ringmaster, Stunting, and other models. Third, top and bottom spars, usually with spar webs, are preferred for wings with large area where excess weight would hamper ultimate aerobatics. In the third case, leading-edge sheeting running back to both top and bottom spars is virtually standard. Scratchbuilders employ tricky spar methods. For example, an "egg crate" construction employs a full-depth sheet spar into which rib notches are cut to half the spar depth from the top; equally deep notches are cut in the ribs, so that the ribs slide into position (like the partitions in an egg crate) with the spar flush with both top and bottom of the wing. For small models, a single thick spar may be located on either the top or bottom of the wing. In many cases, scratchbuilders may skin a wing with sheet balsa. This may be done on Racing machines for strength, or to provide a smooth surface without covering sag between the ribs, on models with big glider wings, for example. The sheeted surface is a good base for covering and/or a painted finish.

SOLID CONTROL-LINE WINGS   For a Profile "quickie" with a 0.049-cu.-in. displacement engine, a wing can be cut from sheet balsa, and the edges rounded with sandpaper. Larger trainers—inexpensive "learning" planes for the inexperienced aeromodeler—use solid balsa wings. In this case, the balsa sheet is thicker and is planed and sanded to a curved top surface or airfoil shape. In a kit this wing is preshaped. For some competition Racing machines (Profile Goodyear types, Rat Racers, etc.), the solid wing is common. For these faster craft, the balsa slab wing is faced with a hard balsa leading edge to minimize denting. In the competition Speed model, which can hit 200 mph plus in some cases, the wood may be something like pine, perhaps with a streamlined airfoil (curved top and bottom).

Control-line Scale model wings generally are built up realistically with the same number and spacing of ribs as on the prototype, though the frame may be balsa-skinned, or skinned foam-core wings may even be employed.

Radio Control Wings

Since "cored" wings occur so often (especially in RC models), a brief description is in order. The Styrofoam core is shaped by a hot cutting wire attached like a string on a wide U-shaped bow or boom. Root and tip templates for the wire to follow are glued to the ends of a foam blank. Household current passing through a model-railroad-type transformer heats the Nichrome wire. Normally two people, one at either end, draw the bow wire along the profiles to remove the excess material (see the photo on p. 56). A short bow can be operated by one person. After balsa edge material is glued to the front of the core, and sometimes to the back, and sanded to match the airfoil curvature of the foam core, wide sheets of soft 1/16-in.-thick butt-joined balsa, or 1/64-in.-thick veneer or plywood are wrapped around the

foam and attached to it with a *compatible* contact cement that does not
"eat" the foam. (Ordinary model glues dissolve foam—as do some contact
cements.) Kits include precut foam cores. Custom-built cores can be purchased; refer to model aviation magazines for companies that advertise them.
You supply the root and tip airfoil templates.

On radio-controlled models, variations of all the wing forms described
(except flat sheet balsa) are employed in numerous combinations. In the primary trainer kits (many ready-to-fly) we may find an unskinned foam wing,
or even an all-foam model (possibly excepting those with sheet-balsa tail surfaces). The foam in these simpler craft is not hot-wire cut, but is of a different
composition with a soft, coarse-grained texture. Referred to as "pop corn"
plastic, because beads of material are placed in a mold and expanded by heat,
the surface has a pebbled but smooth appearance. Although such a wing can
be covered with paper applied with thinned aliphatic glue, or with a low-temperature iron-on film, it is almost always used as it comes from the kit. Subject to dents, it quickly shows battle scars; this does not handicap a trainer,
which some folks say should be considered expendable. With care, such a
wing can last a long time. More expensive ready-to-fly models have a finer
textured, heavier foam, with a smoother, perhaps prepainted, surface. This
type of wing cannot be built at home, but a variety is available by mail order.

Most RC Sport wings are built up, a compromise in weight and strength
between the fragile free-flight wings and built-up types found on advanced CL
stunt craft. The open-frame wing may have only two sturdy edges plus ribs

*Hot-wire-cut foam core being skinned with thin sheet balsa. Both surfaces are thinly
coated with compatible contact cement. The wax paper (foreground) hides the remain-
der of the butt-joined sheet, which will wrap around the top surface of the core. (Fred
Marks photo)*

in very small craft, but a minimum of two spars (one on top, one on bottom) is almost universal. This is true of simple trainers for 0.09 to 0.10 engines, of average Sport planes of 0.15- to 0.40-cu.-in. displacement, and even of large Sport and Scale machines, ranging as big as 12 ft. or so, with engines of 0.60- to 5-cu.-in. displacement. Larger Scale craft, and "monster" planes, in general, employ both front and rear spars the same as many real aircraft.

Wire-cut foam-core sheet-skinned wings are not too common in Sport models, but are found more often in Sport Scale types, such as those made by Top Flite. The foam-core, balsa-sheet or thin ply-skinned wing is common on Pattern and Pylon racing machines.

The core wing usually requires a left- and right-hand panel, joined at the middle. When dihedral is needed, the root ends of the panels are slanted to match at the required angle. For strength across the middle, a 3/32- or 1/8- in.-thick plywood joiner piece, profiled to match the dihedral angle, and, to the same thickness as the core, is inserted into slots cut in each core panel. These joiners, and the centerline joint of the panels, are epoxied together to make a one-piece wing. A strip of thin fiberglass cloth, about 2 in. wide, is epoxied chordwise over the top and bottom of the center joint.

Wing Attachment

Depending on the type and size of model, the wing usually is simply glued in place, attached with rubber bands, or attached with crash-breakable nylon bolts. A rubber-banded wing springs free in a crash to minimize damage. When rubber bands are used, dowels are located through the fuselage with ends projecting so that the requisite number of bands can be stretched crosswise in an X over the wing (shown in the photo on p. 115). Small to modestly sized RC Schoolyard Scale models normally are built as an integral unit. Other RC Sport models, Pylon Racers, and Pattern ships employ nylon bolts to attach a one-piece wing.

Two nylon bolts near the trailing edge engage plywood inserts built into the fuselage frame, the inserts drilled and tapped to take the bolt threads. A short length of dowel built into the wing's leading edge at the centerline projects forward to insert into a hole drilled through the plywood bulkhead just forward of the wing. Thus, the plane may be disassembled for travel.

RC gliders up to about 6 ft. in span may have either one-piece wings or two separate wing panels (right and left). Big gliders of up to 12 and even 15 ft. always have detachable panels. Stabilizers also may be one piece or in left and right panels, usually but not always in two panels on large machines. Lengths of music wire are epoxied into the fuselage and project a number of inches on each side of the fuselage (this varies with the size of the plane, as does the thickness of the wire—say, from 1/8 to 1/4 in. in diameter).

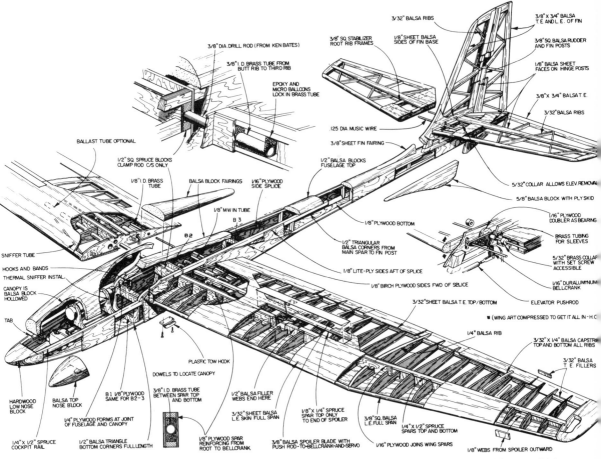

A championship Unlimited class RC sailplane, showing how wing and stabilizer panels slide onto thick steel wire anchors in the fuselage. The thermal sniffer near the nose transmits a signal to the ground receiver so tone pitch indicates climb or descent. (Drawing by Hank Clark, courtesy Model Aviation)

Built into the detachable wing panels are lengths of brass tubing, into which the music wires slide when the panels are pushed into place. The tubing pieces are inclined inside the wing (usually not inclined on tail surfaces) to provide for the dihedral angle or uptilt of the wing (alternately, the music wires may be prebent to the dihedral angle). The tubing is locked in place structurally and epoxied against the wing spars or spar joiners. Detachable panels are required because of transportation problems.

Wing Tips

Kits often provide plastic molded wing tips. If you are going to construct your own, however, there are three basic methods: using shaped soft balsa blocks, segmented sheet-balsa pieces butt-joined together, or laminated thin strips of balsa or spruce. The soft block is cut to its top and side profile, contoured to the cross-section shape, and, if it is large, roughly hollowed with a small gouge for lightness. Left slightly larger than the wing-tip rib, it is glued to the outermost rib, then final-sanded at the same time as the wing frame.

Curved tips are most difficult (viewed from above). The traditional method for achieving a rounded-off tip—which may be circular, a combination of curves, or even elliptical in shape—is to pin down (using waxed paper) about two to five sheet-balsa segments. Each segment has straight ends (cut diagonally) to match the adjoining segment; each has grain running in the long direction. On large models, there may be two to three layers of segments, so arranged that the joints of each layer are staggered for strength. When joined to the wing panel, the wing-tip wood is slanted and/or rounded off where the covering attaches. This is done with a sanding board or block on which several inches of bare plywood extend at one end so as not to abrade the tip rib.

Sanding is done with an assortment of sanding boards and blocks. Here, paper is wrapped around the sanding block to prevent unwanted sanding of ribs as the tip block is sanded to match the wing's airfoil contour. (Randolph photo)

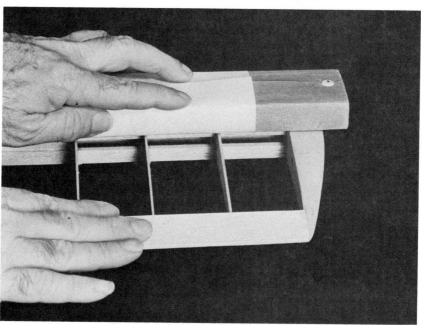

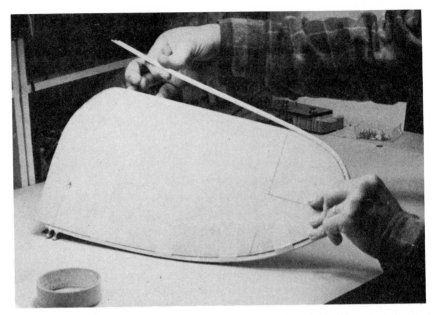

Assembling a laminated wing tip of soaked, glued-together (with thinned white glue) strips, bent around a plywood pattern and held in place with pins and masking tape. It retains its shape when dry.

The bare end slides over the endmost rib, but the sandpapered portion engages the tip pieces, thus ensuring that only the tip is sanded, then rounded off.

The laminated tip, typical of lightweight rubber scale models, some free-flight, and big RC Scale craft, requires a pattern cut from plywood or corrugated cardboard. The pattern matches the shape of the wing as viewed from the top, but is slightly undersized to allow for the accumulated thickness of the laminations. The pattern is pinned or nailed to the bench over waxed paper, which is then wrapped upward and around the outline of the pattern to prevent glue sticking to it (or else make sure that the edge of the pattern is heavily waxed). On very light models, perhaps two laminations will suffice, but big models take three to five, sometimes more.

The wood to be laminated is soaked in hot water or ammonia for at least 15 min. Each lamination is wrapped around the pattern, then held in place by pins driven vertically into the work surface or by small blocks held down with pins. If the model is small, all the laminations can be bent simultaneously. For larger sizes, two laminations are located first, then others added one at a time. The laminations are glued together by thinning aliphatic glue

50-50 with water, then brushing it on the surface of the lamination being added to the one already in place. By working fast, it is possible to assemble any number of laminations in one session, and the work is then allowed to assume shape overnight or until thoroughly dry. The finished "bow" is sanded to the required contours after glueing to the wing frame. The laminates vary in width and thickness according to the nature of the job. Small planes use balsa, large ones spruce, or you can alternate laminations of bass and balsa.

TAIL SURFACES

Winglike in construction, stabilizers and fin rudders employ similar materials but, because these surfaces seem dull to make, there is a tendency among Sport modelers to use simple sheet balsa whenever possible. Sheet balsa is natural for hand-launched gliders, small R.O.G.'s, most CL models, and for RC Sport, whenever the cross section is flat. Thicknesses range from 1/32 to 1/4 in., depending on the size and type of model. Free flight, both powered and soaring types, most often use a built-up frame for lightness. Ultralight construction is imperative and stabilizers in this category often have a "lifting type" cross section—an airfoil rib that contributes to the overall lift of the craft.

All but the smallest of Sport-type control-line and radio-controlled models that have sheet-balsa tails use a hard balsa leading edge butt-joined to the sheet, for cross-grained strength and warp resistance, and to avoid dents. When a movable rudder and elevators are employed on larger models, a hard balsa or spruce square strip along the trailing edge of the stabilizer or fin is added as a spar to prevent breakage close to the fuselage and to provide a firm base for hinging. On larger craft, working elevators and rudders have a hard balsa spar butt-joined along the front edge of the surfaces. In cases where the rudder position compels divided-type elevators (two elevators instead of one long one), this spar (which must be spruce, dowel, etc.) is essential to avoid uneven up-and-down movements of the elevators when the control rod is attached to just one elevator; the force of the airstream thus restricts movement of the other one. If the control horn is attached at the centerline, this problem is eliminated, but many designs do not permit this.

A streamlined cross section, rather than flat sheet balsa, is sometimes preferred for lightness and strength on large CL Stunt ships and RC craft, and always on high-performance RC Pattern ships. In Sport models, the framework of this symmetrical cross-sectioned tail is open construction, with shaped leading and trailing edges, and at least two spars, one top and one bottom.

The Pattern model, which most likely has a molded fiberglass fuselage and a foam-core, sheet-skinned wing, also very likely employs a foam-core, sheet-skinned stabilizer. However, if it has a fiberglass fuselage, the fin is molded as part of the shell as it comes from the kit. In all cases, the movable surfaces are balsa, tapered in cross section toward a thinner trailing edge, with a hard balsa or spruce leading edge for spanwise strength.

An interesting exception to this construction method is the "flying tail." Jet airliners have flying tails, as you will note at the airport. This is a horizontal tail that has no movable elevator. The main spar is located at about 25 percent of the chord, back from the leading edge, and rotates through a bearing in the fuselage or fin. Control is effected by tilting the entire tail around this axis. Seldom used on most models, the flying tail is often employed on large, RC Soaring gliders, and can also be located on top of the fin, a T-tail configuration similar to that of many jet airliners.

LANDING GEAR

Common materials for landing gear are music wire, balsa, spruce, plywood, and sheet aluminum. We shall describe the typical, basic systems employed by Sport fliers.

Free-Flight R.O.G.

For these models, a single piece of thin music wire is bent at the top of the vee with a needlenose pliers to an inverted U-shape, which then slides downward over the motor stick; the joint is wrapped with thread and glued.

Small Free-Flight Cabin

For a rubber-powered model a small sandwich is made by laminating two pieces of sheet balsa and a center piece of plywood the same thickness as the wire (usually 1/16 in.). The plywood piece is smaller in width and depth to allow for the wire thickness. The wire is bent at the top into a wide inverted U-shape that fits around the top and sides of the plywood piece. All these pieces, and the wire, are glued together, and small C-clamps are used to hold the unit until the glue sets. The sandwich then is glued between the fuselage sides at the bottom. (On very small models the wire is bound with thread to a bottom crosspiece and glued.)

For larger rubber-powered or small gas planes, a rectangle of plywood is cut so that its width overlaps the fronts of the side crosspieces of a built-up fuselage flush with the outer surfaces of the sides, and notched at the bottom corners to fit over the longerons. The depth typically is one-fourth to one-third the depth of the fuselage at that point, sometimes full depth. A full-depth plywood bulkhead is not common on rubber-powered models because of its weight and the necessary passageway for the rubber. Before the plywood is installed, the wire is bent with a sharp vee at the top, then attached to the front face of the plywood by means of thread, fine wire, or, on larger gas models, J-bolts (available in hobby shops). If thread or wire is used, two pairs of 1/16-in. holes are drilled for each leg of the vee, and then the thread or wire is sewn back and forth over the landing-gear wire, then glued. If J-bolts are used, three are sufficient, one at the vee at the top and one each close to the bottom of the ply. If the model has an open framework with the plywood resting against the front faces of vertical and bottom crosspieces, triangular balsa gussets reinforce the adjacent uprights of the body. And when the siding is sheet balsa, the plywood mount butts against the inside surface and reinforcing strips are glued to the sides (inside) against the plywood to prevent its breaking loose.

Small Free-Flight and RC Scale

While some models in this category (the Cessna 140 and 195 are typical) have but a single strut as described before, others (North American's Mustang, for example) have that strut running vertically up to the wing rather than to the fuselage, thus requiring two separate struts, one out on each wing. Many types involve double struts (like a vee) on each side of the fuselage. Some have diagonal struts when viewed from the front. Still others (the Spirit of St. Louis and the Robin, for example) have a combination of two struts extending like a vee down to the axle, with another vertical strut from the axle up to a wing strut, extending from that joint upward to the top fuselage longeron. On ultrasmall models (such as Peanuts with maximum wing spans of 13 in.), the struts are simply streamlined by sanding them from hard balsa strips with their upper ends slanted to make flush joints against the fuselage, and are glued in place along the wire legs. This is done after covering, so that tiny scabs of tissue are removed from the fuselage longerons, to allow wood-to-wood contact of the joints.

Most Scale models generally combine thin, bent music wire with balsa streamlining. One piece of wire provides both axles. It runs up to the fuselage corner, straight across the fuselage bottom, and down to the other axle. The second piece for the rear vee strut is more difficult, since its ends adjacent to the axle must be bent to run parallel to the front strut for approximately 1/4 in. This joint is then wrapped with thread and glued, or if more strength is needed, wrapped with a few turns of thin copper wire and soldered for a rigid joint. If there are struts extending from the axle joint to the centerline or far corners of the fuselage bottom on the opposite side, the ends of this third vee are included in the wrapped joint near the axle.

The wood streamlining may simply be a flat piece rounded off or stream-lined at the rear end, grooved along its front edge to fit over the wire, and glued. On large models, silk or thin fiberglass cloth is wrapped around the strut and doped or epoxied. The epoxy may be thinned to creamlike brushing consistency with butyrate dope thinner or epoxy thinner. (It takes a day for this to cure, if thinned.)

Frequently, the area between the front and rear struts is filled in with balsa or plywood. The silk or fiberglass cloth is wrapped around the single strut that results. On large Scale models such struts may have a thick cross sec-tion and balsa or even plywood laminations added to the inside and outside surfaces of the strut; the whole assembly is then streamlined before covering.

Control-Line Models

The most popular plane configuration in this category is the Profile design, and the most common landing gear material is music wire, although sheet-aluminum landing legs with stub axles are also common on competition Pro-file forms, especially Racing models. For smaller Profiles, the landing gear is a single piece of wire, bent similarly to the gear on the small free-flight R.O.G.'s. But, whereas the R.O.G. gear is shaped to an inverted U at the apex of the vee of the gear, the CL Profile gear has a very deep, thin U, correspond-ing in depth to the depth of the fuselage. The wire slides down over the thin fuselage and is held to it by means of soft wire passed through holes drilled through the profile, wrapped several times around the wire, and glued. For larger models, a wire bender is increasingly necessary, but kits supply the wire already formed.

On medium-size Profile ships, the wire is held to the plywood doublers that face the balsa of the fuselage proper by J-bolts or landing-gear straps. The strap is a small ready-shaped piece of nylon or aluminum, with a semicircular portion to fit over the wire and two short tabs through which small screws are inserted into the wood for retention. For larger craft, especially competi-tion forms, two separate aluminum sheet-metal struts butt against each side of the fuselage profile, and are held in place by 3-48 or 4-40 machine screws (bolts), which pass through both gear pieces and the fuselage.

Stub axles either come in the kit, are found at the hobby shop, or can be made from, for example, 1/8-in. (4-40) steel bolts with a nut screwed tight against the outside face of each strut before the wheel is installed. When heavy wire is required, it is possible to use a two-piece gear. Instead of the U-bend at the top of the one-piece gear, each piece has its upper end bent at right angles to insert into a hole drilled into the profile. This prevents the strut from twisting. Struts are held in place by J-bolts or landing-gear straps, as before.

Two-Sided CL Fuselage

Although a music-wire gear similar to some free-flight landing gear described before is common, such wires are subject to bending at the juncture with the fuselage corner. Therefore, a single aluminum sheet-metal-strut gear is often used. The center portion of this one-piece gear is flat to butt to a plywood insert in the fuselage bottom, and is attached by means of two or four (depending on the plane's size) self-tapping sheet-metal screws or small machine screws with nuts on the inside of the plywood foundation piece. If you have the required cutting equipment—such as a Dremel jigsaw—you can cut your own metal gear from sheet aluminum (usually 3/32 to 1/8 in. thick). Hobby shops carry a full range of preformed metal gear and, of course, any kit supplies the gear blank already bent to shape, with only some rounding off (filing) of corners being desirable, though not essential.

Wing-Mounted CL Landing Gear

On small sheet-balsa craft, each wire landing gear strut attaches to the flat side of a thin plywood base that glues into a shallow recess cut in the bottom of the wooden wing. This type of "split" gear is often employed on larger open-frame or foam-core sheeted wings, but the mounting is more substantial than in smaller craft.

On larger craft it is essential to provide torsional action to the wire gear attachment to absorb landing shocks. The best method is to use a hardwood

Torsion shock-absorbing landing gear on a Pilot Model ready-to-fly RC. The wire inserts through a hole in the right-hand side of the hard channel block, free to twist at the strut end.

landing-gear block. This block (in kits or from a hobby shop) has a channeled end-to-end groove to accept the wire. Adjacent to one end of the channel block, a hole is drilled through to the thickness of the wire, perpendicular to the slot. If you do this yourself, place the block in a vise or drill press with the groove upward.

The wire is bent at the upper end of the strut at an angle to match the wing (at a right angle, for example, if the wing has no dihedral), extended for the length of the groove in the block, and then bent upward at the appropriate angle to insert through the hole in the block. Two landing-gear straps across the wire hold it inside the channel in the block; small self-tapping screws hold the straps to the channel block. When the gear sustains a rearward shock upon landing, the portion of the wire in the block channel will twist, but not deform, and it is firmly anchored by the short length of wire that passes through the hole in the block.

In the open-frame wing, notches are cut into the required number of wing ribs to accept the landing-gear channel block; each rib involved is laminated in the vicinity of the block with a short length of 1/32- to 1/16-in. plywood, notched to fit over the block, and matching the neighboring rib contours. Blocks are epoxied in place.

In the case of a foam-core wing, the gear block must be recessed. This requires cutting a rectangular hole to fit the block, through the sheet-balsa skin of the wing panel (or in the foam, if there is no skin). The full depth of the recess is attained by removing the foam with a sharp knife, or better yet, the appropriate X-Acto gouge. Experienced builders attach a shaped wire loop to a soldering gun and remove the foam by sliding the heated loop along the cutout. (Never inhale fumes from foam when cutting by heat.)

Radio Control

While basic landing-gear configurations suffice for many RC craft, the addition of remote control introduces some intriguing gadgetry and full-scale-type features. Most powered models are equipped with a steerable nose wheel for better ground handling, straight takeoff runs, and to avoid nose-overs. The unit usually is supplied with kits that feature a tricycle landing gear, but it is also available by itself at larger hobby shops. Basically, it consists of a single music-wire strut that incorporates a torsion-spring shock absorber, and an adjustable steering arm that is activated by the push-pull action of a pushrod running to the rudder servo. Steering is automatic when the rudder is turned. Construction is involved because the builder has to attach the nylon bearing blocks to a plywood fire wall or nose piece and adjust the strut length and movement.

The retractable landing gear, common on Scale and Pattern-type craft, is

Here's how a shock-absorbing nose-gear strut attaches to the fire wall on an RC model. Nylon bearing blocks allow the strut to steer by means of a tiller arm actuated from the servo inside the fuselage.

the ultimate in realism. "Retracts" are either mechanically or pneumatically operated, and handle both two-wheel and tricycle-wheel arrangements. On Pattern planes and many Scale aircraft, the wing-mounted gear swings inward toward the aircraft centerline to retract, while the nose wheel swings rearward and up into the fuselage. This landing gear is included in certain kits, although the components are also available by mail order or from better hobby shops. Careful work is required for their installation. For example, wheel wells must be accurately prepared, as well as spaces to accommodate folding parts. Wheel-well covers attached to the struts may conceal the retracted wheel, especially on Scale models. For certain Scale craft, such as the P-40 and Corsair, the main gear folds backward instead of sideways, requiring the strut with wheel to rotate as well as fold. Retracts are operated by a special servo, activated by a two-position switch on the transmitter top—that is, "down" and "up." If construction to accommodate retracts is tedious, detailed instructions supplied with these mechanisms do make things clear.

In the case of large Scale craft, full-scale-type shock-absorbing gear is imperative, because otherwise bad landings cause repairs that take weeks. Of course, only experienced builders should tackle such subjects. One really needs to be an all-round old-fashioned craftsman. It is commonplace for such builders to fabricate telescoping tubular shock struts containing tiny coil springs, or to concoct hinged strut attachments with shock loads taken by springs. Such gear is a machinist's delight.

Good construction requires the builder to understand plans and directions before a project is begun. And, above all, hobbyists must discipline themselves not to rush. With patience and care, all things become possible.

chapter six _____

Power Sources

Many forms of power plants and energy have been tried in model airplanes: clockwork, compressed air, carbon dioxide, gasoline, alcohol, rockets, pulse jets, electric motors, rubber strands, gas turbines, steam, and even solar energy. Most of these power sources have proved feasible, and attract modelers with a variety of interests. Most visible is the "gas" engine—but when the hordes of youngsters are considered, it is possible most models in use today are rubber powered. Electric power is solidly established and has a significant future. However, the dropping cost of solar cells interests a handful of experimenters, and carbon dioxide engines also fascinate a growing group of specialists. Rocket power, pulse-jet engines, and compressed-air engines are seen less frequently.

GAS ENGINES

The common gas engine operates by the timed compression and expansion (by explosion) of a vaporized mixture of air with gasoline, alcohol, or kerosene-base fuels, which drives a piston inside a cylinder, rotating a crankshaft to which the propeller is affixed. Modelers most commonly use the two-cycle engine, and sometimes the more costly four-cycle design. The number of cycles relates to how many up-and-down strokes the piston makes inside the cylinder per revolution of the crankshaft. The most popular gas engines are, in order, glow engines, spark-ignition engines, and diesels (compression-ignition engines). (The carbon dioxide engine and the compressed-air engine do not derive power from timed explosions of a fuel vapor; the carbon dioxide or air is compressed to high pressure in a cylindrical container within the fuselage and the piston is driven by expansion of the "gas.")

Technopower's seven-cylinder radial glow-ignition engine in a Sterling Stearman PT-17 model. A four-cycle engine, it has a master connecting rod and overhead valves as in full-scale power plants.

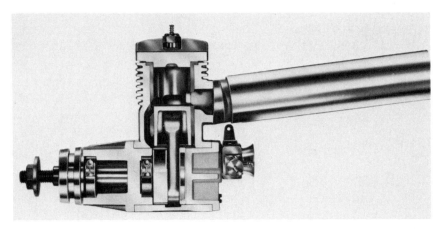

Cutaway of a K&B rear-exhaust Schnuerle-ported engine with rear rotary intake and double ball-bearing (ring-type) crankshaft. This 6.5-cc displacement engine is especially designed for Pylon RC racing.

One hears terms such as Schnuerle, baffle, lapped pistons, and ABC in connection with these engines. The lapped piston is the simplest, having a steel cylinder liner and an aluminum piston, fitted by honing or grinding (by the manufacturer). It requires considerable breaking in before flying. Lapped engines depend on close fits of piston and cylinder for compression, and have more friction between piston and cylinder wall. A piston ring (or rings) in more sophisticated engines than the lapped type provides a seal with less metal-to-metal friction; it requires less breaking in, and attains higher rpm. Schnuerle porting allows very high rpm for maximum speed and power; if you look through the exhaust port of one of these engines, you will note that the piston does not have a fencelike baffle across its top. Non-Schnuerle engines have this baffle. ABC means that the piston is aluminum (A), the cylinder liner is bronze (B), and the liner is chromeplated (C). These metals have a more compatible coefficient of expansion and are less easily damaged from overheating. The ultimate glow engine (much more costly) is an ABC with Schnuerle porting, and ball-bearing-supported shaft rather than a plain bronze bearing.

Engine displacement (size) is not the sole criterion when choosing a power plant. In displacements of 0.049 to 0.051 cu. in. and under, Cox or Testor's engines are universally used. In larger sizes, there are more design variations for the different kinds of flying. Such things as bore-to-stroke ratios, intake opening sizes, and port timing must be taken into account. Control-line Combat, Racing, and Speed models require high rpm engines (well over 20,000 rpm) turning small-diameter, high-pitched propellers. Competition free flight has similar requirements, but low-pitched props. RC Pylon and Pattern

GAS ENGINE PROPELLER SIZES—CONTROL LINE

ENGINE	STUNT/SPORT/ SCALE	COMBAT/CARRIER	SPEED/PROTO	RACING	TEAM RACING
.049	6–3, 6–4		6–5		
.09	7–4, 7–5				
.15	8–4, 8–5	7–4, 7–4·1/2	6–7, 6–7·1/2	7–5, 7–6	7–8, 7–9·1/2
.19–.23	9–4, 9–5, 9–6				
.29	10–6		7–9·1/2, 7–10, 7–10·1/2		8–8, 8–8·1/2
.35	10–6	8·1/2–6·3/4, 9–5, 9–7, 9–8		8–8, 9–6, 9–7	
.40	11–6	9–7, 9–8		8–8, 8–8·1/2, 8–9	
.45	11–6, 12–5				
.60	12–6, 13–5	9–8	9–12·1/2, 9–13, 9–13·1/2		

GAS ENGINE PROPELLER SIZES—FREE FLIGHT

ENGINE	ALL CLASSES
.049	6–3, 6–4
.09	7–3, 7–4
.15	7–4, 8–4
.19	8–4, 8–5, 9–4
.23	8–4, 8–5, 9–4
.29	9–6, 10–4
.35	9–6, 10–4
.40	10–4, 10–5
.60	12–4, 12–5

GAS ENGINE PROPELLER SIZES—RADIO CONTROL

ENGINE	PATTERN/SPORT	SCALE	STUNT/SPORT/ SCALE	PYLON RACING
.049	6–3, 6–4	6–4, 7–3	6–3, 6–4	
.09	7–3, 7–4	7–4, 8–4	7–4, 7–5	
.15	8–4, 8–6, 9–4	8–4, 8–6, 9–4	8–4, 8–5	7–4·1/2, 7–5
.19–.23	9–4, 9–5	9–4, 9–5	9–4, 9–5, 9–6	
.29–.35	9–6, 10–6	10–6, 11–4	10–6	
.40	10–6, 11–4	11–4, 12–4	10–6	8·1/2–6·3/4, 8·1/2–7, 8·1/2–7·1/4
.45	11–4, 11–6	12–4, 12–6	11–6	
.60	11–7, 11–7·1/2, 11–7·3/4	12–6, 13–5, 11–4	11–6, 11–7, 12–6	
.70		14–4, 14–6		
.80		14–4, 14–6		
.90		14–6, 16–6		
1.40		18–6, 18–8		
2.00		20–6, 20–8		

Note: In all columns except ''Engine,'' the first number is diameter; the second number, pitch.

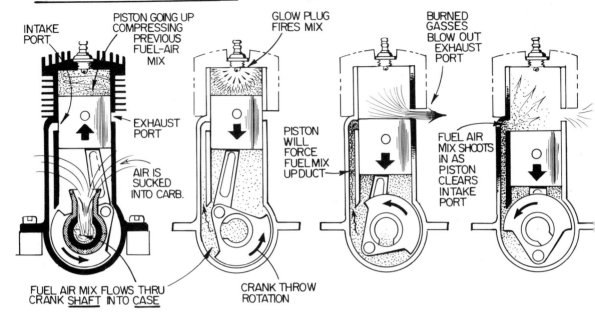

The most common type of engine has glow-plug ignition and operates on the two-cycle principle, delivering a power stroke for each revolution of the crankshaft (four-cycle engines give one power stroke for every two revolutions).

models have high rpm (Schnuerle) engines turning high-pitched propellers of small to medium diameter. RC Sport ships turn average diameter and pitch combinations at, say, 10,000 to 13,000 rpm. CL Stunt ships and many RC Sport and Scale craft emphasize torque, or the brute power to turn larger propellers at somewhat lower rpm. Sport free flight, Oldtimer, and Antique craft use larger diameter, lower pitched propellers turning at relatively low rpm.

Two-Cycle Engines

The fuel/air mixture enters the two-cycle engine by means of a carburetor (think of it as an atomizer) that, on most engines, is located in front of the cylinder. A squarish hole cut into the hollow crankshaft covers and uncovers the fuel-mixture passageway at the bottom of the carburetor in a precisely timed manner as the crankshaft rotates. A bypass(es) within the cylinder block connects the crankcase cavity with the upper cylinder, above the piston. As you turn the propeller a simple operational sequence takes place. An engine with an air intake in front is called a "shaft valve." Some engines have a rear intake and utilize a "rotary" valve, a disk just inside the rear crankcase cover, turned by the crankshaft.

Instead of following traditional descriptions of the two-cycle sequence, we will approach the engine exactly as we find it when we are ready to start it. Assume that a few drops of raw fuel have been injected into the carburetor's venturi opening to "prime" the engine. The normal starting procedure is to turn the propeller a few revolutions (without ignition—either spark or glow—being activated) in order to suck vaporized fuel into the crankcase and to force it through the bypass to the upper cylinder. At this point, attach the booster lead to the glow plug and flip the propeller to start. The piston will be in the lower cylinder. On the first stroke, the piston travels upward toward top dead center. As it does so, it first closes off the intake and then the exhaust openings in the cylinder wall. Additionally, the upward-moving piston creates a partial vacuum within the crankcase, which causes more fuel mixture to be drawn into the case through the carburetor. As the piston reaches top dead center, the heated glow (or spark) plug explodes the compressed vaporized mixture between the piston and cylinder head, driving the piston down for a power stroke. The intake part in the crankshaft closes at this point.

As the piston travels downward it first uncovers the exhaust port, which allows the burned gases to escape, then it uncovers the intake port opening. Since the exhaust port is still open, the inrushing fuel mixture above the downward-moving piston "scavenges" the exhaust, forcing remnants through the exhaust port. Continuing to the bottom of its stroke, the piston acts as a pump to force new fuel up from the crankcase through the bypass to the upper cylinder. As the shaft rotates, the piston drives upward once more. On its way up it again first closes the intake port, then the exhaust port, trapping and compressing the fuel mixture in the upper cylinder, where again the vapor is exploded for another power stroke and repetition of the process.

It will be seen that the piston has two strokes, one up (intake) and one down (power), during a single revolution of the crankshaft. Thus, the two-cycle engine delivers a power stroke for each revolution of the shaft—whereas the four-cycle engine delivers a power stroke on every second revolution.

Four-Cycle Engines

Having intake and exhaust valves at the top of the head, which are mechanically operated like those in most automobile engines, the four-cycle engine delivers a power stroke on every second revolution of the crankshaft, unlike the two-cycle engine, which has a power stroke for every revolution. Much more complex and costly, these engines operate more quietly at lower rpm than the two-cycle, and have greater torque to turn a larger propeller in

The Enya four-stroke 0.40 engine. The mechanism of pushrods, rocker arms, and spring-loaded overhead valves shows clearly. It burns alcohol-based fuel and has glow-plug ignition.

a realistic manner for Scale models. The four-cycle system precisely times the mechanical opening and shutting of intake and exhaust valves (as in an automobile engine) for improved efficiency and thus fuel economy.

On the first stroke as the piston travels downward, the intake valve in the cylinder head opens to admit fresh fuel mixture and the exhaust valve is shut; then, as the piston travels upward (second stroke) both valves are shut, so that when it is at top dead center, the fuel/air mixture is compressed and exploded, driving the piston downward for a power stroke (third stroke). On the upward portion of the fourth stroke, the intake valve remains shut, but the exhaust valve is open to permit the exhaust to escape. Thus, it takes two up-and-down trips (four strokes) of the piston (two revolutions of the shaft) to take in fuel, compress and explode it, and then exhaust.

It is interesting to note that our four-cycle engines often are the glow type, whereas the big chain-saw types are usually two-cycle ignition engines.

Glow Engines

The word "glow" in glow engine comes from the presence of a glow plug rather than a spark plug. The glow plug has a thin platinum wire coil element

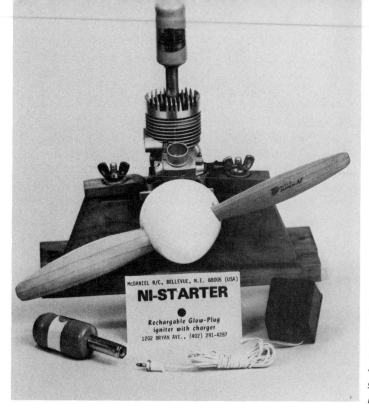

A rechargeable nickel cadmium boost-er battery is most reliable for standard glow plugs. The McDaniel battery in corporates a booster connector that attaches to the plug (by pushing down and turning to lock in place). In the fore-ground is a duplicate unit showing a plug-in charger.

that is heated by an external battery source when starting the engine, but it continues to glow from the heat of the exploding fuel, thus keeping the engine running, after the external booster/starter battery is disconnected.

Glow fuel consists of a mixture of nitromethane (nitro), methanol (alcohol), and a lubricating oil (plus igniters, detergents, etc., blended by the manufac-turer). Common mixtures for Sport flying contain 5 to 10 percent nitro, and approximately 20 percent oil. Racing fuels go to 40 percent or more nitro, but engine and plug wear is then rapid. Nitro improves starting and idling characteristics. Engines will operate without nitro—in Europe nitro is vir-tually unobtainable—though the engine is usually slightly modified for best results. A nitroless F.A.I. fuel is required in international competitions in which engine power is a major factor, except for events in which the diesel is preferred for economy (higher mileage).

The amount of fuel admitted to the engine is governed by a needle valve in the carburetor, which when screwed in reduces the amount of liquid fuel in relation to air, and vice versa. On variable-speed engines common in radio control, the throttle fuel/air mixture is increased and decreased in volume to vary rpm, usually by moving a rotatable barrel, which varies the air opening inside the carburetor, by means of a servo (or by a third line with control-line models). The proportional servo enables a varied choice of power settings between wide open and idle. RC carburetors have a second, "low speed" needle valve or control screw for adjusting the proportion of air and raw fuel, which is different from the one required for full power. Most control-line models are flown wide open, but many have two speeds, open and idle (as in the Navy Carrier event), effected by a third line running to the control handle held in the pilot's hand.

The newcomer to radio-controlled modeling often has difficulty adjusting the low-speed carburetor control. On many of the more economical engines, low speed is adjusted by a small spring-loaded, thread-adjustable knob. On most engines, screwing in this control reduces air flow at low speed, resulting in a richer, not leaner, fuel mixture. However, there is at least one engine that uses this adjustment to reduce fuel flow, so that when the control is screwed in the mixture becomes leaner. For such reasons, you should always follow the engine manufacturer's directions to the letter. Many people learn to operate certain popular types, then assume a replacement engine of another make is necessarily the same. It may not be.

Further, engines that don't have this control but instead have a second needle valve, or a slotted-head adjustment on the side of the carburetor opposite to the one with the high-speed needle, are adjusted for low speed in the same way you would use the high-speed needle. When this needle is screwed in, the fuel supply is reduced for a leaner mixture; when screwed out, the mixture is made richer. In some carburetors, this movement of the low-speed adjustment upsets the setting of the high-speed needle, which then must be readjusted after the low speed has been set. In such cases it is usually necessary to establish the low-speed setting first for proper throttle response, then fine-tune the high-speed setting.

Diesels

In the diesel engine, the two-cycle function is the same, but instead of a glow plug there is an adjustable contra-piston in the cylinder head, which adjusts the compression ratio. The compression ratio-varying lever is located where a glow or spark plug usually is found; in addition to the true diesel, there are special conversion heads (Davis heads) available to change a suitably robust glow engine into a diesel.

Ignition takes place through compression of the fuel mixture as the piston attains top dead center. These more robust engines have a very high compression ratio, ensuring self-ignition (compression-ignition). One common diesel fuel mixture is about one-third kerosene, one-third ether, one-third oil,

A diesel engine burning a kerosene-and-ether-based fuel offers greater torque for larger propellers and fuel economy. Actually, this is a Davis conversion of a .60 glow engine. An Allen-head adjustment screw on the top enables the pilot to get a varying compression ratio to adjust for starting and high rpm. (Preston photo)

and other ingredients, including 1-1/2 to 2 percent amyl nitrate (for antiknock purposes).

The diesel is more difficult to operate than a glow engine because the variable head compression makes for an additional control to adjust. There are infinite combinations of head compression and needle-valve settings that must be quickly matched for optimum rpm and reliable running. Fuel economy makes the diesel supreme in control-line Team Racing.

Spark Ignition

Taking a mixture of unleaded gasoline and oil—say, 20 or more to 1, these engines are used in very large RC craft for power and fuel economy (glow fuel costs much more), and in Oldtimer types with or without radio control, where the builder seeks to duplicate the once-common gas-ignition engines that dominated the scene years ago.

Ignition is achieved by a timed spark across the electrodes of the spark

Model airplane engines have displacements ranging from 0.02 to 3.00 cu. in. or more, the biggest developing as much as 5 horsepower. The 2-c.i.d. Quadra (left) is a two-stroke engine with magneto ignition that runs on a mixture of unleaded gasoline and oil. At right, the glow Cox Pee Wee 0.02 with tank mount. (Preston photo)

plug by means of a spark-coil and condenser system, by a magneto (common on big engines), or by electronic (solid-state) ignition somewhat similar to that found in many automobiles. If a spark coil or magneto ignition is used, "points" are located at the front end of the crankshaft, just behind the propeller. Points are a pair of electrical contacts that come together (close) or separate (open); it is the same principle at work under the distributor cap on many automobiles. They make and break (that is, close and open) by means of a cam on the shaft that controls the timing of a high-voltage spark across the spark-plug electrodes.

Fuel Tanks

Several basic types of fuel tanks provide for free-flight, control-line, and radio-controlled craft, with many variations on each theme. Tanks normally are metal or nylon, and vary in capacity from a fraction of an ounce up to 32 oz. Small engines, such as those by both Cox and Testor's, often have a combination tank/mount built into the engine and no separate tank is necessary.

Pressure Fuel Feed

The purpose of a pressure system is to obtain consistent fuel feed, and/or force a greater volume of fuel to the engine for maximum rpm, or to allow the remote location of a fuel tank (as on the center of gravity) to minimize variations in the plane's balance as fuel is consumed. Pressure systems do not concern the beginner.

Fuel is generally pressurized in the tank by two means, crankcase pressure and muffler pressure. All pressure systems require a sealed tank, which has only two lines (if there is a third line, it must be blocked off before starting): one to admit pressure and the other to supply fuel to the engine. With crankcase pressure, a tap is usually located on the rear crankcase cover for the pressure line. Crankcase pressure rams fuel to the engine, and thus sees use

K&B 0.40 RC engine with Perry pump and carburetor. Fuel pumps are often employed on high-performance Pattern RC machines, and also in cases where a remotely located tank is desirable, especially in scale models. The fuel line from the tank connects to a nipple on the far side of the pump. (K&B Manufacturing photo)

in competition free flight, control-line Speed and Racing types, and on many Pylon Racing and Pattern models in radio control—all of which require maximum rpm. Muffler pressure is lower than crankcase pressure and is easier to install. It requires a pressure tap on the engine muffler—many mufflers come with such a tap. Other unique high-pressure systems are used by competition fliers in free flight and control-line Combat and Speed. Such fliers may use ordinary pen-bladders or baby pacifiers, which are blown up with raw fuel as if they were balloons.

A third form of supplying pressure feed is by the fuel pump; this is most often encountered on RC Pattern craft. The manufactured pump attaches to the rear of the crankcase or into the fuel feed line, and is normally used with a special fine-jet, precision-controlled carburetor, the Perry pump and carburetor, for example. Robart supplies a variety of pumps, with one type capable of returning excess pumped fuel to the tank. Pumps normally are used for engines of 0.40 or larger displacement.

Free-Flight Tanks

The simplest form of tank, for the Sport model, is metal, cubical or rectangular in shape. (See Perfect's display rack at hobby shops.) Fuel capacity is small due to the plane's short engine runs. Brass tubing fuel-line connections are already soldered in place, one for filling, one for venting, and the third to feed the engine. The feed tube enters the tank at the bottom front, extending to the tank's rear; the vent and fill tubes are side by side on the top. As fuel is pumped in, the displaced air escapes through the vent, as does the overflow.

When the plane is launched and climbs, fuel is forced by acceleration and gravity to the back of the tank, where it is sucked in by the feed line. As fuel diminishes, air enters the tank through the vent tube so that a vacuum is not created—in which case, the engine would not draw fuel. External fuel lines are usually clear neoprene, surgical rubber, or silicone tubing pushed over the short brass tubes that project from the tank.

Tank location must be as close to the engine as possible (unless it is a crankcase-pressure, pacifier, or pen-bladder tank) to minimize fuel-draw variations that cause uneven running, and at a height related to the engine's needle valve. In unpressurized tanks, one-third of the fuel level is above an imaginary line running horizontally through the needle valve, and two-thirds of the fuel is below that line. As the fuel level drops and the weight of the fuel decreases, the engine tends to run leaner. The fuel above the line actually creates slight pressure feed, whereas fuel below the line is pulled into the engine by crankcase suction alone. Were the tank below the needle valve, the run would depend entirely on suction, and as the fuel level dropped, the proportion of air to raw fuel would increase at the needle-valve body, leaning out the engine. The length of draw progressively increases as the fuel level drops while the nose is tilted up. The run becomes increasingly "lean" and the engine could stop. Pressure is often used in Free Flight competition.

Free-Flight Timer/Tanks

All free-flight models compel a limitation of engine run. Competition craft are permitted short runs, like 7 or 10 sec. because they climb so high that the total flight time carries them far downwind, necessitating huge flying fields and time-consuming chases that delay the competition, perhaps preventing all competitors from getting in their required number of flights. On Sport models, an untimed engine run means a lost model. Competition craft normally use a mechanical timer (such as those made by Seelig or Tatone) that ticks off the seconds to the selected position that will cut off fuel by pinching the feed line. (These timers also may activate a dethermalizer device, normally set to bring the model down within 3 min., or even adjust a rudder tab—and sometimes the stabilizer angle—to retrim the plane for gliding.)

The Sport free-flighter normally flies small 1/2A-class powered models (0.02- to 0.049-cu.-in. displacement) that require a limited tank capacity (and usually do not have a timer). Some 1/2A engines have combined tank

Dad and son hand-start a Cox 0.049 in a 1/2A free-flight competition model. A booster lead, to heat the glow plug for starting, clips to the glow plug and to a doorbell battery in the field box.

mounts. To limit the run for small sites, a wooden cube or other small object is placed in the tank to reduce its capacity. Clever makeshifts are used: for example, a glass eyedropper, or a coiled length of fuel-line tubing, with the open end upward for filling. These forms of tanks are located so that one-third the fuel level is above the needle-valve position, to prevent lean running and engine failures as the fuel level drops. A trial engine run is timed to determine the correct amount of fuel. (Comparatively rare is the flood-off timed system, used only in competition, by which fuel is injected directly into the venturi, thus stopping the engine.)

Control Line

Since the CL model flies in circles, centrifugal force pushes fuel to the outside of the tank. Additionally, the Stunt model is flown both inverted and right-side up, while doing aerobatics. The fuel line, therefore, is usually located as far as possible toward the outside of the flying circle, and on the same level as the needle valve (so that feed is the same when the plane is inverted). A good example of this is the wedge cross section, the narrow edge of which is toward the outside of the flying circle. The fuel-feed line enters the front of the tank at the extreme outside edge, extending to the rear, also at the outermost corner. Since the tank must perform inverted and upright, the fill tube in a three-line system enters from the top and extends to the bottom, while the overflow extends up through the bottom to the top. No matter what position the tank is in, one or the other tube provides venting. (Of course, a pressure system can also be employed.)

A control-line racing tank with fast-fill plug for pit stops. The plug seals the tank pressure tight with the first flip of the propeller. CL tanks exist for all competition events. (Courtesy Carolina-Taffinder—Taff's and Randy's Custom Tanks)

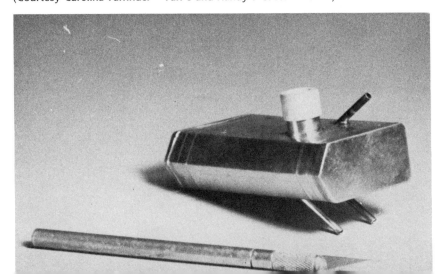

Competition fliers use all sorts of tanks designed for steady fuel feed, as well as variations on the wedge tank. Some tanks have baffles to prevent fuel frothing and surging. In Combat craft, the common pen-bladder or baby-pacifier tank is contained in a spanwise compartment between the wing spar and the leading edge (on the outside wing normally), and extending at right angles to the aircraft centerline; or it can be placed within the fuselage of a Speed model. But for everyday Sport flying, the wedge-type tank is adequate. The tank is always positioned half above and half below the needle valve, and as close as possible to the engine to avoid variations in fuel feed, hence power, as the ship changes between inverted and upright flight. If the tank were too high, the engine would run rich rightside up and lean when inverted.

Radio Control

Small limited-stunting designs powered by 0.02 and 0.049 engines can be flown with a normal free-flight tank or engine tank mount. However, most RC machines are larger and aerobatic. Not only do they fly upright or inverted the same as control-line planes, but they perform rolling maneuvers, and some can climb vertically continuously. Special tank designs have evolved to suit them.

Since fuel is not always pushed by centrifugal force to the outside as in control-line models, but may be forced against the sides, top, or bottom of the tank, in various combinations, the fuel-line pickup necessarily must be flexible inside the tank so that it reaches all spots at the tank rear. The pickup inside the tank is a flexible tube with a weighted end called a "clunk." The clunk position is governed by gravity, and assures fuel flow regardless of the tank position.

Varying in capacity from 1-1/2 to 32 oz.—engines vary from 0.02- to as much as 5-cu.-in. displacement—tanks are usually made of nylon, and may be roughly rectangular, oval, round, or of some other cross section, such as round on top, flat on bottom. After it is purchased, an RC tank requires final assembly—fittings, clunk, and pieces of tubing are in the package. Most tanks provide three exit holes for line connections. One is sealed, and requires opening by the flier if he or she wishes to use a third line. Both three- and two-line systems are common. Many tanks provide brass tubing that must be shaped by grasping both ends of the tubing and bending it around a round object. Don't use pliers—they cause kinks. K&S Engineering and Harry Higley offers simple tubing benders.

All radio-control systems should have a filter (a metal cartridge containing a fine-mesh screen) in the fuel-feed line between tank and engine. Most fliers place a second filter in the fuel line that is connected to the filler bulb or that

An O.S. 0.15 engine mounted on a plywood plate bolted to hardwood motor bearers in the author's Goldberg Eaglet RC trainer. The tank is the three-line nylon Sullivan slant type (the lines are for filling, feed, and muffler pressure). RC tanks come in many shapes and sizes.

A Super Tigre 0.25 Schnuerle-ported engine installed in a Goldberg Falcon 56 RC. Note the silicone tubing lines leading from the Kraft 6-oz. tank, arranged to avoid kinking; the brass tubing transfers through the plywood fire wall; the fuel filler in the feed line; and the A.M.A. acorn-type safety propeller nut. A high-speed needle valve shows below the carburetor venturi; the low-speed needle valve control is on the opposite side. (Preston photo)

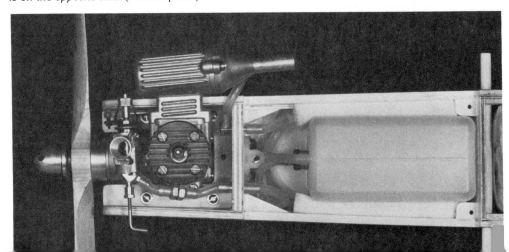

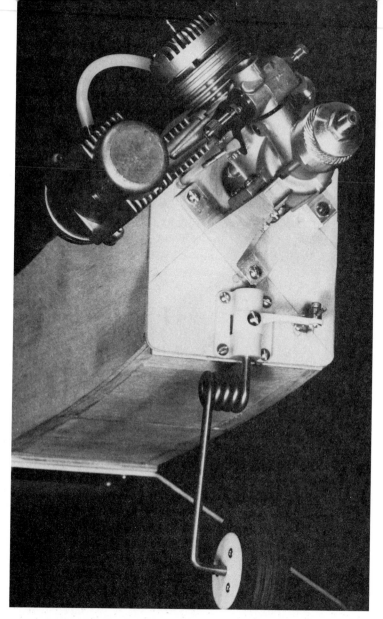

A Super Tigre 0.46 glow engine installed in a Sig Kavalier RC. The muffler location is that typically found on all engines having 0.09 or more displacement. The silicone tube extending from the muffler to the tank supplies pressure for consistent engine runs. Sig divided-type engine mounts are shown, but numerous other types of mounts exist, most being one-piece units made from aluminum, fiberglass-filled nylon, etc. (Preston photo)

drops down to the bottom of the fuel can when a remote pump is used for filling. Otherwise, tiny foreign objects clog the feed hole in the throttle barrel, causing engine failure and/or lean runs. (A lean run can destroy an engine.) Starting becomes difficult and variations in throttle response are encountered. To cure this condition, remove the fuel line from the engine and blow fuel through the needle-valve opening; disassemble the filter to carefully remove debris that clogs the fine screen. Be sure a filter with screw-on ends is tightly assembled to avoid air leaks that cause erratic running.

Muffler pressure is desirable for steady, reliable operation in engines of 0.09 displacement and up. Crankcase pressure is of a higher order, more complex, but it also makes possible the remote and/or lower location of the tank, as for Scale purposes. The radio-control tank normally is located on the aircraft centerline, but with its fuel-feed line about 1/4 in. lower than the needle valve.

When buying a tank and fuel-line tubing, advise the dealer whether it is for glow fuel, gas and oil, or diesel fuel. (Magazine ads show the different varieties.)

Common RC tank sizes for glow engines are: less than 1 oz. for 1/2A (normally a tank-mount engine, but otherwise 1 oz. maximum); 1 to 2 oz. for a 0.09; 2 to 4 oz. for a 0.15; 4 to 6 oz. for a 0.19; 6 to 8 oz. for a 0.23 to .25; 8 oz. for a 0.29 to 0.35; 8 to 10 oz. for a 0.40; 10 to 16 oz. for a 0.60 displacement engine; up to 32 oz. for engines for giant crafts.

CARBON DIOXIDE ENGINES

Less common than gas engines, these attractive little power plants are used in free-flight craft of rubber-powered size, especially for flying Scale. They are realistic in slower flight and run with a pleasant humming noise for about as long as a rubber-band-powered engine. There are several makes and sizes, the biggest of which is about the size of a Cox 0.02 gas engine, the smallest about tie-tack size. The tank is a metal capsule that is charged (filled) from a common soda sparklet held in a special device. The turn of a screw on the holder causes the sparklet to release enough gas to fill the tank. Roughly six to eight flights are obtained from one sparklet. (Much larger filler/chargers are available.)

A thin copper tube runs from the top of the tank to the cylinder head. Inside the head is a tiny ball-check valve. When the propeller is started, the compressed carbon dioxide pushes the piston down, the check valve then closes until the piston moves upward again to the top of the cylinder. A bump on top of the piston unseats the check valve, causing it to open momentarily every time the piston reaches top dead center. The exhaust port is a hole (or

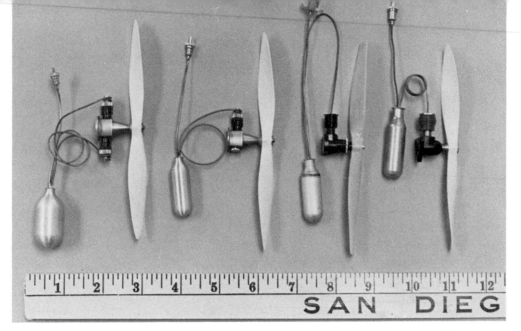

Carbon dioxode (CO_2) motors distributed by Peck Polymers (left to right): Brown M5-140 Twin, Brown MJ-70, Telco, and Shark. The tanks are filled under pressure from special cartridges that come in various capacities.

holes) at the base of the cylinder that is covered and uncovered by the up-and-down stroke of the piston. The carbon dioxide craft can be adjusted to circle and climb in large gyms, auditoriums, armories, and so on, and may be enjoyed both indoors and out.

COMPRESSED-AIR ENGINES

Seldom seen these days but widely used many years ago when gas engines were home-built affairs, these unique power plants are occasionally employed to duplicate some historic model to be flown in Oldtimer or Antique competition. Compressed-air engines operate much like carbon dioxide engines, but the fuel tank is a thin-walled rolled cylindrical metal tube, perhaps several inches in diameter and as much as 2 ft. or so in length, and may withstand air pressure up to 150 lbs. per square inch. The compressed-air engine can propel craft 6 ft. in span or larger. Equipment is scratchbuilt—something for the specialist/expert.

RUBBER POWER

Millions of models are flown by the energy of twisted rubber strands. Youngsters in particular enjoy them. However, people of all ages are devoted to many forms of such models, either for fun or for competitions at the club level, special contests, and even at the National and World Championships. Catering to experts who may never build anything other than a rubber-powered craft are small specialist suppliers of rubber, rubber winders, and accessories—a "cottage industry" through which items may be ordered by mail.

Tens of thousands of outlets sell little ready-to-fly models, but most of these outlets (not hobby shops) do not handle model supplies and it's almost impossible for customers to replace rubber or parts. Rubber strands are almost always available at a hobby shop, where rubber is bought by the foot from large spools. Specialist suppliers even sell entire spools in various thicknesses and/or widths of rubber.

Rubber strands, approximately 1/32 in. thick, come in various widths, typically 3/32, 1/8, 3/16, and 1/4 in. Bigger models require more "power" than smaller ones, so that propellers range from, say, 4 in. of molded plastic (plastic propellers come in many sizes) up to giants of 10 to 16 in. or more, which are carved at home from balsa-wood blocks, or are cambered thin plywood blades.

A motor consists of a single loop of rubber with its ends tied by a square knot (other knots slip). The knot is located close to the rear rubber hook or peg in the plane, so that it does not interfere with smooth running. The loop itself is a calculated length so that it can be doubled over, tripled, etc., to constitute a 4-, 6-, 8-strand or more motor. The knowing builder rubs the dry rubber (after knotting) with rubber lube—typically a mixture of green soap and glycerine. This decreases chafing or nicking, which would eventually

Stretch winding a rubber motor in a Comet 50-in. Taylor craft. Using a converted hand drill winder, the flier walks slowly toward the model as the rubber turns approach the maximum, for a flight lasting about 1 1/2 min. (Tom Schmitt photo)

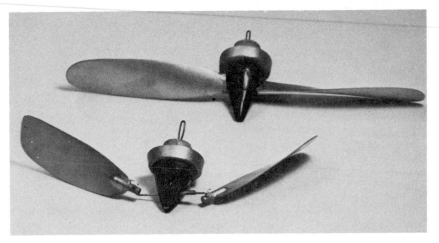

Typical large rubber-powered model propellers used on a Nationals Scale winner. At top, a freewheeling one-piece; below, a folding propeller for best glide. Inside the spinner on the shaft of the latter is a tiny coil spring that slides the propeller forward as the rubber winds down. The rubber hook then engages a stop to prevent rotation, which allows for extremely long rubber motors.

mean that the motor would snap when well wound. By using lube, more turns can be achieved.

Since the objective is the greatest number of turns for maximum propeller runs and duration, the "stretch winding" technique is common. The longer the rubber motor, the more turns achieved—sometimes the rubber motor length is double or more the distance between the propeller shaft hook and the rear rubber anchoring hook or peg. You will note that the simple store-bought stick model has a single loop of rubber that equals the distance between those hooks—if it were longer, it would fall off as turns wind down, dragging the model earthward. When a flier winds a short motor he or she turns the propeller until a row of knots appears.

Stretch winding more than doubles the available turns. A rubber winder is required. This winder has a small hook to engage the rubber, which is detached from the propeller shaft during winding. The helper holds the model at the projecting ends of the rear anchor dowel or tube, with its nose facing the person doing the winding; the latter stretches the rubber to three times its length, then winds steadily, slowly walking toward the model after he has gained, say, 50 to 75 percent of the turns. When he reaches the model, he detaches the rubber from the winder, and attaches it to the propeller hook. To get it off the winder, he holds the rubber close to the winder, and allows the winder to run freely backward a few turns, so that he can grasp the rubber to make the transfer. The winder has a crank that is geared to the winding hook—normally at a 5-to-1 ratio (though this varies). Thus, one turn of the winder yields five turns on the rubber.

On large models other methods may be used. The hook on the winder may

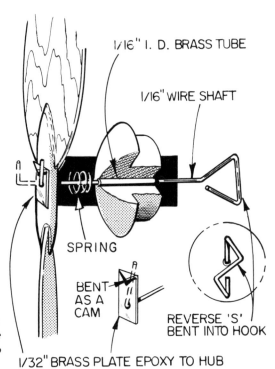

1/16" I. D. BRASS TUBE

1/16" WIRE SHAFT

SPRING

BENT AS A CAM

REVERSE 'S' BENT INTO HOOK

1/32" BRASS PLATE EPOXY TO HUB

How a freewheeling propeller works on rubber models. The hub is a dowel sanded to match the blades. The reverse-S hook prevents rubber knots from climbing onto the hook.

attach to a wire loop on the front of the prop hub (the end of the propeller shaft) and the propeller left in place as winding takes place. Usually, a protective winding tube is employed so the model is not broken if the rubber breaks. The tube slides over the rubber and is pushed back inside the model. An extremely long shank is used on the hook, which is part of the winder. When the rubber is fully wound, the tube slides forward, off the rubber, and over the long winder hook. The rubber then is detached from the winder hook and placed over the propeller shaft hook.

For overlength motors, "tensioning" is required to maintain the nearly unwound rubber motor to a length approximately the distance between hooks. The braided motor is one solution. Before the long loop of rubber is doubled over, redoubled, etc., for the desired number of strands, the loop is braided. This technique requires two people. The helper grasps the single giant loop at its midpoint, the loop being doubled back toward the winder, resulting in two loops half the length of the original. Each loop is given up to twenty-five turns of the winder, and then the two loops, side by side, are grasped between thumb and forefinger and rubbed together with a kneading action from end to end. The rubber then becomes a single group of lightly twisted strands whose length roughly equals the distance between hooks.

After this motor is stretch-wound, and expends its energy in flights, the rubber will not fall off the hook or gravitate toward the nose during the glide—which causes a dive or series of stalls.

Experts may use a mechanical tensioner. A light coil spring is located on the propeller shaft so that as the rubber winds down and decreases its pull between hooks, the spring moves the propeller and shaft slightly forward. As this happens, the specially bent end of the rubber hook engages the head of a small wood screw or wire pin placed in the back of the nose block. This prevents further unwinding, and the rubber is retained sufficiently taut between hooks to prevent its bunching up or becoming detached.

To extend the glide, either a "freewheeling" propeller or one with hinged folding blades is used. The freewheeler, found on small Scale and Sport models, has a simple ratchet mounted on the front of the propeller. The shaft is bent at right angles so it engages the raised tooth of the ratchet while the propeller is unwinding. When unwound, the airflow windmills the propeller, and the bent shaft end simply rides freely over the ratchet tooth. The folder is found on virtually all competition rubber-powered planes, especially Wakefield and Unlimited models. When the rubber winds down and the tensioner engages the stop on the back of the nose block, the propeller stops turning. Since its centrifugal force disappears, the airflow blows back the hinged blades to fit snugly against the fuselage sides.

Competition Indoor and most Scale—Indoor or Outdoor—models have no such gadgetry. The trick is to determine the size and length of the rubber and the number of turns that carry the craft to its cruising altitude without striking the ceiling, then let it descend slowly under power with a few turns remaining as the craft touches the floor or ground. This condition yields maximum power duration. Indoor models (except gliders) are considered overpowered if they glide.

When rubber lube is used, a small amount is placed in the palm of one hand and the rubber motor balled up and rubbed well between the hands. The excess moisture is then wiped off with tissue. Rubber knots must be tied before the motor is lubed because the slippery strands will slip the knot if it is made afterward. Once the model is adjusted to fly properly, the good rubber flier will experiment with slightly thicker and/or longer strands to achieve maximum power and endurance.

ELECTRIC POWER

Capable of motor runs of 6 to 8 min., the radio-controlled electric airplane, depending on its design, can perform a full range of aerobatics and match the flight duration of the largest sailplanes. Large Scale models with wing spans of 6 ft. or more make flights approaching 10 min. duration. Electricity works well in Sport free-flight models and competition Antique and Oldtimer events. It occasionally is seen in control line—for fun. It is effective in free flight, but here we will talk about popular radio control.

Several manufacturers make electric flight systems and sponsor major contests. Compared to gas engines, electric motors may seem less popular, but progress is so rapid that the future is unpredictable. The man-carrying Solar Challenger flew the English Channel using a large Astro Flight hobby-type motor, integrated with an elaborate gearing arrangement and powered by a vast array of solar cells.

Since motor-run times and power both have increased by 50 percent during the time this book was being written, we are reporting the state of the art as of spring 1983. Electric power has special advantages and some disadvantages. There is no starting problem, or the mess of exhausted fuel. You simply switch the current on and the motor runs. These relatively quiet craft can be flown in many places where a noisy gas engine would not be permitted. Small planes can be operated from schoolyards and parking lots. Using expensive high-technology one-shot batteries, some experts have kept electric models airborne for over 90 min. in indoor sports arenas. The disadvantage is the weight of the batteries, which comprise a significant percentage (about half) of the craft's gross weight. Electric models must be lightly built, although they are not necessarily fragile.

Until quite recently other handicaps of electric power made the modeling public cautious. For example, if the propeller was snagged in weeds while the power remained on, either the motor or the batteries, or both, would burn out in a few seconds. A rarer problem, encountered on long soaring flights when the power was exhausted, was the windmilling propeller, which ran down the batteries below a safe minimum. The result was a burned out battery pack on the next fast charge. These problems are avoided by the following practices.

A fuse should always be located between the motor and battery pack. Common on all ready-to-fly models, this fuse eliminates burnouts. The fuse is a common type, and replacements are available through such outlets as Radio Shack. There are simple on/off mechanical switches—available from the system manufacturer—that are actuated by movement of the throttle stick on the radio transmitter. During prolonged soaring, the motor can be switched on and off as many times as desired. The plane may descend or cruise with the power off, then resume its climb when the power is turned back on. If a mishap snags the propeller, the motor is instantly switched off

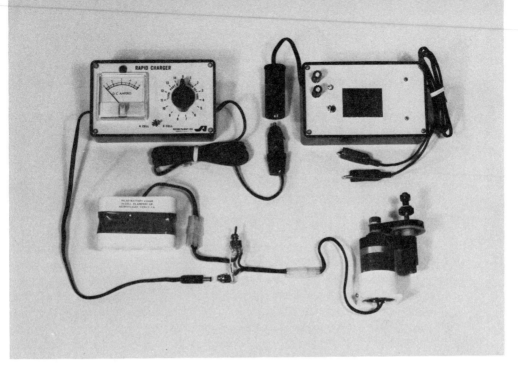

A belt-reduction Astro 15 electric motor for 12- or 13-in. propellers with 8-in. pitch. The charger is top left; beneath it, a 16-cell (0.55-amp./hr. capacity) nickel cadmium airborne battery pack. Top right is a voltage booster, required for large electric motors needing 24- to 30-V charging (a car battery is only 12 V). The motor itself is at bottom right. Most motors are smaller than this, and don't require a booster. (Preston photo)

from the transmitter to protect the motor and/or batteries; the fuse is a backup if the system is damaged. Another choice is the electronic switch control which feeds power to the motor in proportion to the movement of the throttle servo. A variation of the on/off switch is the three-position switch that, incorporating a dropping resistor, yields a selected cruise rpm in its midposition.

Electric motors usually are identified by numbers that relate them (roughly) to gas-engine sizes, such as 02, 035, 05, 075, 15, 25, and 40. The power source is a pack of rechargeable nickel cadmium batteries, the number of cells, sizes, and capacities varying with the size of the motor. The electric system includes a charger that works from a 12-V battery (motorcycle, gel cell, etc.) or directly from the automobile battery. The charger indicates the charging rate, time of charge, and so on. Some systems include a voltage booster (which looks somewhat like the charger) that steps up the 12-V automobile battery current to about 24 or 30 V, which is required by the bigger packs and motors. Usually, the charge takes about 15 min. after waiting for the battery pack to cool off if the plane was just flown.

This Eastcraft on-board electric starter placed in a 1/4-scale Stinson with a Quadra engine is operated by radio control. Note the toothed drive belt to the engine from the starter shaft.

Electric multimotor planes provide equal power to all motors and eliminate risks of motor failure with loss of control due to asymmetric thrust conditions, or "engine" failures. Two, three, or even four motors start simultaneously with the flick of a switch, and all respond alike to throttling. Scale experts achieve realistic cruise flight and longer duration by switching off two of three or four motors in flight whenever desired. Because of its weight, the power pack is located at, or close to, the aircraft's center of gravity, and a free flow of air for cooling purposes must be provided over both motors and batteries.

Another exciting mode is the geared motor, which drives a toothed belt running over reduction gears on the motor shaft, and on the propeller countershaft. Different ratios are available. If 2 to 1, the motor turns the full rpm, but the propeller rotates at only half that speed. This mechanical advantage allows the use of huge propellers turning at lower speeds, ideal for aircraft spanning 5 or 6 ft. An Astro Flight 2-to-1 ratio reduction belt drive (which is typical) allows a 12- to 13-in.-diameter propeller with an 8-in. pitch—on only a 15-size motor!

What about propeller sizes? Here are three examples: An Astro Flight 035XL turns a 6-in.-diameter, 3-in.-pitch propeller at over 14,000 rpm, which is perfect for a Goldberg Junior Falcon, Airtronics Q-Tee, Flyline kits, etc. Their 05XL swings a 6 × 4 prop at over 13,000 rpm, delivering 8 to 10 min. of power for 300- to 350-sq.-in. wing area Sport and Scale, or for 2-m span powered gliders, such as the Gentle Lady. The 075XL turns a 6 × 4 prop at 14,500 rpm, or a 7 × 4 prop at 13,500 rpm. It attains a 1,000-ft. altitude on models normally powered by gas engines of 0.10 displacement, or sailplanes of 100 in. or so span. The Leisure "hot wind" 05 is also is excellent for fast, Aerobatic craft; this firm specializes in sophisticated chargers and is adding other motor sizes as this is written. Capable of turning an 11 × 8 prop, the geared version of this 05 is excellent for Free Flight RC Assist, especially Oldtimers, of roughly 60-in. wing spans.

chapter seven

Covering and Painting

There is a saying in aeromodeling that "covering covers a multitude of sins." But any structure not reasonably prepared for covering and/or painting makes a plane look like the devil when finished. Conversely, the most craftsmanlike structure does not result in a classy-looking product if covering or painting is botched. It is hoped that this chapter will provide a good beginning and a happy ending.

Taken as a whole, the varieties of materials and methods of their use can seem bewildering. No modeler knows everything about the entire subject. But modelers need not know the characteristics of every material, and every finishing product, or even all the tricks of the trade. Why? Simply because nobody builds every type of model—there are hundreds of them. One does not live long enough to become proficient in every aspect of this hobby. Everybody gravitates to one—sometimes several—flying category. To be reasonably proficient, the reader may become adept in perhaps only 10 percent of the across-the-board methods to be described.

The fly-for-fun modeler, who comprises at least 80 percent of the total, can build a fine craft of any type (except Indoor) using just the traditional cements and dopes; he or she need not possess airbrushes or become involved in intricate techniques. So don't feel intimidated by the more exotic information that has been included here for completeness. Indeed, some respected experts who have won national contests have deliberately remained at a low-key level.

Understanding the representative examples that follow, you can choose methods that apply to your immediate requirements. It is emphasized that by granting equal space to each of these methods, equal popularity of each is not implied. The overwhelming majority of older hobbyists are engaged in radio control, and favor the quickly done, brilliantly colored, iron-on film cov-

Magazine columnist Bob Beckman shrinks iron-on film using a Top Flite heat gun, which avoids scratching. (Preston photo)

ering method using materials such as MonoKote, Coverite, and Solarfilm. The following discussion relates almost exclusively to Outdoor machines (see page 164 for information on Indoor).

PAPER COVERINGS

Two kinds of paper coverings are used on models: Japanese tissue and SilkSpan. Japanese tissue is lighter, has a very close "weave," and comes in white and assorted colors so that the models it covers usually are not painted. SilkSpan, similar to tea-bag paper, comes in two weights (for rubber and gas models). It is tougher but more porous, and it is whitish. It may or may not be painted, depending on the desired weight and finish. Japanese tissue is essential for most small, light craft. It is common for rubber-powered, but is often used on quite large rubber- and gas-powered competition free-flight craft. It is more prone to puncturing and rips more easily than SilkSpan in minor mishaps—though this is of concern only on bigger, faster machines. Both materials are always applied with the grain lengthwise to the structure—spanwise on wings and tails (if it is applied with the grain chordwise, the covering dips between ribs). Tear a corner of the sheet to establish its grain direction.

Japanese Tissue

Simple rubber-powered models are purchased by the hundreds of thousands from hobby departments in all sorts of retail shops, as well as from hobby shops, and many youngsters find that covering with the Japanese tissue provided in such kits is difficult. Often the photos or diagrams illustrating the technique are inadequate. (Keep in mind that Japanese tissue is widely used by more experienced modelers on small rubber-powered, gas-powered, electric-powered, and CO_2-powered scale models, and on competition gas- and rubber-powered free flights of a wide variety of designs.) Therefore, we will discuss Japanese tissue in depth and, since wings and tails are more tedious to cover than bodies, we shall consider them in greater detail.

The ultrasimple rubber-powered, tissue-covered model is typified by the A.M.A. Delta Dart. The tissue that comes with the kit is imprinted to show the outlines of the flying surfaces. The balsa-wood edges of those surfaces—there are no spars—are coated lightly with white glue (such as Elmer's) and pinned down on the outlines, with waxed paper between the paper and the workboard. When the model is dry, the covered frame is finished—nothing more is done to the covering. It is not doped; in this small model there is so

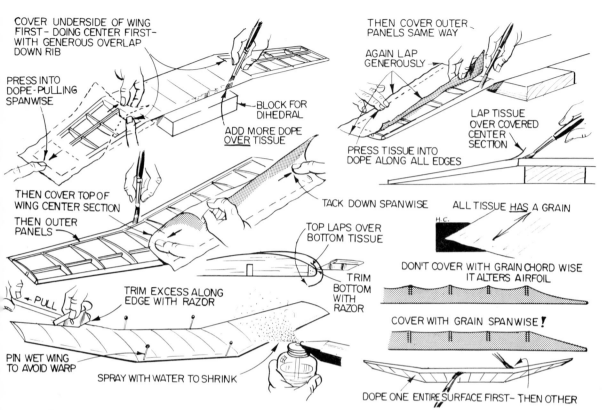

COVER UNDERSIDE OF WING FIRST – DOING CENTER FIRST – WITH GENEROUS OVERLAP DOWN RIB

PRESS INTO DOPE – PULLING SPANWISE

BLOCK FOR DIHEDRAL

ADD MORE DOPE OVER TISSUE

THEN COVER OUTER PANELS SAME WAY

AGAIN LAP GENEROUSLY

PRESS TISSUE INTO DOPE ALONG ALL EDGES

LAP TISSUE OVER COVERED CENTER SECTION

THEN COVER TOP OF WING CENTER SECTION

THEN OUTER PANELS

TACK DOWN SPANWISE

ALL TISSUE HAS A GRAIN

TOP LAPS OVER BOTTOM TISSUE

TRIM BOTTOM WITH RAZOR

DON'T COVER WITH GRAIN CHORD WISE IT ALTERS AIRFOIL

TRIM EXCESS ALONG EDGE WITH RAZOR

COVER WITH GRAIN SPANWISE !

PULL

PIN WET WING TO AVOID WARP

SPRAY WITH WATER TO SHRINK

DOPE ONE ENTIRE SURFACE FIRST – THEN OTHER

Covering a wing with Japanese tissue or SilkSpan. SilkSpan also can be wet with water just before each panel is applied, and it will shrink tightly with fewer wrinkles. Silk and other cloths are applied in basically the same manner, but usually are wet before application. Tail surfaces and fuselages are covered with the grain of the material running in the long direction.

little air-pressure differential between the top and bottom of the wing that air does not leak through the covering. (While hundreds of thousands of Delta Darts have been built, its design is an exception to common practice, because it was intended to be built by a group in a short session and to be flown immediately afterward. Other open-framework models covered with paper invariably are lightly doped after the covering is preshrunk.)

Most kits do not supply printed tissue. The frame is built first, then tissue is applied to major components before they are assembled into the complete flying machine. Usually the flying surfaces are simple, squarish, and sometimes sparless frames. Before covering, the framework is smoothed using a sanding board with a fine-grade sandpaper. The frame is rested flat on the workboard and the sandpaper block swept gently over it to remove glue bumps, surface fuzziness, and uneven joints—all of which are conspicuous after covering. Turn the frame over several times while sanding, because the pressure and frictional heat of prolonged sanding otherwise will bow the wood.

Model airplane dope is brushed onto the outer frame edges of the top panel of the wing (such little wings are single surface, not covered on both sides), the tissue laid in place, and the paper rubbed onto the wet-doped wood with a forefinger. While the dope is wet, the paper is stretched lightly to remove wrinkles. If the dope sets before the job is complete, soften the seams with dope where necessary. (Tiny, sparless wings and tails such as those found on R.O.G.'s are not doped all over because such fragile wings warp disastrously.) When dry, the overhanging edges of the tissue are trimmed away with a single-edge razor blade. Go over the papered edges with a fine dope brush and rub down any fringes to ensure a neat and tight smooth seal all around the frame.

How do we shrink the paper? With small, flat frames, one must be extremely careful. While the paper frame is held flat to the bench—if dihedral, do one panel at a time—it is lightly sprayed (misted, really) with water or alcohol in an atomizer. Spray from a distance so that a mist of liquid merely moistens the material. As it dries, it shrinks taut. The wetted, flat panel can be placed under a straight piece of wood, such as plywood, with a weight on top to guard against warps when shrinking (this will take several hours or perhaps overnight). The paper will not stick to the bench, but waxed paper between bench and paper is a precaution against snagging.

Larger rubber-powered models and gas-powered free flights have cambered ribbed (airfoil cross-section) wings, and almost always have one or more spars. Such open-frame wings and tails are covered top and bottom. Craft in roughly the 15-to-50-in.-span group require at least two coats of clear dope thinned 50-50 to seal the shrunk paper. Cover all bottom panels first, then the top surfaces. The water spraying and doping are not done until all panels are covered. Some wing designs may have polyhedral (more than one dihedral break), tiphedral (modeler's slang for a wing with no dihedral at the center, but with the outermost section of each wing tipped up at a severe dihedral), or vee dihedral (a single dihedral break at centerline, then both panels tilting moderately upward). In these cases, each panel is covered, starting on the bottom at the center, with an individual piece of tissue for just that panel. Don't try to cover with one piece tip to tip.

More care is necessary with these more complicated (and larger) wings. First, the wood surface is carefully fine-sanded. A wrung-out damp rag is passed over the wood surfaces that contact the paper (don't soak!). This raises dents and causes fuzziness to stand out, after which a final sanding with very fine paper produces a sheen to the wood. Surfaces that will touch paper are given a coat of dope (two on big models) that penetrates the wood. When covering, dope used to stick down the paper will penetrate the paper to soften the dope already on the wood and make a tight bond, especially desirable on the narrow top and bottom edges of the ribs. At this stage the tissue has been doped only where it sticks to the wood. Some builders stick the tissue only to the outer edges of a panel—that is, at its two ends and at the leading and trailing edges. Then, when the entire surface is doped, the dope again penetrates the paper to soften the dope previously applied to the top and bottom edges of the ribs, and the tissue is again bonded to the ribs.

To apply tissue to a panel, stick the paper at the highest point of the center rib, then to a similar point on the rib nearest the tip, and pull gently spanwise to remove sagging. (If you need to rework the placement, resoften the second spot with dope.) The doped portion of the tip and center rib is progressively expanded toward the leading and trailing edges while you continue to stretch the paper spanwise. Approaching those edges, dope the paper along them and gently pull out any spanwise ripples by stretching chordwise. Remaining local wrinkles can be eliminated by resoftening the edge with dope and pulling the material tighter. This method also applies to SilkSpan, silk, nylon, and other clothlike materials.

The tissue is moisture sprayed as before, but, since the frame has greater strength (due to its thickness), it need not be weighted down; instead, rest it flat on the bench. When it is dry, apply the first coat of surface dope spanwise, the second chordwise. Don't go over either coat until it is thoroughly dry. Rubber Scale modelers prefer to test-fly and adjust models before paint-

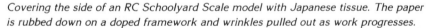

Covering the side of an RC Schoolyard Scale model with Japanese tissue. The paper is rubbed down on a doped framework and wrinkles pulled out as work progresses.

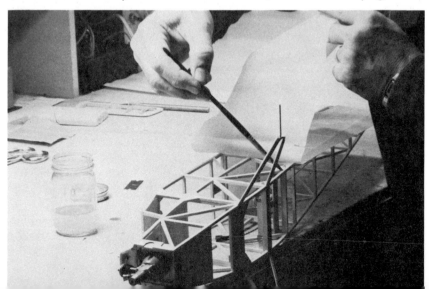

After the Japanese tissue is in place, overhanging edges are trimmed off with a single-edge razor blade.

Finished tissue covering is shrunk tight by a fine-spray misting of water or alcohol. After drying, the tissue is clear doped.

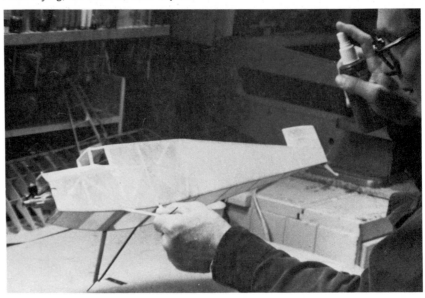

ing. They often use white tissue and then mist-spray one coat of color over the one or two coats of thinned clear dope.

A fuselage with flat sides, top, and bottom is covered with four separate pieces of either Japanese tissue or SilkSpan—usually tissue regardless of size for rubber-powered craft, SilkSpan for some bigger gas-powered craft. When a fuselage has rounded-off surfaces—of stringer and former construc-tion mostly—the covering material is cut into narrow strips, wide enough to cover between as many stringers as possible without wrinkles.

SilkSpan

Stronger and heavier than Japanese tissue, SilkSpan can be applied dry like tissue—or, as old hands often do, by a wet-covering method. Its tough texture allows it to be water soaked before application, a less wrinkle-prone method (wet-covering can also be used with silk, nylon, and Silron—see page 155). SilkSpan is good for large free-flights, medium-size Sport models of all kinds—where the builders may prefer not to use popular iron-on films—and on open-framework wings of those control-line planes on which some heavier cloth-type covering is not essential.

Covering the wing of a Sterling Ringmaster control-line model with SilkSpan paper. SilkSpan is soaked first with water, laid in place, and then the wrinkles are pulled out and the edges doped down.

The covering is pulled tightly around a shaped wing-tip block, doping as necessary until edges are evenly applied.

Finished Silkspan covering, now shrunk dry, is given two or more coats of clear dope thinned 50-50.

To wet-cover, the SilkSpan is folded until it fits in a shallow flat pan partially filled with water. The wet material is laid briefly on a soft towel to rid it of excess water, then unfolded, laid in place over the predoped frame and pulled tight enough to eliminate wrinkles. Dope it to the perimeter of the frame area before doping it to ribs or crosspieces. If wrinkles remain near corners and joints, the dope should be softened by an application of thinned dope, the wrinkles pulled out, and the loose edges rubbed down while wet with dope. If the covering shows any dry spots before the job is complete, rewet it with a swab of cotton or with an atomizer.

Because SilkSpan is used on more heavily loaded, faster-flying craft, more lift is exerted, and air pressure is therefore more likely to leak through pores not properly filled. After drying, SilkSpan surfaces require anywhere from two to four coats of clear dope. Since paint weight is less critical than with small tissue-covered machines, two coats of colored dope thinned 50-50 can be applied without penalty over the clear dope.

CLOTH COVERINGS

Silk, Nylon, Silron

These materials are applied, either wet or dry, as described for SilkSpan. Silk is a thing of beauty when it is not hidden by opaque paints and is favored by many experienced modelers who will never change their ways. It can be used on any model with sufficiently strong structure from about 36-in. span on up. Nylon and Silron are much stronger than silk and somewhat heavier, and thus are favored on larger Sport and Scale models (but not on big free flights, where minimum weight is paramount).

Silk requires that the framework be sanded to perfection, because the material snags when pulled. Because of its relatively open weave it may require a minimum of four coats of thinned clear dope before the pores are sealed. From two to four coats of colored dope thinned 50-50 may then be applied. If white or natural-colored silk is not to be painted, five or six coats of clear dope may be required. Woven materials are harder to trim neatly than tissue or SilkSpan, because frayed ends are common. These are brushed and rubbed down with clear dope before painting. If clear dope is extended roughly 1/2 in. beyond the edges of the frame as the material is first applied, the overhanging material trims neatly when dry.

In addition to being heavier than silk, nylon and Silron are also stiffer. Strands of these materials do not absorb dope or moisture. Both are virtually impervious to rips and punctures. The author prefers to wet-cover when using all such materials. Since nylon does not remain wet very long, it must be remoistened several times with a cotton swab when large areas are being covered. Silron is similar to nylon, but has a tendency to creep along the wooden frame edges when it is first doped down. Do not depend on a narrow band of dope to hold it. If it creeps, pull on the excess material outside the frame while rubbing down the wet dope with a fingertip until it sticks.

When covering fuselages with cloth materials, attach the covering at one end, stretch it tight to the other end, and only then attach it to the longerons, at which point lengthwise wrinkles can be pulled out. Silk works very well around compound curves, since it stretches in all directions. With other materials, special pieces may have to be cut for difficult areas, such as around the nose, or over stringers that follow a curve while simultaneously tapering with the fuselage width.

Polyesters

A favored material for very large RC models (especially large Scale), polyester cloth gives superior results when applied wet and then heatshrunk (after drying) at a low temperature. (Heat-shrinking is described on page 158.) After shrinking, two to three coats of clear dope thinned 50-50 seal the weave, providing a base for two coats of either thinned colored dope or hobby-type paint. Its tough strands make it more difficult to work around sharp compound curves and to stick down its edges after trimming. Because it is an ideal material for doping and painting, it is not essential to use any special sealers other than the dope itself, but super finishes result if an automobile-body filler, such as Duco, is brushed on after clear doping and before painting to hide seams where this thicker cloth overlaps. Follow this up with a sanding using very fine wet-and-dry paper. This is a good treatment for large Scale models.

The combination of wet-covering and heat-shrinking creates a drumlike surface, and further shrinking is not desired. Hence, low-shrink dopes, such as Sig Lite Coat, are recommended.

IRON-ON FILMS

Some iron-on films, such as MonoKote or Solarfilm, have a backing that is peeled off prior to application. The side to be stuck to the frame is not sticky to the touch; the adhesive is activated by the iron. Others, such as FabriKote and Micafilm, have no backing and require that the structure be painted with a special, heat-sensitive adhesive such as Coverite or Balsanite. Coverite's Micafilm can be applied with either side down, depending on whether a shiny

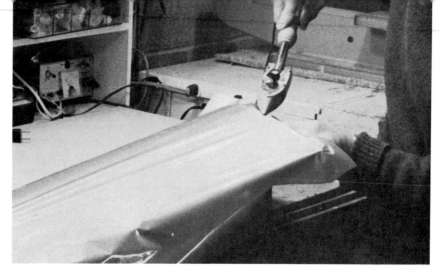

Spotting down Mono-Kote silver iron-on, heat-shrinkable film at the root and tip ends of a wing.

or clothlike surface is preferred. (When in doubt, the adhesive side of a film can be detected by touching a corner with the iron.)

Iron-ons may be applied to raw wood sanded reasonably smooth, not to a supersmooth finish. However, adhesion is improved if the wood is first coated with Coverite's Balsarite, which penetrates the wood and sticks to the film when heat is applied.* Iron-ons are first attached to the framework edges, then shrunk by gentle circular movements of a hobby iron, or by a hobby-type heat gun, which resembles a hair dryer but operates at a higher temperature, which is adjustable (Top Flite makes popular irons and heat guns). The heat gun avoids tiny scratches that may occur from heavy applications of the Teflon-coated heating-iron shoe.

Covering sharp compound curves takes patience. Small areas of the material are applied over wing-tip blocks, etc., while pulling the covering as tight as possible. When covering a wing, attach the material at a spot at the high point of the camber at the center section, and at a corresponding spot on the tip rib, and pull it tight spanwise. Then spot the material down at each of the four corners of the frame, pulling it taut diagonally to remove as many wrinkles as possible. A series of spots at the extreme rear edge of the trailing edge, and the top of the leading edge, are then tacked down, the spaces between adhered by rubbing the iron chordwise (in a direction away from the edges) around these edges. The entire surface is then heatshrunk lightly, and

*Coverite markets three special-purpose liquids, including Balsarite. In addition to an improved bond with iron-on films—and paper, silk, nylon, etc.—Balsarite inhibits fuel creep through iron-on seams, especially in the nose compartment. Quik Stik can be used as an adhesive to stick down covering edges, and with iron-ons to improve bonding to wood, among other things. Glas-kote is a clear finish applied over (never under) any type of paint and all Coverite coverings. It resists scuffing, oils, and high-nitromethane-content fuels.

gone over again two or three times to produce maximum shrinking. At first, the material appears hopelessly loose, but its shrinking ability is enormous. When trapped air causes bubbles under the film (where it touches wide wooden pieces), prick the bubbles with a pin one or more times to allow air to escape. The bottom surfaces of the wing and tail are covered first, then the top surface is allowed to extend over the edges to overlap the bottom by about 1/4 in.

Cover the bottom of the fuselage first, then the sides, and finally the top. The intent is to overlap seams downward so that exhaust residue fuel cannot seep into the seams. Similarly, vertical seams are overlapped in a rearward direction. When the material is wrapped and ironed around very sharp, curved edges, such as the sides of the nose, it is slit where necessary to readily overlap rather than wrinkle.

Be careful when using iron-on films with Styrofoam. High temperatures melt foam, although MonoKote films, among others, can be applied over a sheet-balsa-skinned foam-core wing if the iron is not set too high. A low-temperature film, such as Pactra Solarfilm, generally is preferred with unskinned Styrofoam, because the iron is set at a low temperature. A heat gun can wreck low-temperature film, so it should be held at a suitable distance with a low temperature setting. Film should never be applied over doped wood because the dope melts from the iron or heat gun.

Coverite offers a family of special iron-on, heat-sensitive materials, including impregnated color and camouflage; procedures may vary somewhat with each but the instructions that come with the materials are clear. Generally, these woven polyesters require much higher temperature settings. Although Micafilm, which is extremely light and strong, does have a spun polyester

After the four corners have been pulled tight, the Mono-Kote is ironed down on the wing edges; meanwhile the film is pulled tightly in place. The finished covering is shrunk tight by rubbing lightly with the iron.

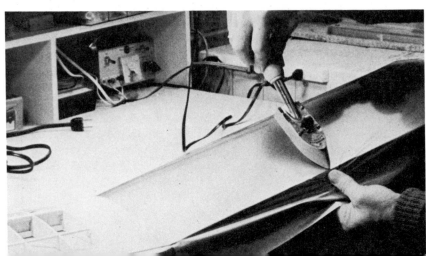

fiber bonded to it, it is in a category with MonoKote and Solarfilm as far as application is concerned. It is not a high-temperature material.

FABRIC IRON-ONS

This category of materials includes such products as Top Flite's FabriKote and Coverite's Coverite, Super Coverite, and Silkspun Coverite. All of these have different manufacturing techniques and ingredients, but basically they have a wovenlike texture, and most are polyester-type fabrics. They are also tougher than pure plastic film. Since required iron temperatures vary somewhat, directions for such materials must be followed closely. All are worked with a common hobby iron, which, in some cases—with some Coverite materials, for example—must be slightly modified as described in the material's instructions to provide higher temperatures. These textured materials take a wide variety of hobby-type paints. Most can take two coats of clear dope thinned 50-50 as a sealer before painting. Always test samples of your materials for compatability.

FINISHING AND PAINTING

Everybody loves to paint. The trouble is that many of us (especially the first time around) are "paintaholics." Before the first coat dries, or if it doesn't look immediately beautiful, we apply coat upon coat. The result? A gooey mess and an overweight plane, or one so out of balance that only a great chunk of lead in the nose saves the day (we hope!). Most of the surface area of an airplane lies behind the center of gravity and the more paint that is used unwisely, the greater the disaster.

The overwhelming majority of planes are not supposed to be painted. Many others should be painted only very lightly, without the intricate business of working for weeks to achieve a super finish. On the other hand, competition craft that involve appearance points in judging are painstakingly painted, finished, and decorated. Expert Scale builders treat their subjects like a Rolls-Royce, laboriously sealing, filling, and finish coating—sometimes dozens of coats—topped off by buffing and waxing.

The factors to consider in finishing and painting are the nature of the covering material, whether or not the structure is open-framed or has a solid surface, the choice of paints, whether to brush or spray, the compatibility of liquids, and the procedures of sealing, filling, and finishing. A perfectly acceptable job can be done with high-quality soft brushes. A small airbrush is a good choice for superlight rubber Scale models, for which the builder wants the maximum in-flight duration as well as realistic decorations that match the full-size aircraft. Spray-painting may be used on larger models, particularly RC and CL Scale craft where perhaps only two coats, depending on the type of paint (epoxy paint, for example), result in an even finish that can be quickly applied.

A new brush must be broken in by painting any convenient object, such as a tin can (loose bristles will come out), and then thoroughly cleaned by dipping in a compatible thinner and wiping with a soft cloth or folded-over paper napkin. If an airbrush is used, it must always be thoroughly cleaned after each usage according to directions.

Although "exotic" paints such as epoxy paint and acrylic enamel are frequently used by skilled modelers, the average hobbyist favors simple aircraft butyrate dopes.

Safety Measures

Before discussing the painting system, it is imperative to consider the work area and safety measures. For fifty years or more, modelers stupidly filled their shops, and entire houses, with noxious dope fumes. We joked about it, but it was no joking matter. Today, thousands of products are widely used in the home—including some designed for modeling—that contain chemicals that could potentially be dangerous to eyes, skin, lungs, and so on. But with care, the proper equipment, and attention to instructions, these products can be handled safely.

Your shop or work area must be well ventilated. Cross-ventilation, provided by two windows, is desirable. When spraying anything but a small object with butyrate dope for a very brief time, you should have at least one window exhaust fan working (two fans are recommended for prolonged airbrushing). I take all large objects to be sprayed outdoors on a warm, dry day when the wind is not blowing. The object is hung by a bent coat hanger, or the like, from a convenient branch or beam.

When painting or spraying you must always wear a spray-protective mask (respirator). The cheap, common breathing mask (often made of paper) picked up in a hardware store is safe only for dust, not paint mist. Suitable respirators have a charcoal filter that is changed whenever breathing becomes difficult, irritation is noticed, or you start to smell the dope through the mask. One relatively inexpensive respirator approved by the government for paints that give off organic vapors, as well as for protection from dusts and mists, is the 3M No. 8741 Spray Paint Respirator Assembly.

Use only products made for modeling purposes—leave the strange paints and preparations you may stumble upon in hardware, automobile supply, and paint stores for the professionals. Polyester catalysts, for example, are extremely hazardous for amateur or hobbyist use. One drop in the eye can destroy vision. Imron, intended primarily for the super finishes on automobiles, is notoriously dangerous, and professionals who use it do so under strict conditions of ventilation and special respirator protection. You should not use it under any circumstances.

Work must not be performed in the vicinity of an open flame, such as the pilot light on a water heater, gas dryer, or furnace. And you certainly should not smoke while doping or painting.

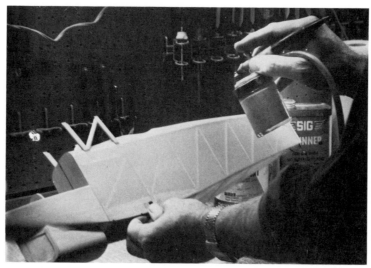

One light coat of silver dope being sprayed on a Japanese tissue-covered Kawasaki pre-World War II biplane fighter, an RC model.

To spray on the red Japanese sun over the finished silver fuselage, a paper mask is held in place.

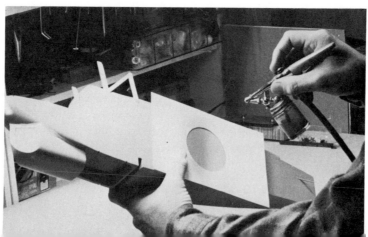

Painting and spraying can be eliminated by using iron-on film, and ventilation is not then required unless some chemically prepared liquid is used on the wood as a bonding agent. Don't breathe any vapors, such as the fumes from curing epoxy mixes. *Always* read the precautionary notices on containers of all kinds, including glues—especially "instant" glues.

It is strongly advised that young and inexperienced hobbyists stick with butyrate dopes, model airplane cements, and aliphatic glues, such as Elmer's, until they have the expertise necessary to use the chemical preparations that must be handled with extra care.

Open-Framework Models and Colored Dopes

For rubber- and gas-powered free-flight types, as well as small Schoolyard RC models, colored tissue and silk may eliminate painting—but do note that the clear dope both fills and seals the covering, the final coats of dope producing a pleasant sheen. Builders of rubber-powered and small RC Scale models do use an airbrush for lightweight colored finishes of 50-50 thinned dope, even though the covering is Japanese tissue or SilkSpan.

Since SilkSpan is white and can be soaked in water (as for wet-covering), it can also be easily dyed, as can silk. It is not worthwhile to strive for super paint jobs with SilkSpan on open frameworks, because although tougher than Japanese tissue, it is easily torn and punctured. If you must paint, SilkSpan used on the average Sport model should need only two or three coats of thinned color. When the first coat is brushed on over the clear doped covering, the appearance is uneven and reveals brush strokes. The second coat, and perhaps a third, will achieve an even finish. Brush marks level off when dry. Apply the second coat at right angles to the first, always brushing the unpainted portion toward and overlapping the already painted area. Don't paint long narrow pathways, but progress evenly from, for example, the wing root toward the wing tip. Each coat must dry thoroughly before the next coat is applied. Don't be tempted to touch up spots or try to remove brush marks with more paint while a coat is still wet or soft. (Incidentally, free-flight experts often double-cover when using tissue. After the first covering is shrunk and doped tight, a second covering layer is placed over it, with the grain running at 90 degrees to the first layer—strength is much improved.)

For open-frame wings on Sport control-line craft and some radio-controlled models, a bit more weight is tolerable and a third or even fourth coat of thinned color may be desirable, notably over silk and other relatively open-weave materials.

Some models present structures that have large sheet-balsa or shaped block areas, or wings that are balsa or plywood skinned; these are considered solid structures for painting.

Sealing and Painting

Painting usually requires four stages: the preparation of the structural sur-face (using sealers), the covering (using fillers), the undercoating (using seal-ers), and the painting itself. The first step for a good paint job is to sand the wood surfaces of the framework. Dents, small openings, etc., are filled with Dap spackling compound before sanding. The surface must then be sealed. For years modelers mixed clear dope with talcum powder, five parts to one, when they were sealing wood. Or they simply used clear dope by itself. Pac-tra then introduced bottled sanding sealer, which is brushed on like dope. All three methods are fine. For the truly expert there are finishing resins found in families of paints by K&B, Pactra, Sig, etc.—do read the labels carefully and follow instructions to the letter.

Consider the airfoil balsa wing of a hand-launched glider. For this type of model, brush on successive coats of clear dope (or dope mixed 5 to 1 with talc), or sanding sealer, allowing each coat to dry hard before sanding with fine paper. The purpose is to reduce high spots. If the object is held at a slant to a bright light, low areas will be discerned. The first sanding with fine wet-and-dry paper will reveal raw wood at high spots, but the "valleys" remain untouched. Successive sealer coats fill these hollows, sanding after each coat, until eventually the surface is smooth. It will shine and feel satiny to the touch. The final sealer coat is not sanded. A hand-launched glider is not painted.

If larger "solid" surfaces are to be painted, as on an exhibition-type Scale model, this smoothed surface is covered with light-grade silk or SilkSpan, and sealer coats of clear dope are applied over the covering, sanding between each coat, until the covering material is satiny to the touch. To thoroughly seal, at least two more coats of clear dope are applied without sanding. This prevents the color coats that follow from penetrating through to the sealed wood, which could soften it. At least two, and possibly three or four, under-coats of colored dope, thinned 50-50, are brushed on, sanding after each is dried. Finally, at least two finishing coats are applied, by brush or with an airbrush.

An airbrush must be held far enough away so that it does not deposit excess paint that runs, and the path of the brush must be in a straight line along the surface—don't fan the brush, because uneven shadings result. Practice on scrap materials until you get the hang of it. Test all paints to be used over each other for compatibility, also using scraps.

The following system works well when a super finish is desired on a large aircraft whose entire surface is wood, such as a Pattern or monster Scale plane.

The wood surface is sanded as smooth as possible. The sealing is provided by covering with 3/4-oz.-weight fiberglass cloth, which is comparable to silk in thickness but far stronger. The "glass" cloth is applied like silk by brushing it on with modeling clear-satin brushing epoxy, which yields a flat matte-like finish. The material is then sanded with fine paper, and a second coat of brushing epoxy is applied and sanded when dry. A third coat is then applied but not sanded. This base is now compatible with virtually any type of paint. Before painting, two spray coats of either modeling epoxy primer or Duco acrylic automobile primer are applied. Then spray on several coats of paint: lacquer, thinned colored dope (a form of lacquer), enamel, epoxy, etc. Acrylic enamels are cheaper than epoxy paints. Each color coat is fine-sanded, except the last.

We do not mean to imply that the inexperienced modeler who has never used any colored dopes or paints realistically has a choice of all the materials. If you have used colored dopes, and already know something about the kinds and sizes of models on which special finishes may be used, you are ready to explore epoxy- and acrylic-type paints and associated materials. For those to whom painting is a new experience, it is suggested that butyrate colored dopes be used. Many experts prefer such dopes. The truly experienced modeler in search of especially hard and glossy finishes frequently opts for epoxies or acrylics. We do not wish to recommend one brand over another, since so many exist, but in the popular epoxy-type paints both K&B and Hobbypoxy products are widely used.

Experts sometimes use many different methods and products. One system that should not be overlooked eliminates the need to cover the "solid" wood with any kind of paper, silk, or glass cloth. It relies on a polyester-resin wood sealer that stabilizes and strengthens the wood, then accepts whatever fillers and paints are selected.

Hobbypoxy has a four-page booklet that describes their many products, the proper groups to use for various applications, and well-detailed instructions for achieving a first-class job. Also, there is a definitive work on paints and finishes, *There Are No Secrets,* written and published by columnist Harry Higley (see page 283).

INDOOR MODELS

While perhaps only 1 percent of the millions of modelers specialize in Indoor, one can see where the fascination lies after watching these amazing machines in slow-motion activity. All but hand-launched gliders are open frameworks, covered with ultralight materials—applied by entirely different methods than those previously described—and never painted (except for

Scale). Beginner's models and flying Scale types are covered with Japanese tissue, either white or colored. In general, and depending on the performance category, other covering materials used are condenser paper, Micro Lite (polycarbonate film), and microfilm. Tan and nonporous, condenser paper weighs 0.008 to 0.011 oz. per 100 sq. in., is preshrunk on a wooden frame, then applied with shellac, sugar water, acetate-type cements, or water-base glues, and even saliva. The open surface is not coated with anything.

The "adhesive" is applied simultaneously to the edges of the covering material and the frame, after laying the covering material over the frame. Sugar water is a mixture of water and sugar to a very thin, adhesivelike consistency. Saliva, the liquid once traditionally used to apply microfilm (see below), is still often used. Again a fine-pointed brush is employed, or a wetted finger. The framework is not licked! For some odd reason, saliva makes a perfect adhesive for ultrathin covering materials.

Micro Lite, which weighs roughly 0.005 oz. per 100 sq. in., is either clear or has an aluminized finish. It is applied with shellac or rubber-base contact cement, and trimmed with a fine brush and a plastic solvent, such as MEK (methyl ethyl ketone). Difficult to apply, it is held in position by a wooden frame while it is attached to the structure.

The ultimate covering is microfilm, a nitrocellulose film prepared by pouring a solution of lacquer or clear dope (with thinners and plasticizers) onto the surface of water in a shallow tank. The film floats and, after hardening, is lifted from the water with a balsa frame of wire hoop coated with rubber cement. It is applied to the model's frame with distilled water or saliva. *Building & Flying Indoor Model Airplanes,* by Ron Williams, is the definitive book on the subject (see page 284). Indicative of the science of Indoor flying is Williams's remark that microfilm covering is a book in itself.

Control-surface outlines of ailerons, rudders, elevators, flaps, and trim tabs are done with fine-tipped marking pens on a lightweight Curtiss Owl rubber-powered model.

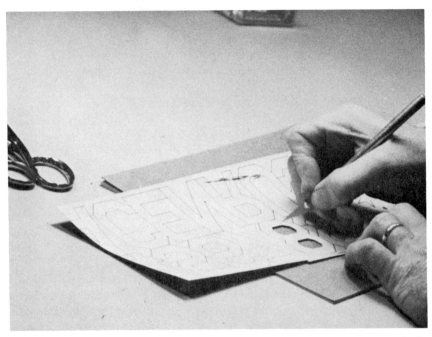

Numerals, letters, etc., printed on the back of Trim-Film sheets, provide a guide for cutting with a No. 11 X-Acto balsa knife blade.

For multicolored designs over iron-on film, shapes cut from Trim-Film sheets are pressed in position. Large trim shapes can also be cut from a sheet of iron-on material.

DECORATIONS

Decals are available as letters, numerals, and devices. Attach them by wetting according to the directions, then sliding them off their film backing into position. They are preferred on tissue and silk with ordinary doped surfaces, Cover with a thin coat of clear dope to seal. Decals do not take well on some iron-on films, and experts consider them unsightly on first-class painted surfaces as well.

For iron-ons, Top Flite has colored Trim-Sheet with letter and numeral patterns printed on the removable backing; these are cut out, then ironed on. Wide Trim-Sheet allows you to make various designs. Coverite Graphics include numerals, letters, and decorations such as stars. These are die-cut, 100 percent cast vinyl, and are simply pressed on. Goldberg Striping Tape is available in many colors and is used for numerous decorative effects.

Deluxe paint finishes really require preparing your own patterns by making masks from sticky-backed vinyl shelf paper, and airbrushing the areas to be painted. Outlines of many different designs can also be readily marked on the painted surface, then masked off with vinyl tape, which is less thick than old-fashioned masking tape (which also leaves visible edges and requires sealing). Tape folded-over newspaper to the surrounding areas to avoid overspraying or overbrushing.

To put all this into perspective, it is foolish for anyone who is not an expert flier or a scale model craftsman to invest time and money in exotic finishes. Most of us find our flying models take a beating. It makes no sense to work for months on a fantastic finish and then damage or destroy the plane. That surely will turn you off!

Applying Goldberg Striping Tape, available in many colors. The splotches on the red cut-out design over the white wing are light reflections. For fabric-covered, doped wings, mask off desired areas with thin vinyl tape to be painted for trim schemes or numerals, letters, and devices. The masking tape marks outlines to be painted and protects remaining areas from unwanted painting.

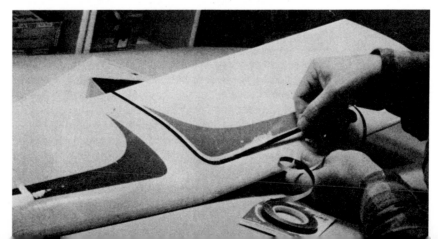

chapter eight

Free-Flight Techniques

When a beginner tosses a hand-launched glider it often stalls, loops, twists, or dives. When an expert flier sends an engine-powered free-flight model high in the sky to soar like an eagle, he makes it look easy. But in the beginning he too struggled with small gliders and rubber-powered Stick models; although he probably did not study aerodynamics, he had to learn why and how an airplane flies.

Understanding enables the experts to control from the ground flying models with which they have no physical link. Unlike control-line craft, which are restrained by control wires running to a handle held by the pilot, or radio-controlled machines, which respond to the movements of a transmitter stick, the free-flight model seems to be totally independent of its creator. But one can tame a wild falcon. Successful free-flighters preprogram their planes to execute desired flight patterns. Modelers call this "adjusting." Carried to the ultimate by an expert, adjusting appears mysterious. But even simple craft fly immeasurably better when crudely adjusted.

The first objective of free flight is to make the plane fly in any fashion— achieving a bridgehead, in military terms. After that, the wonder of prepro-grammed flight unfolds. Once hobbyists make their jaunty craft fly and land without smashing, they come to grips with the basic principles that make the craft do their bidding.

Space: to the astronaut space is infinity; to the free-flighter, it is painfully finite. A flying area limited by trees, terrain, buildings, and the ground. An area in which the model must be confined if it is not to be lost in the distance or fall victim to menacing obstacles. Free flight is a challenge even to an expert. Even when it is perfectly adjusted, a model may drift quickly with the wind or be caught in a powerful thermal which, if precautions are not taken, will carry it out of sight, perhaps directly overhead!

Mario Rocca of Italy is lifted on the shoulders of jubilant teammates after winning the flyoffs for the World Championship gas-powered flight. He ran off perfect scores on seven successive official flights—as did eight who tied him—but topped all on his tenth flight with 360 sec. (Cynthia Sabransky photo from Free Flight Digest)

Melanie Sanford launches her rubber-powered P-30 class model during the 1979 A.M.A. Nationals at Lincoln, Nebraska. (John Oldenkamp photo)

The child who manages to fly a glider or small rubber-powered model in circles can have fun in a cul-de-sac without having his or her dream ship roost in a tree or land on a roof. A tiny rubber-powered model can circle in a rec room, possibly bouncing off a wall undamaged. But staying away from walls is a problem that quickly teaches the beginner to control his or her craft in rudimentary fashion. Expert indoor fliers achieve astounding times with their gossamer-light craft, usually without striking the walls or ceiling. In fact, they learn just how much rubber to use, and how many turns to give it to stay below a ceiling that may be anywhere from 20 to 100 ft. high. (Competition categories for Indoor models are determined by ceiling heights; World-class Indoor craft may float around for more than 50 min. in a sports arena or dirigible dock.)

Large, efficient Outdoor models—including towline gliders—require wide-open spaces regardless of how well they are preprogrammed. A slow-flying, lightweight rubber Scale model flying in circles of 100 ft. diameter may drift across a 1/4-mi. field in the barely perceptible evening breeze! Years ago, when unlimited endurance was the criterion, gas models sometimes meandered over state lines, soaring for hours, even though they had a limited fuel allotment. One traveled from the Bronx to Montauk Point in New York, or a distance of about 130 mi.; another hit the mast of a ship 4 mi. at sea.

Obviously, the free-flight craft must circle to stay in the vicinity. Techniques vary because, like people, no two of these models are alike. According to the accidents of its design, the model may be more inclined to turn one way than the other. We sometimes see them climb straight ahead, then transition into a circling glide, either to the right or the left. The modeler "goes with the airplane"; that is, he or she bases adjustments upon the model's natural turning inclinations.

How do modelers protect their planes from flying out of sight? How do they rescue their craft from a thermal or "boomer"? And since the competition Outdoor model must remain aloft sufficiently long to win, isn't there a conflict between the need to protect the craft from drifting off and allowing it to go for maximum duration?

All competition free-flight models—including some hand-launched gliders—are equipped with a timed dethermalizer (D.T.) device to terminate the flight. All sorts of Rube Goldberg gadgets have been tried, including drag par-

Indoor rubber-powered scale models delight young and old alike. This model is a Monocoupe built to A.M.A. Scale rules, which reward precision. (Linstrum photo)

Bill Gieseking makes a typical, strenuous javelin launch at a steep angle of climb of an F.A.I. free-flight gas-powered model. F.A.I. is flown under international rules. (Laird Jackson photo)

achutes, but the standard is the "pop-up" tail. The stabilizer is pivoted at its leading edge so that when a slow-burning fuse or clockwork-type timer releases a trip at the trailing edge, the rubber-band-loaded stabilizer instantly assumes a 45-degree angle negative to the flight path. This forces the craft to assume a steep, nose-high attitude, after which it descends like an elevator.

In the case of gas models, the engine run must be limited, or otherwise the craft would simply vanish into the blue. In the mid-1930s, fuel was limited to

1/4 oz. per pound of airplane, then to 1/8 oz. As performance improved, it became necessary to switch to a timed motor-run limitation, at first 30 sec., then 20, and ultimately to as little as 7. Normally, the engine run is terminated by a mechanical timer that pinches off the fuel line, or that allows raw fuel to inject into the engine's air-intake opening—the "flood off." Expensive mechanical timers will shut off the engine, then after a desired interval, activate the dethermalizer. Some experts also operate rudder and elevator trim changes (from the same timer) to transition from the power climb to the gliding mode, which requires slower, tighter circling flight. World-class fliers may use a propeller brake to lock the propeller still in a split second. (Due to the time it takes sound to reach the ground—yes, they get that high!—judges sometimes erroneously decree engine "overruns.")

Competition is conducted according to A.M.A. (American) and F.A.I. (International) rules. In the Outdoor gas-power, rubber-power, and towline glider events, these rules afford interesting insights. In the gas-powered category, A.M.A. rules consider variations in flying-site size by setting timed limits for three categories of 2, 3, and 5 min. (Surplus time is not counted.) Corresponding engine-run time limits are 7, 9, and 12 sec. Three official flights are permitted, and when ties result, flyoffs reduce engine runs with each ensuing flight until a winner is determined. Since rubber model "engine runs" (or

The simplest dethermalizer uses a slow-burning fuse in a safety snuffer tube (it stops burning after the rubber band over the wire hooks burns through). The tension of the rubber band at the front of the stabilizer swings it to a 45-degree angle for forced elevatorlike descent.

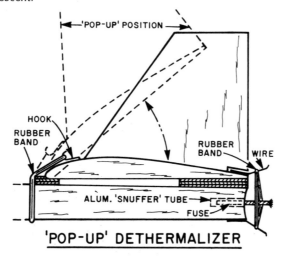

'POP-UP' DETHERMALIZER

glider launching) cannot be time controlled, ties are broken by adding minutes of duration allowed, for successive flights, until a winner results. Competition towline gliders usually compete under the F.A.I. system, which is strikingly different.

F.A.I. rules call for rounds, seven flights permitted, each limited to 3 min. (Duration beyond 3 min. is not counted.) When ties result—as many as thirty-three people tied at one World Championship event—the allowable flight time is increased by 1 min. on each ensuing flight, until a winner is determined by a process of elimination. A round is flown within a certain time period, all entrants making their first flight, and so on. Obviously, the model

Bob White, one of the top fliers of rubber-powered models in the world, with an Unlimited class plane. The white pole behind the model has a long, thin streamer to detect wind conditions. What appears to be a camera tripod in the distance behind White's left arm is a thermistor device that detects passing thermals.

A Satellite gassie makes a vertical takeoff at sunrise. Free-flight models usually are hand-launched, but V.T.O.s are sometimes allowed. Note the multispar construction with ribs and diagonals for lightness and rigidity. (Meuser photo)

must be retrieved quickly enough for the following round—the prime reason for the 3-min. limit and, of course, for the 7-sec. engine run permissible in F.A.I. gas-powered events (greater times were once permitted, but the contests became unmanageable).

For Indoor competition, we have both A.M.A. and F.A.I. rules. Traditional events (hence model types) have been with us for years. But to attract more people to a field that commands less public attention, special events (and simpler models) evolved, some now official, others provisional (in Purgatory, so to speak), and others still a novelty. Because sport activities evolve into provisional and occasionally official events under A.M.A. rules, one really must obtain the *A.M.A Official Rule Book* to be aware of all that goes on.

If free flight sounds forbidding, it also can be simple sport. We have only to master the ABCs of the child's hand-tossed glider and its first cousin, the rubber-powered rise-off-ground model (R.O.G.) (if it has a landing gear, it is an R.O.G.; if not, it is a Stick model).

Sharlene Chase releases a Rogue R.O.G. designed by
Dave Linstrum. (Linstrum photo)

THE DYNAMICS OF FLIGHT

The name of the free-flight game is stability. Stability means the aircraft
will return automatically to its flight path when disturbed by an upsetting
force, such as a gust of wind. Stability keeps the machine flying smoothly.

Unlike a car or boat, a plane operates in three dimensions. An aircraft can
rotate around three axes: the vertical or yaw axis, around which it steers; the
lateral or pitch axis, around which it noses up or down; and the longitudinal
or roll axis (see the diagram, next page). An aircraft is rotatable simultaneously around all three axes, in an infinity of combinations. While the craft
is stable about each control axis, the free-flighter establishes a fixed degree
of rotation around these axes when adjusting the model. He or she controls
its angles of climb and glide, and causes it to bank and turn. Because the
machine is stable, it remains in the desired flight pattern provided the pilot
does not exceed its stability limits.

Stability is not a magic constant. There have been instances of a full-size light aircraft taking off and even landing without a pilot (after he had started the engine and before he could get back into the cabin). That is maximum stability. A fighter pilot, on the other hand, does not wish maximum stability because it works against his efforts to violently maneuver the machine; were he not in the cockpit, and the machine not on automatic pilot, it would fall from the sky like a thunderbolt.

We think of stability as positive, neutral, and negative. Aircraft designers avoid negative stability. Such a plane requires constant controlling—if indeed it can be controlled. We need positive stability in free-flight models. Neutral stability is desirable in some forms of control-line and radio-controlled models, which are linked to the pilot. The neutrally stable craft does not recover when upset, but remains where it is pointed.

Four basic aerodynamic forces are always present in flight: thrust, lift, drag (air resistance), and gravity (weight). Thrust offsets drag and lift offsets weight. The greater the thrust, the faster the machine will fly. More speed increases wing lift; it becomes greater than weight, hence the aircraft climbs.

The three axes around which an airplane yaws, pitches, or rolls.

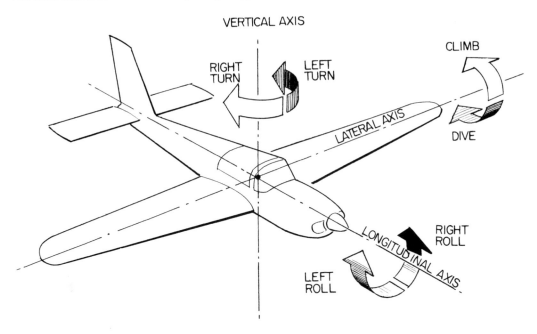

VERTICAL AXIS

RIGHT TURN   LEFT TURN

CLIMB

LATERAL AXIS

DIVE

LONGITUDINAL AXIS

RIGHT ROLL

LEFT ROLL

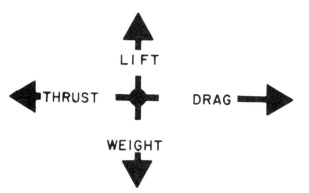

FOUR FORCES ACTING ON PLANE

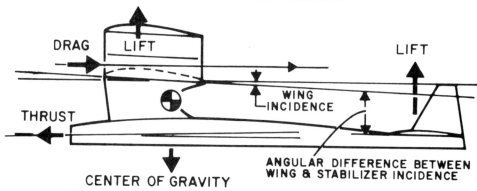

TYPICAL PYLON COMPETITION GAS

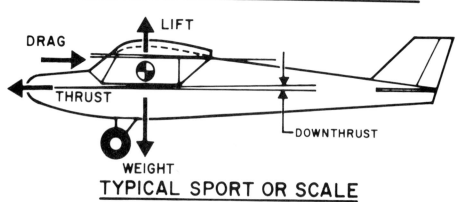

TYPICAL SPORT OR SCALE

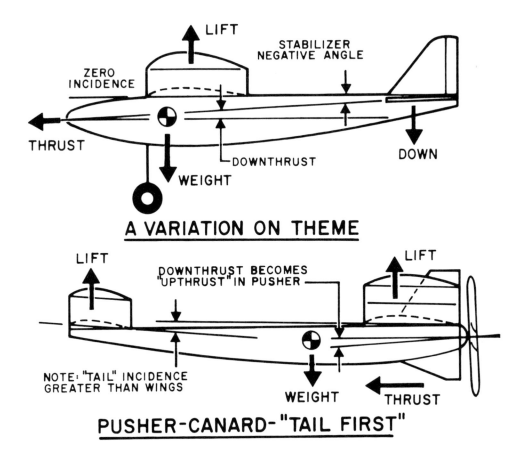

A VARIATION ON THEME

PUSHER-CANARD-"TAIL FIRST"

Drag also is a function of airspeed, and at a certain speed it will counter any amount of thrust—the machine can't fly faster.

All four forces act through invisible levers (we call them "moment arms"). Weight is a downward force concentrated at one point, the center of gravity (C.G.). If the other three forces always acted through the C.G., there would be few upsetting influences. But in the free-flight model, the line of thrust may lie above, or below, the C.G. The center of lift is well above the C.G. (creating a "pendulum" stability effect), and the wing usually is located well above the thrust line. Most of the drag of a plane (about two-thirds of it) is in its wing. Drag in a free-flight model is exerted rearward at a point far above the C.G. Thus thrust, lift, and drag exert leverage around the C.G., all creating

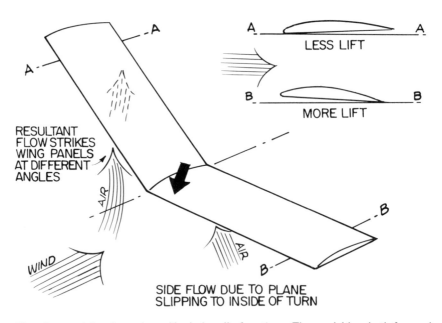

■ HOW DIHEDRAL AFFECTS LIFT
  (BANKED LEFT TURN SHOWN)

A - - A
A - - A
LESS LIFT

B - - B
B - - B
MORE LIFT

A - - A

RESULTANT
FLOW STRIKES
WING PANELS
AT DIFFERENT
ANGLES

AIR

AIR

- - B

WIND

B - -

SIDE FLOW DUE TO PLANE
SLIPPING TO INSIDE OF TURN

*Very few modelers know how dihedral really functions. The model has both forward-
and sideslipping speeds, and the relative airflow that results varies the effective angle
of attack of both wing panels. Detail, upper right, shows resultant angles of attack at
two points on the wing. (They do not imply that the wing frame is twisted.)*

upsetting moments that are controlled by "adjusting" the model. The thrust
line, lying below the center of drag, also exerts leverage around the drag center, as well as the C.G. Free-flight kits and plans harness these forces, and
provide adjustment information suited to the particular design. It is up to the
builder to fine-tune the adjustments to ensure the intended flight pattern.

The vertical axis involves the "weathervane principle." If sufficient side
area lies aft of the C.G., the plane is directionally stable—like an arrow.

Stability about the rolling (lengthwise) axis is ensured by the incorporation
of dihedral in the wing. There are many explanations; the simplest is that the
airplane slips sideways when tilted, and that the center of the side (include
the side view of the wing) area, being above the C.G., exerts a leverage to
right the machine. This is a half-truth at best. The machine has forward

motion (airspeed), and is turning and rolling simultaneously (banking). As the diagram shows, this causes the wing on the outside of the circle to meet the air at a smaller angle of attack than the wing on the inside of the circle. Thus the lowered wing exerts more lift, helping the machine to roll back to level flight.

Pitch-axis stability most affects our first attempts at free flight. For example, if the C.G. is too far forward of the center of lift, the plane is nose-heavy; it dives. If the center of lift is too far in front of the C.G., the plane is tail-heavy; it stalls and loops. A simple analogy is the child's seesaw, where the pivot or fulcrum is the C.G. The weights of two children determine their distance from the fulcrum to maintain balance. The heavier child represents the lift force, and the lighter child, much farther from the fulcrum, the stabilizing force. The modeler varies these weights and distances to balance his or her model. As the model flies, the forces represented by the children on the seesaw do vary. (We already know that changes in thrust, lift, and drag have related effects.)

A vitally important variable is the airfoil, or cross section, of the wing. Lift is exerted at one point on the wing—such as one-third of the chord (wing width) back from the leading edge. With increases in the angle of attack of the wing (quite large if the plane mushes along in a slow flight), the center of lift (also called the center of pressure, or C.P.) shifts toward the leading edge. In increasing the distance of the center of lift in front of the C.G., a corresponding increase in the leverage through which the lift acts destabilizes the machine. In plain English, a typical airfoil is unstable. This is why we have a stabilizer, itself a winglike surface. Some airfoils minimize this center of lift or C.P. travel, but they are not suited to the kind of performance required of a free-flight model—a combination of high climb rate and slow, floating glide.

The free-flight design compensates for this destabilizing influence by having the stabilizer fixed at a smaller angle of incidence (incidence relative to the plane, not to flight) than that of the wing. The angular difference between the two may be anything from 1 degree to 6 degrees. Too great an angular difference is counterproductive when the craft gathers airspeed; the lift generated by a wing section increases greatly with each added degree. Under high power, the model could loop. And since drag also increases with airspeed and a greater angle of attack, glide becomes too slow, with a high rate of sink.

How does this angular difference work? Consider that a typical wing stalls at roughly a 16-degree angle of attack. When the wing stalls, the airflow over its top surface breaks into severe turbulence and lift is destroyed. The stabilizer, set at a smaller angle to begin with, does not reach the angle at which it stalls until after the wing is stalled. Thus, wing lift is gone but the stabilizer

These examples show typical free-flight wing structures. The top two sections are used in competition gas and gliders, the second one down mostly for F.A.I. types. Both are thin and have a high lift-to-drag ratio under high power. The second section is sometimes favored for high lift at slow gliding speed as well. The sport or scale section is thicker, to develop more lift at slower flying speeds. The single-surface rib is for smaller designs using sheet balsa as the primary structure; ribs are widely spaced chord-wise members that retain shape in the wing. If its bottom surface is also sheet-balsa-covered, the wing is stronger and more efficient but would be used on somewhat larger models. The flat section is favored on extremely small hand-launched gliders and R.O.G.s, and develops lift only when the model flies at a slight angle of attack (a condition forced by setting the stabilizer angle at a slight negative angle). The Jedelsky section is also a single-surface wing, for models falling between simple beginner craft and medium-performance sport planes. When sheeted on the bottom as well to make a double-surface wing, it is used in some competition gas models and tow-line gliders.

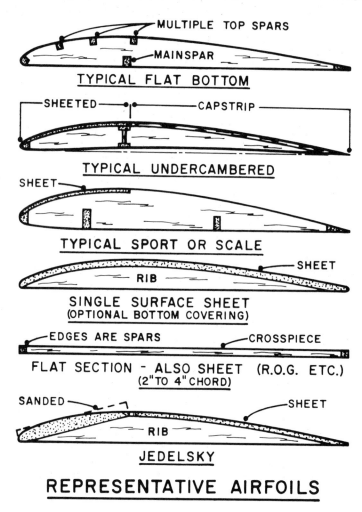

MULTIPLE TOP SPARS

MAINSPAR

TYPICAL FLAT BOTTOM

SHEETED — CAPSTRIP

TYPICAL UNDERCAMBERED

SHEET

TYPICAL SPORT OR SCALE

SHEET

RIB

SINGLE SURFACE SHEET
(OPTIONAL BOTTOM COVERING)

EDGES ARE SPARS — CROSSPIECE

FLAT SECTION - ALSO SHEET (R.O.G. ETC.)
(2" TO 4" CHORD)

SANDED — SHEET

RIB

JEDELSKY

REPRESENTATIVE AIRFOILS

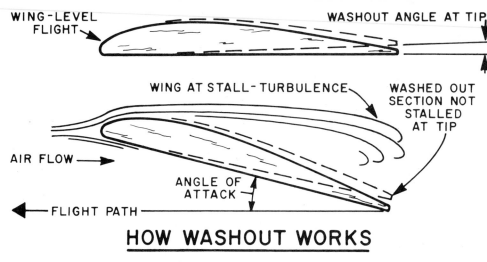

WING-LEVEL FLIGHT

WASHOUT ANGLE AT TIP

WING AT STALL-TURBULENCE

WASHED OUT SECTION NOT STALLED AT TIP

AIR FLOW →

ANGLE OF ATTACK

← FLIGHT PATH

HOW WASHOUT WORKS

Washout or negative twist to the outer wing is commonplace, but few people understand how it works. It prevents wing-tip stall in a slow glide—when a tip stalls, the model enters a spin.

still lifts, causing the tail to rise and forcing the wing to a lower angle of attack, at which point its lift is restored.

The terms *washin* and *washout* are often heard, as is the slang word *twist,* which is a less exact term for these two. If you twist a wing tip so that its leading edge is higher than its trailing edge, it has washin; if the leading edge is twisted down to be lower than the trailing edge of the wing, washout exists. Washout is used to improve lateral stability at lower flying speeds. It is used on competition free-flight models, Scale craft, and Sport radio-controlled models. Washin always makes the wing tip stall first, often causing a crash and a spiral dive or spin; it is unstable. (Incidentally, warped wings may have excessive washout or undesirable washin.)

How does washout benefit stability? It delays the stall at the wing tip, so that the main portion of the wing stalls first. The machine then stalls straight ahead. Without washout, a wing tip stalls before the center of the wing, then the tip drops abruptly and the plane "falls off."

An average wing stalls at approximately a 16-degree angle of attack. Now, if the wing tip were twisted to, say, 2 degrees of washout, the tip would have reached only a 14-degree angle of attack when the center of the wing has reached 16 degrees and stalled. Thus, the wing tip still has available 2 more degrees of angle of attack before it stalls. Because the tip is still "flying" it tends to keep level as the craft stalls.

In rigid wing structures, washout must be built into the frame during assembly. If open-framed, the wing can be purposely warped the desired amount after covering. If paper or cloth covering is used, the wing section is heated over steam from a kettle, then twisted and held in the desired position. If an iron-on film covering is used, the film is softened with the heat gun, the wing twisted and held in the desired position while it cools.

ADJUSTING THE MODEL

Adjustments are concerned first with the gliding aspects, then with power-on aspects, and ultimately are blended for a perfect pattern. A flight pattern has two parts, the power-on and glide. Generally, we seek to keep the craft circling close to its launching point. The diameter of the circles may be small or large, depending on the flier's wishes or his aircraft's flying characteristics. As we will see later, both power and glide portions may circle in the same direction, right-hand or left, or the glide circle may be in the opposite direction to a left- or right-hand power-on circle; the combination is largely determined by the characteristics of different aircraft configurations. The drawings on pages 190–91 show popular patterns used for Sport models (expert fliers resort to many variations on these themes).

First the model must be physically balanced. When it is supported by a fingertip under each wing panel at the designated C.G. location, it should hang level. If not, either the wing must be shifted fore or aft until it does, or weight added to either nose or tail (the latter is unlikely). If the wing is fixed in position, the only recourse is to shift the C.G. location by adding ballast, bits of clay, lead shot, solder, or some other convenient material. (Ballast also is used by RC glider fliers, not to correct balance, but to make the plane heavier for windy conditions; the ballast is added at the C.G. position.)

The Hand-Launched Glider

For our immediate purpose the ready-to-fly hand-launched glider is an adequate example. This glider will already have the required nose weight attached when it is purchased. Its wing can be moved fore or aft, as it is located in a slot in the body or attached by a plastic clip to the fuselage. The stabilizer is already set at a slight negative angle relative to that of the wing. If we made a glider from scratch, all these things would have to be ascertained by trial and error.

Adjustments always begin with hand-glide tests. Grasp the ready-to-fly glider between thumb and index finger close to the rear of the wing. To launch, aim it at a spot on the ground about 15 ft. away, and throw it with a *gentle* dartlike motion. Such tests should be made over grass or a soft surface. The nose is never pointed up at this stage. The correct glide path is string-straight, and the plane should show no diving or stalling tendencies. If a dive or stall is evident, first increase or decrease launching speed to make sure the throwing velocity is correct. The flight path is not correct if the glider seems to swoop too gracefully to a perfect landing. That swoop is "flared out"; the glider is still tail-heavy. Nor should the path be undulating, the nose rising and then sinking, through one or more cycles. That means the model is even more tail-heavy.

The correction is to shift the wing forward a bit at a time to cure a dive, or backward to correct tail-heaviness. If the glide path turns right or left, the probable cause is a wing or tail warp. When one wing panel has its leading edge warped upward, both lift and drag are increased on that side of the craft (vice versa if the edge is warped downward). The added lift on one side is more effective at higher speeds—such as immediately after launching—and the drag more effective at very low speed when the lift is naturally diminished. You will probably note only the lift effect, since the glider contacts the ground (in hand-glide tests only) before speed fades away. At low speed the warped wing acts like an asymmetrical brake. But if the glider did attain a higher altitude, you might see that drag of a warped panel reverses the direction of the turn late in the flight. Warps can have unpredictable effects, which are exaggerated with speed. Bad warps are fatal to all free-flight craft. A high-performance machine would be dashed to bits if the warp were not first removed. On our plastic-foam or sheet-balsa-winged glider, the warp is removed by breathing on the offending surface, simultaneously twisting it in the opposite direction until it retains the proper setting. (Open-frame wings covered with paper, cloth, or an iron-on film can be unwarped by holding the frame over a steam kettle or heating with the iron, as the case may be, and twisting as described.)

Once balanced and successfully hand-glide tested, the glider will stall or loop when thrown hard directly ahead. This is characteristic of all free-flight craft, and is due to excessive flying speed. When throwing the glider we actually give it "power." At the launch, power is excessive, airspeed high, lift more than is needed (although the lift will be correct after launching velocity is lost). This excess lift is harnessed by making the model turn. In a banked turn, the lift force is not vertical to the earth but tilted to one side, at right angles to the wing. If we visualize the glider in a vertical bank, we see that the lift is exerted parallel to the ground. It cannot support the plane, which then spirals earthward. So we "preprogram" the glider by launching it in a slightly banked position, throwing it a bit side-armed rather than straight ahead like a dart. It circles. If the circle is so wide that the glider rolls back to level and stalls, we increase the angle of bank at the launching. If the glider circles too tightly and spirals downward, we impart less bank angle at the launch.

For full-fledged flights the glider is thrown quite hard. In fact, experts throw robust balsa gliders as hard as they would a baseball.

Finer adjustments are possible as launching velocity is increased. For a

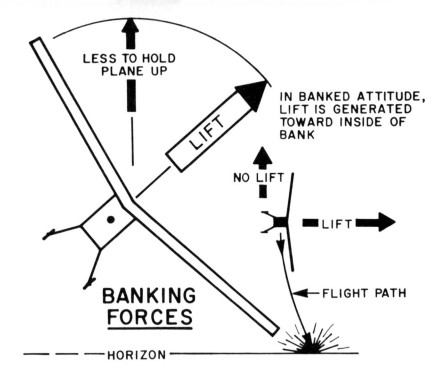

LESS TO HOLD
PLANE UP

LIFT

IN BANKED ATTITUDE,
LIFT IS GENERATED
TOWARD INSIDE OF
BANK

NO LIFT

LIFT

**BANKING
FORCES**

FLIGHT PATH

——   —   ——HORIZON———

glider thrown to the right (if you are right-handed—it would be thrown to the left if you are left-handed), washin is imparted to the right wing. The glider then can be thrown in hard tight turns, and the added lift resulting from the washin prevents a spiral dive. Or the fin/rudder can be ever so slightly warped—to the right to tighten the circle (impart less bank on launching), to the left to open it (this also allows a left glide circle after velocity fades).

A competition hand-launched glider has a wing section carved from thicker sheet balsa to form an airfoil. Since the thicker wood is difficult to warp, a dab of clay may be added to one wing tip or the other to achieve special turning trim effects.

Rubber- and Gas-Powered Models

Now suppose our glider is instead a read-to-fly rubber-powered R.O.G. or Stick model. Adjustments now involve power as well as glide. Power adjustments are made by tilting the thrust line. Usually, this adjustment involves downthrust (pointing the propeller and thus the thrust line down), and often side thrust as well—usually toward the right (right thrust). In our ready-to-fly model the plastic propeller bearing incorporates both these angles; if the model were built from scratch, thrust-line adjustments would have to be determined by a series of power-test flights, while gradually adding turns to the rubber. (If the model uses gas power, we would begin with a short engine run, possibly running quite "rich" to avoid maximum power.)

The thrust of a rubber-powered motor or gas engine continues through the

A Seelig multifunction timer on a competition gas model. It terminates the engine run, adjusts rudder position and stabilizer incidence for glide trim, and operates the de-thermalizer to bring the model down.

Two of the more subtle forces exerted on a model. Both forces are in opposition, and the experienced flier plays them against each other when adjusting his or her model. Propeller slipstream is most pronounced on high-wing configurations—as with cabin or pylon wing mount.

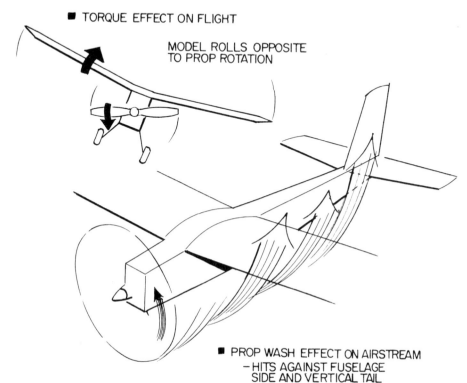

■ TORQUE EFFECT ON FLIGHT

MODEL ROLLS OPPOSITE
TO PROP ROTATION

■ PROP WASH EFFECT ON AIRSTREAM
— HITS AGAINST FUSELAGE
SIDE AND VERTICAL TAIL

For a one-man operation, this flier prepares his Jumbo Scale rubber-powered model for stretch winding. The upright arm of the stooge attaches to the rear rubber tube or dowel, which runs through the fuselage. (Tom Schmitt photo)

"motor run" to propel the craft faster than its gliding speed; the excess lift is converted into climb, harnessed by causing the machine to circle. Sometimes, it tends to stall regardless. Downthrust is incorporated to help hold down the nose.

The propeller introduces two factors not found in a glider. One is torque, the tendency of the model to roll in a direction opposite to that of the propeller rotation—to the left, in other words. Right thrust offsets torque. Enough right thrust is used to ensure that the craft turns right under power, or that it doesn't turn so sharply left that a spiral dive results. The other factor is "prop wash," the twisting slipstream of air behind the propeller that strikes against the side profile of the machine. Prop wash is especially noticeable when the fuselage has a high cabin profile, or the wing is mounted parasol fashion on a pylon. (A pylon in this connection is a finlike structure that extends from the top of the fuselage up to the wing's centerline. A wing mounted parasol fashion is mounted above the fuselage, either on a pylon or on struts.) Since the typical R.O.G. usually is just a motorstick with a wing and tail, it offers no side area (other than the vertical tail) for the prop wash to strike. In more advanced powered models, however, prop wash can be a potent factor.

Although we are using right-hand turns in this discussion, you will find that some models also can be adjusted to fly to the left or in combinations of left- or right-hand circles while under power or in the glide. Experts have terms for such flight patterns: right/right; right/left; left/left; etc., the first word representing the power mode, the second the glide mode.

After the R.O.G. is checked for balance by hand-glide tests, a series of hand-launched progressive power-test flights is made, beginning with, say, twenty-five turns in the rubber, and working up to full winds. Most likely, the R.O.G. will turn left under power because of the propeller torque. If the circle is too tight and the plane loses altitude, the rudder is bent (or a rudder tab, if there is one, is set) slightly right to open the turn to a greater diameter. It is probably safe to try enough right rudder to make this R.O.G. turn right. The launch is made straight ahead with the nose aimed at the horizon, never upward. Stalls and dives or erratic flights are corrected in the same manner as was done on the hand-launched glider. This method of launching is not to be confused with the "javelin" launch, used by expert competition fliers to project their craft upward at a steep angle at high velocity.

More advanced rubber-powered models provide more options for determining a desired flight pattern. The propeller is large in relation to the model size—its diameter is one-third or more of the wing span. The rubber motor may have two, four, six, eight, or more loops, instead of the one loop on the R.O.G. Thrust is dramatically greater, and increased torque becomes something to fear. Almost invariably, generous right thrust of 2 to 3 degrees becomes necessary. By mastering the simple hand-launched glider and the R.O.G., new modelers establish a solid foundation for the more elaborate, "tricky" stuff they encounter later.

If you want to become a competition flier, it is a distinct advantage to know someone involved in this phase of activity, to visit a flying site, if possible (rather difficult because free-flighters are a clannish bunch who drive great distances to out-of-the-way open places), to join the A.M.A. and obtain a rule book, to subscribe to one or more general modeling magazines, to join the

Don Srull launches a rubber-powered scale model of a British Gloster Gannett that was flown in an ultralight competition in England in the early 1920s. (Tom Schmitt photo)

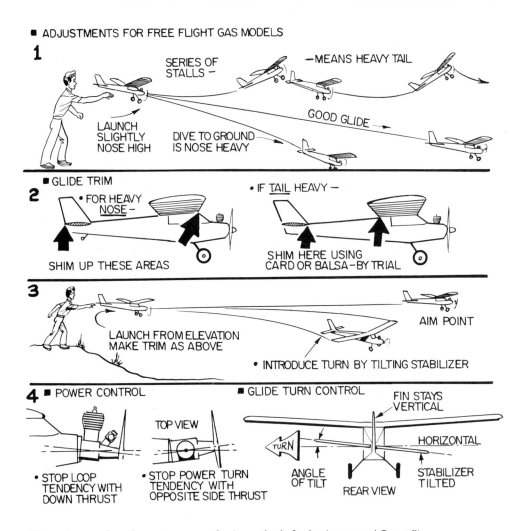

■ ADJUSTMENTS FOR FREE FLIGHT GAS MODELS

1

SERIES OF STALLS –

–MEANS HEAVY TAIL

LAUNCH SLIGHTLY NOSE HIGH

DIVE TO GROUND IS NOSE HEAVY

GOOD GLIDE →

2 ■ GLIDE TRIM

• FOR HEAVY NOSE –

SHIM UP THESE AREAS

• IF TAIL HEAVY –

SHIM HERE USING CARD OR BALSA–BY TRIAL

3

LAUNCH FROM ELEVATION MAKE TRIM AS ABOVE

AIM POINT

• INTRODUCE TURN BY TILTING STABILIZER

4 ■ POWER CONTROL   ■ GLIDE TURN CONTROL

TOP VIEW

• STOP LOOP TENDENCY WITH DOWN THRUST

• STOP POWER TURN TENDENCY WITH OPPOSITE SIDE THRUST

TURN

ANGLE OF TILT

REAR VIEW

FIN STAYS VERTICAL

HORIZONTAL

STABILIZER TILTED

Shown here and on the next page are basic methods for beginners and Sport fliers.

Free Flight Association (through the A.M.A.), and to obtain the remarkable books available through these organizations.

Although they are basically similar to "beginner" models, getting involved with the bigger high-performance craft is akin to stepping up from the family automobile to an exhilarating sports car that demands polished driving technique. Power is so much greater! Things happen quickly; adjustments must be meticulously made. The rudder is extremely effective at higher speeds, so it is cautiously used, if at all, to force a turn. The solution to this problem is ingenious and simple. Instead of bending the rudder to control the glide circle, many fliers prefer to tilt the stabilizer.

Looking at the ship from the rear, if one tip of the stabilizer is elevated about 1/4 in., and the opposite side depressed, the model always glides in

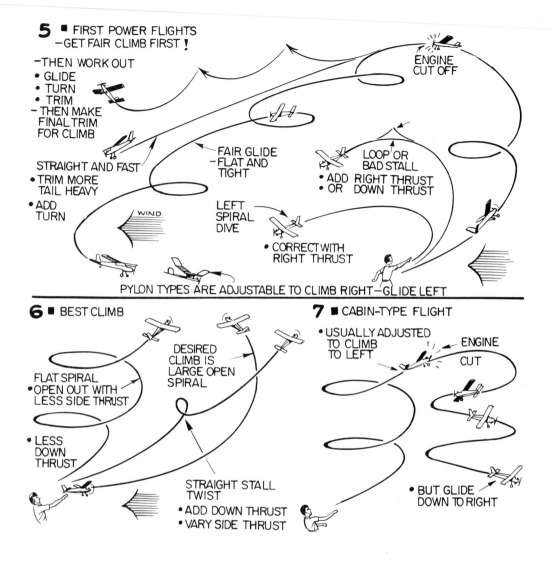

5 ■ FIRST POWER FLIGHTS
—GET FAIR CLIMB FIRST **!**

—THEN WORK OUT
- GLIDE
- TURN
- TRIM
—THEN MAKE
FINAL TRIM
FOR CLIMB

ENGINE
CUT OFF

STRAIGHT AND FAST
- TRIM MORE
TAIL HEAVY
- ADD
TURN

FAIR GLIDE
—FLAT AND
TIGHT

LOOP OR
BAD STALL
- ADD RIGHT THRUST
- OR DOWN THRUST

LEFT
SPIRAL
DIVE

WIND

- CORRECT WITH
RIGHT THRUST

PYLON TYPES ARE ADJUSTABLE TO CLIMB RIGHT—GLIDE LEFT

6 ■ BEST CLIMB

DESIRED
CLIMB IS
LARGE OPEN
SPIRAL

FLAT SPIRAL
- OPEN OUT WITH
LESS SIDE THRUST

- LESS
DOWN
THRUST

STRAIGHT STALL
TWIST
- ADD DOWN THRUST
- VARY SIDE THRUST

7 ■ CABIN-TYPE FLIGHT

- USUALLY ADJUSTED
TO CLIMB
TO LEFT

ENGINE
CUT

- BUT GLIDE
DOWN TO RIGHT

the direction of the stabilizer's high side (see step 4 of the diagram). This tilted stabilizer has little effect on the power mode, so the tilt is safely used to establish whatever direction and diameter of glide turn are desired.

In making the initial hand-glide tests, the flier discovers that these bigger machines, particularly the gas-powered models that have tiny propellers compared to rubber-powered craft, easily glide a long distance when hand launched. It helps if test glides are made on high ground. Launched "dead stick" (without power) from a knoll, the craft glides still greater distances, offering the observer a longer period for evaluating the gliding attitude, radius of glide turn, and so on.

The difference between the design that merely flies successfully and one that climbs smoothly to great altitude, then transitions into a flat circle glide without dips, and stalls when the power stops, lies in the "finishing touch." Invariably, significant improvements can be made by anyone who looks for tiny flight-pattern flaws. There is the opportunity to diagnose both the power and glide modes separately when the machine finally climbs high enough so that you can watch how it glides. The most important factor is: Does the craft seem to be stalling, perhaps ever so slightly, or gliding too steeply? First, is the glide circle tight enough, remembering that turning flight is an antistall factor? Or perhaps the glide circle is too tight—opening this circle may remove the dive tendency.

If the wing can be moved fore and aft, slide it rearward, perhaps an 1/8 in. at a time, to correct for the stall; move it forward to correct the dive. Advanced designs very likely have the wing position fixed, so in virtually all cases, a stall is corrected by decreasing the angular difference between wing and tail settings, using a 1/64- to 1/32-in.-thick plywood shim under the wing's trailing edge or the stabilizer's leading edge—and vice versa for the dive (see the diagram, step 2). Several shims sometimes are required (they are glued in place once the adjusting is complete), but never to the point where the stabilizer incidence angle is more than that of the wing. The glide turn diameter is varied by increasing or decreasing the amount of stabilizer tilt, or by changing the rudder position if rudder is being used to control turn.

By speeding up or slowing down the glide with incidence changes, the powered model once more has a corresponding tendency to nose up under power or not to climb steeply enough, the latter probably exhibited in a fast, tight power turn that can become a disastrous power dive. (This is why we use a *series* of thin shims for partial, trial corrections.) If the glide was slowed up, the downthrust might then have to be increased to control thrust, or the diameter of the power circle tightened up. If the glide was speeded up, downthrust may have to be decreased, or the power circle opened up a bit. Never use upthrust—it makes a plane stall like crazy. Competition fliers may use slight washin on the wing inside the power circle to avoid "spiraling in." In this final stage, it is of paramount importance to keep power and glide adjustments separate and not to make more than one adjustment at a time.

Towline Gliders

The towline glider poses a fascinating riddle, fortunately easily solved. When it is pulled high in the sky by the towline, the glider climbs straight ahead. Although the towline imparts a speed higher than that at which the machine slowly glides after release, the downward force component of the line prevents that excess speed from stalling the glider. But we wish the glider

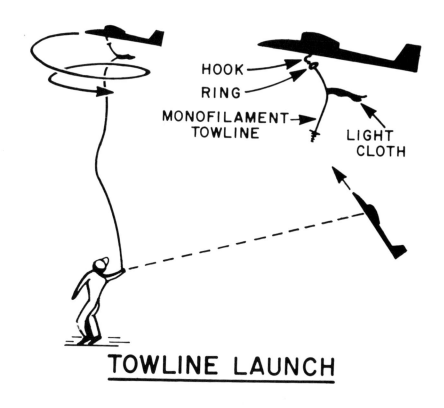

HOOK
RING
MONOFILAMENT TOWLINE
LIGHT CLOTH

TOWLINE LAUNCH

To position the glider rudder for circling after release from the towline, an auto-rudder is held straight during the tow by the pull on the towline.

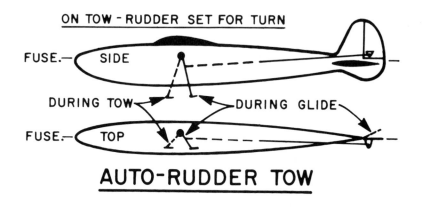

ON TOW - RUDDER SET FOR TURN

FUSE.— SIDE

DURING TOW DURING GLIDE

FUSE.— TOP

AUTO-RUDDER TOW

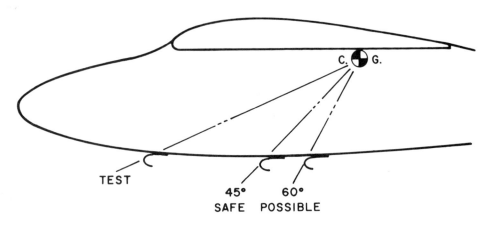

TEST

45°
SAFE

60°
POSSIBLE

TOW HOOK LOCATIONS

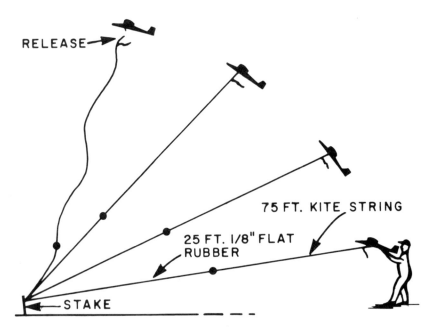

RELEASE→

75 FT. KITE STRING

25 FT. 1/8" FLAT
RUBBER

←STAKE

'HI-START' LAUNCH

How to tow-launch your own Sport glider without running. When the rubber is stretched tight, the model climbs to great heights. The black dots roughly indicate how much the rubber is stretched.

At free-flight contests motorbikes are often used to chase and retrieve. Grandma Meuser helps Marnie Meuser retrieve a winning A-1-class Nordic glider, a Xenakis-designed Tadpole. Marnie holds a reeled-up towline in her left hand. The peculiar flat object appearing above the top of the wing is the stabilizer in its pop-up dethermalizing position. (Meuser photo)

to circle slowly once released. In competition, the skilled flier employs an automatic rudder (auto-rudder), held straight by a line attached to the tow hook under the fuselage in such a manner that, as the towline falls away from the hook at the apogee of the launch, the rubber-band- or spring-loaded rudder swings slightly in the direction of the desired turn. World-class fliers carry this to fantastic lengths. They use extremely complicated tow hooks that permit them to actually tow the model in circles and release it at will by a final tug that also imparts a zoom to gain additional altitude as the plane comes off the line. For general purposes, the simple auto-rudder is quite adequate.

A towline glider has a power mode, the pull provided by the towing. Towing adjustments are controlled by the position of the hook under the belly. If the hook is too far back, the craft persists in spiral diving similar to a kite— one handles this the same as a kite, easing off towing pressure for attempted recovery, then resuming tow. The correction is to move the hook forward, more in front of the C.G. Actually, many fliers employ two hooks, sometimes three, one behind the other, to provide choices. Wind also affects hook position. The more wind, the more forward the hook needs to be—another reason for multiple hooks.

Adjustable hooks are available, the hook sliding fore or aft in a mount so that it can be locked in the correct position for the ship's requirements and the wind conditions. The towline makes an angle of 40 to 60 degrees to the C.G. when the hook is properly located.

Adjusting the free-flight model is a time-consuming process, but every sport requires expertise. Compare the child on a fishing trip using a bent pin hook and a worm for bait, and the skilled fisherman with many lures. Free flight can be sublime, offering great fulfillment. It is worth the effort.

Al Rabe puts his semi-Scale Mustang P-51 into an inside loop during the 1978 World Championships for control-line models. (Laird Jackson photo)

chapter nine

Control-Line Flight Techniques

It is difficult now to comprehend the intensity with which youth in simpler times, without the distractions of today's environment, pursued the dream of flight. All models were free flight. Prior to the early 1920s, the excited flier measured in feet how far his model had flown. At early contests a measuring wheel on a stick was used. But, as we saw in the previous chapter, free-flight craft began to travel for such distances that duration became the yardstick of a performance. Then, during the 1930s and 1940s, the urban sprawl deprived increasing thousands of a place to fly (today, contest experts drive 50 to 100 mi. out of town to test fly their formidable free-flight machines). By 1940, fame and riches awaited anyone with the ingenuity to find a better "mouse trap." That answer proved to be the control-line model, because it could be operated in small, close-in flying sites. If the appearance of the manufactured gas engine in the early 1930s attracted hordes of new hobbyists, the advent of the control-line machine was a quantum leap in the growth of the activity.

When, in the late 1930s, American Junior introduced the realistic Fireball model with an Ohlsson 0.23 engine, the stage was set for a major revolution that could be delayed only by World War II. In 1946 the U-Control system in Jim Walker's Fireball took the nation by storm and even today, thanks to large manufacturers such as Cox, plastic read-to-fly control-line models are sold by the millions. These beginner's models are found at thousands of outlets over and above the normal model airplane distribution system. The older hobbyist, however, is involved with many forms of bigger, more powerful control-line models flown for specific purposes—such as stunting, speed, racing, and combat—and it is appropriate therefore that we pick up where the little ready-to-fly planes leave off.

All control-line craft, from the youngster's plastic models to a World Champion's stunt plane, share basic principles.

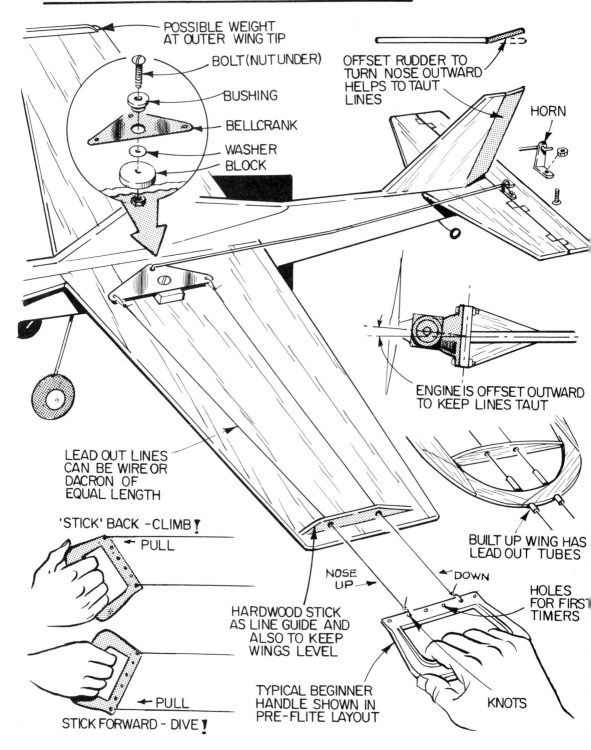

POSSIBLE WEIGHT AT OUTER WING TIP

BOLT (NUT UNDER)

BUSHING

BELLCRANK

WASHER

BLOCK

OFFSET RUDDER TO TURN NOSE OUTWARD HELPS TO TAUT LINES

HORN

ENGINE IS OFFSET OUTWARD TO KEEP LINES TAUT

LEAD OUT LINES CAN BE WIRE OR DACRON OF EQUAL LENGTH

'STICK' BACK - CLIMB!

PULL

BUILT UP WING HAS LEAD OUT TUBES

NOSE UP

DOWN

HOLES FOR FIRST TIMERS

HARDWOOD STICK AS LINE GUIDE AND ALSO TO KEEP WINGS LEVEL

PULL

TYPICAL BEGINNER HANDLE SHOWN IN PRE-FLITE LAYOUT

KNOTS

STICK FORWARD - DIVE!

THE BASIC SYSTEM

The heart of the system is a bellcrank firmly mounted in the aircraft. The bellcrank is T-shaped, with the top of the T facing the pilot, who flies the plane in circles with himself at the center. From each end of the bellcrank, a piece of music wire or thin steel cable (called a leadout) extends along, or inside of, one wing panel and beyond the wing tip, connecting to long steel control lines, which in turn connect to the ends of a control handle held by the pilot. From the upright of the T (facing away from the flier), a stiff wire pushrod extends rearward to the plane's tail, attaching to a control horn fastened to the movable elevator(s). When the handle is tilted back or forward by the flier, pull is exerted on one of the two lines, causing the bellcrank to pivot to pull or push on the pushrod. The pushrod in turn causes the elevator to move up or down. Generally, the line running from the top of the control handle to the front end of the bellcrank (via the leadout) is the "up" line, and when the handle is tilted back at the top, the end result is that the elevator tilts up to make the plane climb. The line from the bottom of the handle is generally the "down" line. In the basic, simple craft, no other controls are present. Advanced and special-mission craft do have additional controls, as we will see.

Most kit makers and designers of magazine projects take the pushrod for granted. After all, it is only a length of stiff music wire. This wire varies in diameter from roughly 1/32 to 1/16 in., depending on the model size (plans and directions will specify). There are, however, two troublesome points. The wire must be rigid; if it bows under compression (it is under tension in one direction, compression in the other), control response is mushy or even ineffective. To keep the wire rigid, a "fairlead" is employed. This may be a staple-shaped piece of music wire, placed over the midpoint of the pushrod and inserted and glued into the fuselage side (common on Profile-type craft). Or it may be a screw eye, or a piece of plywood through which a hole is bored for the pushrod, the plywood glued into a slot cut in the balsa. For built-up planes—those with two fuselage sides as with a full-size aircraft—one or more plywood fairleads are glued internally to crosspieces between the two fuselage sides.

A most devilish task is making the special bend, a kind of jog or step in the wire, that enables the pushrod to slip through the bellcrank hole (from the top) in such a fashion that it won't detach, and without its end jamming against the adjacent structure. Kits usually include prebent pushrods, but it is inevitable that you will want to make your own. To simplify things, obtain two wheel collars (these are made to retain wheels on axles), then bend the ends of the pushrod at right angles to pass upward through the bellcrank

Pitman Jed Kusick has the quick style that gains seconds for his team in F.A.I. team racing. The fuel-stingy diesel engine in this model shuts down by abrupt elevator movement to operate the mechanical shut-off trip. The pitman wears a fuel can and pressure bulb on his arm and has a device at his fingertips for rapid tank filling. (Laird Jackson photo)

hole, and sideways through the elevator-horn hole. After the pushrod is installed, use the wheel collars to retain the wire in place.

In the ready-to-fly model, such crucial matters as balance point and degree of control response are automatically provided for. But in general, just as a free-flighter must adjust the craft for truly successful flight, so must the control-line flier deal with variations in basic principles. The balance point (C.G. location) and degree of movement of the system parts, and consequently the amount of control response, must suit his or her particular needs, which vary widely with the kind of model flown.

Where is the C.G. located? These models normally balance with the C.G. located within a fore-and-aft range, whose most forward position is on a vertical line with the attachment of the front line to the bellcrank, to a rearward position located roughly between the front line and the pivot point of the bellcrank. Normal is midway between these two points. The bellcrank pivot point generally is located at one-third the wing width back from the leading edge. The more forward the C.G. position, the steadier the model flies, and the less sensitive the effect of its elevators. It is easier to fly, but not highly maneuverable. The more aft the C.G., the more sensitive and responsive the craft becomes to control inputs. (Too far aft makes the model uncontrollable.)

Novices require minimum control response until they master flying. The less "jumpy" the model, the better their chances of success. Speed and Racing pilots flying in competition also wish minimum responses. The Aerobatic pilot who performs exotic maneuvers, such as figure eights, requires a more sensitive plane with strong control response; so does a Combat flier. The C.G. on a stunt machine usually is located halfway between the front bellcrank line and the bellcrank pivot point. Trainer models—also those that fly at high speeds—have relatively small elevators, while the stunt machine has big elevators.

The second vital factor that determines the degree of control response is the choice of holes in the bellcrank for line and pushrod attachment, the choice of holes in the elevator control horn for the pushrod, and the choice of line attachment points on the control handle (narrow- or wide-spaced). Don't feel intimidated; it is really quite simple.

Let's begin with the control handle, move on to the bellcrank, and then the elevator control horn.

Two versions of an especially fine universal handle, the Sullivan Insta-Just, are pictured here. The handle on the right has a metal bar to which leadouts may be attached; it permits a choice of two settings, for maximum or minimum movements of the elevators. This handle also provides adjustment of the leadouts for both the amount of movement and for setting elevator neutral. The handle on the left in the photo allows only for setting elevator neu-

Two types of Sullivan Pylon brand control handles and Sullivan flexible steel wire cables on the reel provided. Snaps (left) attach lines to the model and handle. The ends of these lines and the handle cables have convenient eyelets for attachment. The handle at left provides only for adjusting leadout lengths, whereas the one on the right also gives the flier a choice of holes on the bar to allow minimum or maximum elevator response.

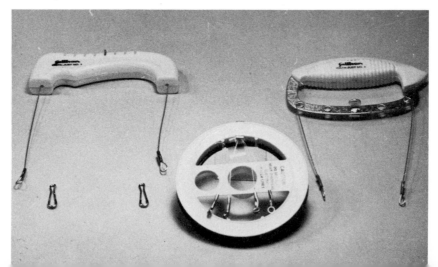

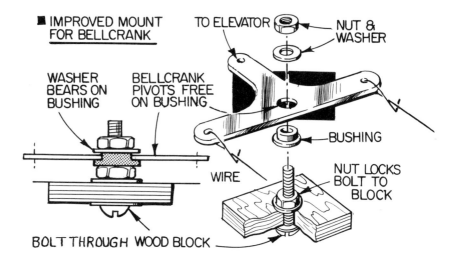

■ IMPROVED MOUNT FOR BELLCRANK

TO ELEVATOR

NUT & WASHER

WASHER BEARS ON BUSHING

BELLCRANK PIVOTS FREE ON BUSHING

BUSHING

WIRE

NUT LOCKS BOLT TO BLOCK

BOLT THROUGH WOOD BLOCK

tral. The short cable (Indent-A-Line) shown has color-coded prefabricated ends for attaching the control lines, and is locked in place on the handle at its center. By loosening the locking device, the cable may be moved more toward the top or bottom of the handle, so that one end or the other of the cable projects farther out from the handle toward the plane. This feature allows the flier to compensate for an elevator that rests in up or down position, rather than in neutral, when the handle is held vertically. Without this adjustable cable the builder has a devilish time altering the pushrod length to neutralize the elevator if he or she erred during construction. This handle has several line attachment points at varying distances from its center to allow decreasing elevator response. The innermost holes reduce control response, the outer holes provide maximum elevator movement. The inner holes are used for small planes, and any holes for larger planes according to the pilot's desired "feel." The beginner would use the innermost holes to minimize overcontrolling—which would make the plane behave like a jackrabbit!

The typical bellcrank is metal, with a brass bearing on which it pivots. Most bellcranks have three holes, one near each end of the crossarm of the T, a third near the end of the stem of the T. The control lines (or leadouts to which control lines fasten—see below) attach to the holes in the top or crossarm of the T. The pushrod attaches to the hole in the stem of the T. In small ready-to-fly craft or other 1/2 A models, the bellcrank may be plastic or plywood. In larger kits, or bigger original designs, builders often must buy their own bellcranks (kits indicate size). Sizes range from about 2 to 4 in., measured between the holes on the top of the T. In large bellcranks, two sets of holes are usually provided in the crossarm of the T. By attaching the lines (or leadouts) to the holes nearest the pivot point, control response is increased. The pushrod hole nearest the pivot point reduces the linear movement of the pushrod, resulting in less elevator movement.

Although elevator control horns vary in size, material, and method of attachment, a horn is nothing but a short arm extending at right angles from the top or bottom of the elevator at the hinge line. The horn is located at the centerline of the stabilizer, or as close to it as possible. In ready-to-fly plastic models the horn may be molded in place. In other small models (1/2 As) it usually is a roughly triangular piece of thin plywood or aluminum, bent at right angles at its base to provide a tab for attachment to the elevator. For original designs, and larger craft in general, many builders prefer a nylon radio-control horn.

Since planes vary in design, some have one long elevator that extends from tip to tip of the stabilizer, whereas others have two elevators, one on each side of the fin/rudder. When two split-type elevators are used, a short piece of hardwood or steel music wire is attached to the front edge of the elevators to join them together. On any but the smallest craft, both elevators may not move a similar distance when the horn is attached to just one elevator. The force of the airstream retards movement of the elevator without the horn. Therefore, the music-wire centerpiece (typical on most large ships) is bent back at right angles at either end, and the arms of the resulting U-shaped piece are then inserted and glued into holes punched or drilled in the front of the elevators.

Typical small horns have a hole drilled close to the outer end of the arm. The pushrod—its end bent at a right angle—inserts through this hole. Larger control horns generally have two or three holes, providing the easiest method for varying elevator movement. The hole closest to the hinge line provides *maximum* elevator movement; the one closest to the end of horn arm the least elevator movement.

All control-line craft require a leadout guide, through which run either the control lines or the leadouts to which the lines attach (see the drawing on page 198). This guide is affixed to, or close to, the wing tip. In ready-to-fly and some small craft, Dacron lines tie to the bellcrank and to the control handle. In all larger machines, the lines do not connect directly to the bellcrank. Instead, leadouts—which may be thin music wire (such as 1/32 in.) or flexible steel cable (available in hobby shops with diagramed instructions)—attach to the bellcrank and extend out through the leadout guide, and past the wing tip. The control lines attach to the outer ends of the leadouts.

Leadouts permit easy replacement of the lines when they become kinked or worn, or for their detachment after flying is finished, which makes for easy transportation and storage. If steel wire or cable control lines were extended through the wing and permanently affixed to the bellcrank, replacement could be impossible, especially when the bellcrank is buried in the structure.

Leadout wire, which can be found in the Perfect brand display racks (Sullivan also has leadout sets), is a 5-ft.-long multistrand 60-lb.-test steel cable that can be cut into desired lengths for two leadouts. This is tough material, so large diagonal or electrician's pliers are necessary to cut it.

All sorts of things are used for leadout guides. A small plastic model has the guide molded in place. Other simple balsa models use a piece of Popsicle stick (or plywood) cemented on edge into a groove cut chordwise on the bottom—or sometimes the top—of the wing. Two holes corresponding to the distance between the two control lines or leadouts, as the case may be, provide passage for either. Without the guide the plane could not fly with its wings level. In more advanced models, notably those with built-up framed wings, the leadouts almost always are internal and pass through holes in the wing ribs to reach the bellcrank. In this case, short lengths of brass tubing are glued into holes drilled through the wing-tip block. Competition fliers, notably in Aerobatic events, who are sensitive to the way a plane feels at different points of its maneuvers, as well as how it "corners," prefer adjust-

Helper Gary Frost launches a Combat model for pilot Bill Harris (far right background). Harris's opponent controls the model already aloft. The prime purpose is to cut or sever the streamer trailing each model—visible on the craft being launched. The duel is breathtaking, but stringent safety requirements govern all competition events. (Charlie Johnson photo)

During the Team Race event at the Nationals things get close at the circle center as pilots "Doc" Jackson, Stu Willoughby, and John Ballard whirl around while looking in three directions. Ballard (right) is in the act of passing Willoughby's model.

able leadout guides. The guide moves fore and aft on a track and can be locked in any desired position.

While Dacron lines are sufficient for ready-to-fly small craft, stronger lines are essential for all other models. Control lines are either single- or multi-strand cable, thin steel wire of the length and thickness required for the size and type of model. Whereas the little plastic model can be flown on Dacron lines 15 to perhaps 25 ft. long, wire control lines generally range from about 25 to 70 ft. in length.

Although both single-strand and cable lines are acceptable, the latter have important advantages. A line that kinks is subject to failure, and stranded cables are less easily kinked. They also are less likely to jam when a careless flier performs too many loops in one direction (the two wires then wrap around each other—five or six loops in one direction are regarded as the safe limit). Loops in the opposite direction unwrap the lines.

For diameters and lengths of lines, the table on the next page (based on Sullivan seven-strand cable wire) covers the entire range.

DIAMETER (in.)	SIZE (cu. in.) OF ENGINE	LENGTH (ft.) OF LINE
0.008	0.05 to 0.075	26.3
0.012	0.09	35
0.015	0.19	52.6
0.015	0.29	60
0.018	0.29	60
0.018	0.49	60
0.018	0.49	70
0.021	0.60	70

When control-line sets are bought, they are wound on a convenient reel. (Many fliers make their own reels with features more to their liking.) When not in use, lines must be rewound on the reel to avoid snarling or kinking. Since the lines are wound off the reel in order to fly, then wound back on the reel after flying, two sets of snaps are attached to the ends of the lines, one set at the airplane end (they hook onto the leadouts), the other attaching to the cable on the handle. Common fishing swivel-type snaps are never used— they may pull apart at the swivel joint.

In the photo of the Sullivan handles and reel (page 201), you may note that the attachment eyelets are already in place on all wire ends, so you are

As his model whirls around him, former World Speed Champion Ugo Dusi of Italy races around the pylon to keep up, grasping it with one hand while the hand with the control handle rests in a rotatable U at the top. Speed is a highly specialized event flown only in competition by experts.

spared the tedious task of fabricating such details. The proper snaps for attachment are included. For those interested in competition, the A.M.A. rule book diagrams techniques necessary to fulfill safety requirements.

Another factor affecting line tension in flight is the weight of the lines and leadouts themselves. This line weight hanging on the inside wing tip tends to bank the model toward the flier. The inside wing is "heavier." To correct this a lead weight is built into the tip of the outside wing. Kits and plans include or specify the amount of weight.

HOW THE SYSTEM OPERATES

Flight of a control-line craft depends on centrifugal force. (It is possible to "whip" a model with the engine not running, like swinging a brick on the end of a string.) The propeller thrust pulls the craft at a speed that generates sufficient centrifugal force to maintain significant tension ("pull") on the lines. With insufficient centrifugal force, the lines lose tension and sag. When this happens it is impossible to move the elevators. The model "comes in" on the lines, helplessly, and crashes. When lines begin to lose tension, the pilot steps rapidly backward to restore tension to them. Line tension is increased by certain adjustments to the model.

The most common measure of line tension is inclining the rudder toward the outside of the circle. This steers the model away from the flier, creating greater pull on the lines, and helps assure that tension won't be lost. In most cases, the engine thrust line is tilted toward the outside of the circle so that the resulting offset thrust also increases the pull on the lines, helping to maintain line tension while the engine is running during maneuvers.

Line tension is also affected by the location of the craft in the hemisphere of space in which a control-liner maneuvers. The higher the ship is above the ground, the less centrifugal force and line tension it has. In a wind, there is always more line tension when the craft is downwind from the flier. This is why maneuvers are executed downwind from the pilot. For example, if the ship is looped, it is at a greater distance from the ground at the top of the loop and, if there is wind, the greater the tendency of the ship to lose line tension and control when the maneuver is executed upwind. The control-liner also must take off downwind, never into the wind. Were it to take off into the wind, it would be vulnerable to being blown toward the pilot, coming in on the lines, and crashing. Beginners should keep their models at a low altitude, in level flight, on the upwind half of the circle, and to attempt climbs, loops, and the like as the plane approaches the downwind side. Failure to do this is the greatest reason why youngsters crash their first airplanes.

Note: Kits, plans, accessories and magazines constantly warn the user not to fly control-line models in the vicinity of power lines. Even a simple-looking line may carry a high voltage. Never be tempted to seek out cleared areas beneath or even adjacent to power lines. The model does not have to touch a power line for the current to jump across the intervening airspace. The person with feet on the earth is GROUNDED, and electrical currents always seek the shortest point to the ground. Nonmetallic control lines, such as cord, are NOT a protection. Once an electrical current acquires a direction it can jump like lightning. As the A.M.A. Safety Code advises, "Do not fly close to power lines."

The biggest surprise to the beginner is that his first attempt is not a cinch. He "overcontrols." No one expects to drive an auto blithely down the freeway the first time behind the wheel. But the beginning flier thinks he is Snoopy chasing the Red Baron. He applies "up" to takeoff and, not having the feel of things, he causes the craft to zoom, then instantly applies down-elevator to try to gain level flight. But he overdoes it and the plane dives abruptly. After a few up-and-down gyrations, the craft dives into the ground. Successive tries lessen overcontrolling. The plane flounders around the circle, alternately diving and zooming but eventually managing to remain airborne. The new flier is so busy he has no idea where the model is in the circle in relation to surroundings, upwind or down, and may get the craft too high on the upwind side of the circle, losing line tension and control. As soon as he masters this bucking bronco and flies a few glorious laps, he finds he becomes disastrously dizzy. This, too, passes quickly. His impression then is that the background is a blur against which he sees the model clearly. Watch the model and try to ignore the background.

There is a simple trick in learning to fly that instructions seldom mention. Given a small trainer-type craft, the flier should not at first tilt the handle to make the plane go up or down. If the arm is held rigidly, pointed at the model, then raised, the handle tilts a small amount so that the craft climbs slightly. If the arm is pointed downward, the resulting automatic tilting of the handle causes a gradual descent. The flier avoids overcontrolling by merely raising or lowering his or her arm, keeping the elbow and wrist locked. Very soon the pilot can begin to add control by tilting the handle ever so slightly using wrist action.

To prepare for flying, a simple procedure is followed. A helper retains the ship before takeoff. First, after attaching the lines to the airplane, place the

Two former World Champions in Aerobatics show how it is done, as Les McDonald launches for Bob Hunt. (Laird Jackson photo)

control handle in the center of the flying circle. Then the lines are "walked out" from the handle to the plane, as you hold one line in each hand to keep them separated. Second, the flier returns to center circle, picks up the handle and with the helper holding the ship (whose engine is not yet running), the pilot tilts the handle for up-elevator and calls "Up!" to the helper. The helper confirms that it is indeed up and not down, which would mean that the lines were reversed. The flier can see the control movement, but many people have taken off and crashed with reversed lines or with the handle held upside down. Third, the pilot returns to the model, starts the engine (or a qualified helper can do this) and adjusts the needle valve, then returns to the center of the circle, picks up the handle, and waves to the helper to release the ship. The helper does so with the nose pointed out slightly from the circle to ensure line tension from the instant the takeoff roll begins.

Control line, like radio control, involves stages of learning like those found in training for full-scale aircraft, whereas free flight is a bit like learning to swim by jumping into the water. A procedure is followed in free flight, but the flier improves by observation and logical analysis. In both CL and RC, there is the initial business of physical conditioning requiring coordination of eye and hand. In the primary stage, corresponding to soloing a trainer in full-scale flying, the flier masters taking off, keeping the plane safely aloft, and landing. As with full-scale, the modeler then progresses to a higher level of piloting technique. At this basic level one learns simple aerobatics. It is as if

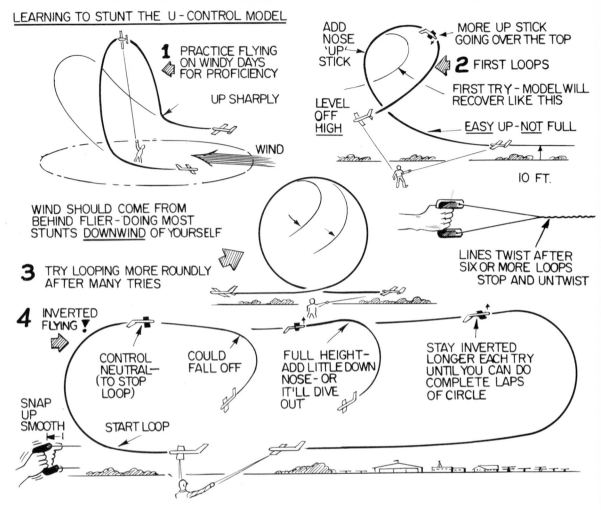

LEARNING TO STUNT THE U-CONTROL MODEL

1 PRACTICE FLYING ON WINDY DAYS FOR PROFICIENCY

UP SHARPLY

WIND

ADD NOSE 'UP' STICK

MORE UP STICK GOING OVER THE TOP

2 FIRST LOOPS

FIRST TRY – MODEL WILL RECOVER LIKE THIS

LEVEL OFF HIGH

EASY UP – NOT FULL

10 FT.

WIND SHOULD COME FROM BEHIND FLIER – DOING MOST STUNTS DOWNWIND OF YOURSELF

3 TRY LOOPING MORE ROUNDLY AFTER MANY TRIES

LINES TWIST AFTER SIX OR MORE LOOPS STOP AND UNTWIST

4 INVERTED FLYING !

CONTROL NEUTRAL – (TO STOP LOOP)

COULD FALL OFF

FULL HEIGHT – ADD LITTLE DOWN NOSE – OR IT'LL DIVE OUT

STAY INVERTED LONGER EACH TRY UNTIL YOU CAN DO COMPLETE LAPS OF CIRCLE

SNAP UP SMOOTH

START LOOP

The sequence of learning procedures developed by the late Cal Smith. The biggest hurdle for beginner/Sport fliers is inverted flight. These maneuvers should not be confused with the formal, more demanding aerobatic sequence illustrated in the A.M.A. rule book for competition fliers.

one had graduated from grade school into high school. With a more experienced modeler to help, a beginner actually may master flying safely around the circle in from one to five flights. Achieving full aerobatic ability is another story—that's college level.

The initial step is to attempt gentle climbs and descents. The climb is begun as the model enters the downwind portion of the circle; the return to level flight occurs at the beginning of the upwind side. With practice the steepness of climb and dive is gradually increased, until eventually a complete wingover is performed with sharp up-elevator entry and pullout. The wingover is the foundation for more complicated maneuvers. Following the

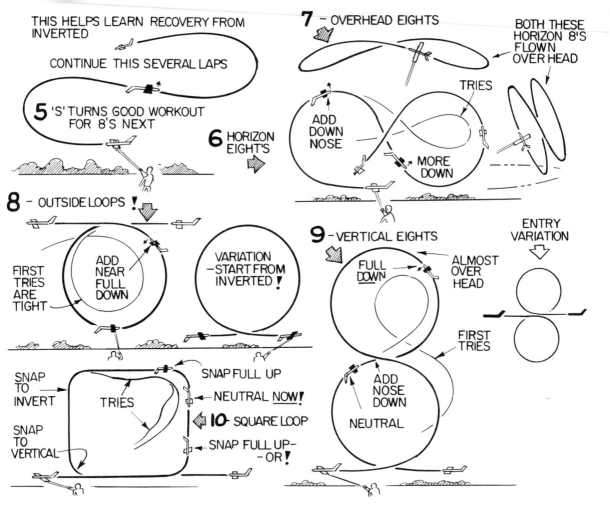

THIS HELPS LEARN RECOVERY FROM INVERTED

CONTINUE THIS SEVERAL LAPS

5 'S' TURNS GOOD WORKOUT FOR 8'S NEXT

6 HORIZON EIGHT'S

7 – OVERHEAD EIGHTS

BOTH THESE HORIZON 8'S FLOWN OVER HEAD

TRIES

ADD DOWN NOSE

MORE DOWN

8 – OUTSIDE LOOPS !

FIRST TRIES ARE TIGHT

ADD NEAR FULL DOWN

VARIATION –START FROM INVERTED !

9 – VERTICAL EIGHTS

ALMOST OVER HEAD

FULL DOWN

ENTRY VARIATION

FIRST TRIES

SNAP TO INVERT

TRIES

SNAP TO VERTICAL

SNAP FULL UP

NEUTRAL NOW!

10 – SQUARE LOOP

SNAP FULL UP– –OR !

ADD NOSE DOWN

NEUTRAL

step-by-step illustrations, each added maneuver is practiced until the flier is letter-perfect at that step. The big hurdle is learning to fly inverted, because after the half-loop entry, the elevator control becomes reversed—up is down, down is up. Sometimes there is a mental block. Things happen too quickly to allow the luxury of reasoning. Eventually, the correct control application becomes an instinctive reflex.

This control reversal must be mastered before advanced maneuvers are possible. How difficult, or easy, this proves to be depends on mental attitude as much as physical coordination. J. C. "Madman" Yates, probably the most spectacular stunt flier ever, smashed fourteen planes before he managed

The Top Flite Tutor is typical of Profile Aerobatic planes flown by Sport modelers.

inverted flight. On the other hand, one of my sons flew inverted on his first attempt, and polished off the flight with inside and outside loops and figure eights. Asked how he had managed this, he explained that, finding his plane upside down after a spectacular, overcontrolled half-loop takeoff, he had watched the wheels and applied down every time he saw the wheels pointed skyward!

Mastering inverted flight is not essential for many competition events—including Speed, Racing, and Carrier—because stunts and inverted flight are not performed in such events.

Sport fliers choose not to go beyond the kind of flying so far described. However, some become deeply involved in competition and, virtually always, become specialists in a single event. To them, that event becomes their hobby. An athlete may be a runner, hurdler, high-jumper, or pole vaulter. So it is with the many-faceted world of control-line flying.

Specialization accounts for the distinct differences between species of control-line models. Other significant differences—invisible to the unpracticed eye—exist in truly amazing control-system devices.

For example, the ultimate Aerobatic machines invariably have wing flaps as well as elevators. When the elevators go down, the flaps go up, and vice versa. "Sharper" corners in some maneuvers are but one advantage. A push-rod extends from the bellcrank to a long control horn on, or near to, the centerline of the flaps, and a second pushrod extends from this horn to the elevator horn. If the handle is tilted back for "up," the flaps go down to increase lift, whereas the elevators tilt up to execute the pullup.

Even more intriguing is the three-line control system used for many scale models and Carrier craft. Two lines provide for up and down as usual, but the third line, operated by a trigger on the control handle, throttles the engine from high to low, and vice versa.

For additional controls special bellcranks are necessary. Inventive modelers come up with all kinds of home-brewed items. At least two three-line system bellcranks and a special handle are manufactured. For the three-line system the functions of two bellcranks are combined into a single unit that

Flaps and elevators are usually linked in Aerobatic models. Flaps move down with up-elevator, and up with down-elevator. This increases the plane's ability to "corner" sharply.

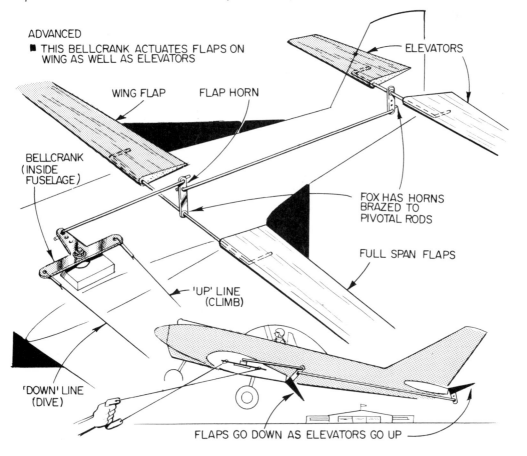

ADVANCED
■ THIS BELLCRANK ACTUATES FLAPS ON WING AS WELL AS ELEVATORS

ELEVATORS

WING FLAP   FLAP HORN

BELLCRANK (INSIDE FUSELAGE)

FOX HAS HORNS BRAZED TO PIVOTAL RODS

FULL SPAN FLAPS

'UP' LINE (CLIMB)

'DOWN' LINE (DIVE)

FLAPS GO DOWN AS ELEVATORS GO UP

The three-line control system with special double bell-crank permits varying the engine rpm and other functions according to the builder's ingenuity. (Bob Smurthwaite photo)

LR Products' three-line system, installed in Mike Gretz's world-class competition Fairchild PT-22 scale model. The pushrod (left) attaches to the throttle, and also operates the two microswitches shown to raise and lower wing flaps by means of a radio-control-type servo. (Mike Gretz photo)

With wing flaps lowered for slow flight or landing, Gretz's Fairchild makes a slow pass for the camera.

Launching a Navy Carrier-type model from a scalelike flight deck. Flown by three-line systems, such models are timed for high and low speeds, and must land on deck, the releasable arresting hook snagging lines across the deck attached to small sandbags. If it misses the deck, the model is said to be "in the drink." (Dick Perry photo)

can handle more than simple up-and-down commands. In a Scale model, engine-speed control is the major option—the engine has a radio-control-type carburetor. In the Carrier-type model, the first, and essential, option is engine throttling, plus extension of the tail hook that snags the carrier deck's restraining lines. The Carrier model usually has wing flaps as well, to permit extremely slow flight—models are timed for both high- and low-speed runs— and for ultraslow landings on the small deck. Such models can hang on the propeller, nose held extremely high, at little forward speed.

Expert Carrier fliers add other devices. They may even use an adjustable leadout guide that can be actuated in flight. Sometimes when flaps are lowered a mechanical catch will allow an aileron on the outer wing to raise. This helps keep that wing down, maintaining line tension, as the plane slows up. Normally, the engine is throttled back by the third control line. Then, by imparting an abrupt, brief, downward control on the elevators, a trip on the pushrod causes the spring-loaded tail hook, flaps, and tip aileron to deploy.

The Scale modeler employs the three-line system, plus additional lines as required, to actuate not only the throttle and flaps, but to retract and extend the landing gear, open a bomb bay door and drop bombs, turn on lights, and so on. This is heady stuff indeed. Multipurpose control handles and bell-cranks are ingenious products of individual effort. The super-Scale expert may concoct wondrous handles with five or six lines. Special control devices display such a stunning range of effects that intricate descriptions are counterproductive. Such machines are largely limited to contests, but details often appear in control-line columns in some major magazines.

There is a less widely used single-line system known as Monoline. Extending from the end of the control handle is a spirally twisted strip of metal. On it rides a knoblike grip, which is slid along the metal strip by the free hand to provide up-and-down controls. This action causes the single-wire line (thicker than the usual control lines to safely withstand the pull of the model in flight) to rotate. In doing so it actuates a worm gear and cam arrangement inside the model's wing, which in turn moves the elevator push rod to position the elevators.

For the overwhelming majority of us, the model normally flown on two control lines is the ultimate in simplicity—and an adequate challenge. Control line attracts a devoted group of modelers who enjoy the intricacies and physical involvement of this type of flight. It is easy to see its appeal.

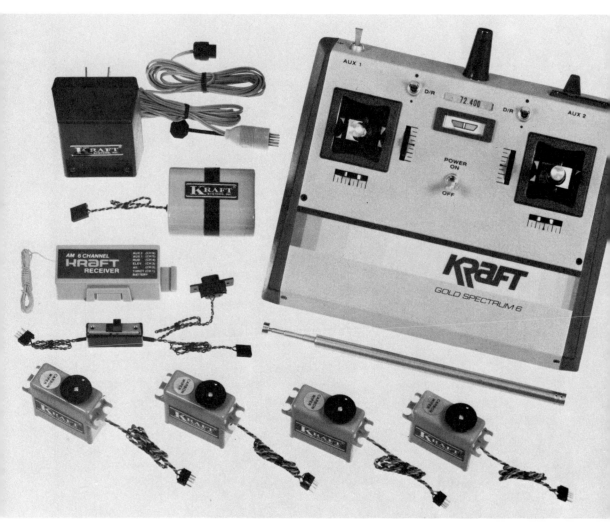

A complete radio system. Counterclockwise from upper left: wall charger handles transmitter and airborne battery packs simultaneously (the red LEDs lights indicate when they are charging); airborne battery pack (with nickel cadmium batteries); receiver; switch harness; servos; telescoping transmitter antenna; transmitter. (Bill Butterfield photo)

chapter ten

Radio Control Systems

Before 1949, the year in which the Academy of Model Aeronautics (A.M.A.) gained approval from the Federal Communications Commission (FCC) for an examination-free frequency (27.255:megahertz [mHz]) for remote control of model aircraft, radio control was considered a "black art" practiced by a mere handful of experimenters who were regarded with awe. Before 1949, one had to obtain a "ham" license from the FCC, which required passing a technical quiz and a code test.

Things are simpler now, but there are legal requirements. You must be an American citizen, at least 12 years of age. Except for "toy" radio systems with less than 100-milliwatts (mW) output (they operate on 49 mHz), you require a station license. To obtain it, you must have read Part 95 of the FCC regulations, then fill out application Form 505. No examination is required and at present there is no fee. Part 95 rules are obtained from the FCC, Washington, DC 20544, or in convenient extracted form from the Academy of Model Aeronautics, 1810 Samuel Morse Dr., Reston, VA 22090. They are also available from the Government Printing Office, 710 North Capitol St., Washington, DC 20401. Form 505 is obtained from either the FCC or the A.M.A., and usually is included with your newly purchased radio system. It is mailed to the FCC, Gettysburg, PA 17236. (Note: At the time of writing, the FCC was proposing to eliminate licenses for RC activities, so these requirements may no longer be in effect.)

Within approved radio frequency bands, individual frequencies allow a number of planes to operate simultaneously without interference between them. Appropriate color pennants (they come with your system and can also be purchased in hobby shops) attach to transmitter antennas to designate the frequency—important when you fly with others.

Until well into the 1950s the typical radio system was about as complicated as something a youngster would whip together today for a science

Radio Control Frequencies

Effective January 1, 1983, the Federal Communications Commission approved the use of new frequencies for radio-controlled models. The new frequencies have been authorized in several stages, to make it easier for modelers to adapt to them and to allow manufacturers to introduce gradually the improved, more selective equipment that will be required while not abruptly obsoleting hundreds of thousands of radio systems already in use. On January 1, 1991, the last of the new frequencies will be introduced and there will be a total of 50 new 72 MegaHertz channels for model aircraft use.

Frequency Choices

27 MHz Band   Available for all types of models (including boats and cars) are the following frequencies: 26.995, 27.045, 27.095, 27.145, 27.195, 27.255. These are not now widely used for model aircraft because of interference from Citizen's Band radios.

49 MHz Band   A license-free band available for all types of models, restricted to very low output power: 49.930, 49.845, 49.860, 49.875, 49.890. Normally used for ready-to-operate models primarily in the toy field, this band's radio range is too short for more typical sport and competition aircraft.

72-75 MHz Frequencies   At the time of writing these are the most commonly used frequencies, and they will continue to be available for all types of models until the end of 1987, at which time they will be elminated (or converted to the new frequencies). Aircraft only: 72.08, 72.24, 72.40, 75.64. All types (including aircraft): 72.16, 72.32, 72.96.

Newly authorized 72 MHz Frequencies

These channels for model aircraft only: 72.03, 72.55, 72.59, 72.63, 72.67, 72.71, 72.75, 72.79, 72.83, 72.87, 72.91. They are compatible with the old frequencies and are the only new channels authorized for use before January 1, 1988. Additional channels will be added after that date and all new channels will continue for the next three years. On January 1, 1991, still more new channels will be added for a total of 50 new 72 MHz frequencies authorized for model aircraft.

Amateur Radio Service 50-54 MHz (Six Meter) Band

An amateur radio license of Technician Class or higher is required to use this band. The RC frequencies listed here are "A.M.A. suggested," since the FCC does not designate individual frequencies for specific uses on Amateur Radio Service bands as it does on other RC bands. At the time of writing (spring 1983) frequencies were available for all types of models: 53.10, 53.20, 53.30, 53.40, 53.50.

Further information and details on licensing are available at no charge from the Academy of Model Aeronautics, 1810 Samuel Morse Dr., Reston, VA 22090.

class demonstration. When the operator pressed a switch, the transmitter emitted a steady carrier wave that caused a plate current change in a vacuum tube in the receiver. The resulting current change opened or closed a relay which, in turn, actuated the magnetic coil in an escapement device to cause the rudder to move to a fixed position for either a left or right turn. That was it! Today's highly sophisticated equipment is tiny and light by comparison, and capable of interpreting transmitter stick movements to cause proportional response of rudder, elevators, throttle, and ailerons, and may have additional capability for operating wing flaps, retractable landing gear, and other special-purpose devices.

A radio-controlled (RC) system consists of a transmitter, a receiver, and one or more servos that move the control surfaces in response to transmitted commands. Power for the transmitter and for the "airborne pack" (receiver, servos, and their power supply) may be either dry batteries or rechargeable nickel cadmium batteries. Because of superior reliability, lower eventual cost (due to the recharging feature that allows the same batteries to be used for a year or more), and greater capacity that permits five or more flights on a given day, the nickel cadmium battery supply is far superior to dry batteries, and hence is virtually standardized.

Modelers think in terms of the number of "channels," one, two, three, or as many as seven. Each channel may be simply described as an encoded transmitted path of intelligence that governs the direction of rotation (after decoding by the receiver) of a tiny electric motor in a servo(s), which in turn moves a control surface either left or right, up or down.

In present-day radios, the carrier wave (the radio frequency, or RF) is modulated, that is, a modulated audio frequency is imposed upon the carrier wave and the control intelligence provided via the various channels, as attained by variations in the pattern of modulation varied by control stick movements.

There is one ultrasimple system, different from all others, made by Ace R/C. The transmitter has a single stick that moves only right and left. The airborne equipment includes a single-channel receiver, batteries, and a magnetic actuator instead of a servo. The transmitter emits a pulsed signal that causes the actuator to swing back and forth from full left to full right, and vice versa. The rudder wiggles rapidly. When the control stick is moved, the arc through which the actuator and rudder swing is similarly moved to one side or the other of the neutral position of the rudder, and proportional steering results. This inexpensive equipment is used only in small models powered by engines of from 0.02 to 0.049 cu. in. displacement.

In conventional two-channel systems, a single stick on the transmitter can be moved forward and backward (for up- and down-elevator), as well as left

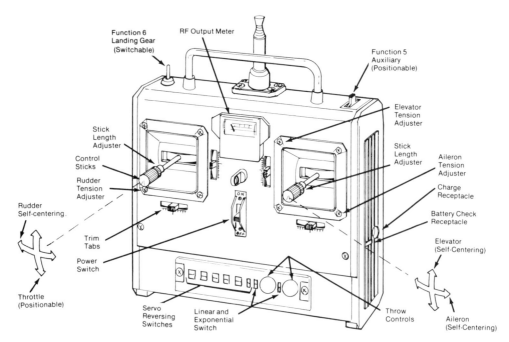

Function 6
Landing Gear
(Switchable)

RF Output Meter

Function 5
Auxiliary
(Positionable)

Elevator
Tension
Adjuster

Stick
Length
Adjuster

Stick
Length
Adjuster

Aileron
Tension
Adjuster

Control
Sticks

Rudder
Tension
Adjuster

Charge
Receptacle

Rudder
Self-centering

Battery Check
Receptacle

Trim
Tabs

Elevator
(Self-Centering)

Power
Switch

Throttle
(Positionable)

Servo
Reversing
Switches

Linear and
Exponential
Switch

Throw
Controls

Aileron
(Self-Centering)

Typical features are depicted in this six-channel Airtronics XL transmitter. The control stick on the left is for throttle and rudder, the one on the right for aileron and elevators. Only the throttle is positionable, both sticks otherwise moving freely for blending infinite combinations of control surfaces. Each of these four primary controls has trim tabs adjacent to the sticks to adjust flight characteristics. The retractable landing gear function (No. 6) is a two-position switch. Function No. 5, for wing flaps, is positionable. The panel at the bottom allows for preflight servo reversing and choice of normal elevator and aileron movements or exponential, which diminishes servo movement near neutral positions for precision control. Some transmitters offer a choice of exponential or rate features (rate is for increasing control movements); both are not simultaneously available.

and right for rudder or aileron control, or in any combination of movements that blend simultaneous action of both controls being used, in any degree desired by the pilot.

On some two-channel transmitters, a smaller lever is located toward the left, independent of the single control stick at the right that operates the rudder only, so that the throttle can be worked with the left hand. The same arrangement sometimes is found on some three-channel transmitters, the single stick operating both rudder and elevator. (Aileron may be substituted for rudder.) Control response is proportional. That is, the surface on the plane (also the throttle) is displaced in an amount proportional to the degree of movement of the control sticks.

In many three-channel systems and most others having more channels, two transmitter sticks are usual, one toward the right side of the transmitter face, the other toward the left. With three channels, the stick on the right normally controls rudder and elevator, while the one on the left governs the throttle position for more or less power. If the right stick is moved toward the right, the rudder turns the plane to the right, and vice versa; if it is moved forward, the plane dives, and if it is moved rearward, the plane noses up. If the left-hand stick is pushed forward, the power is increased, if it is pulled back, power is decreased. The throttle stick has a ratcher-type of locking device that automatically allows it to remain in position until changed by the pilot. Occasionally, the right-hand stick is used for ailerons instead of rudder—rudder then being absent—and for elevators.

On the four-channel system, the throttle stick can be moved left or right for the fourth control, normally rudder. With four channels, there is a distinct change in the aircraft controls. Normally, the right-hand stick is moved left and right to actuate ailerons for banking the craft, and fore and aft for elevator control. But the left-hand stick now controls rudder, when moved left or right, as well as throttle, when moved fore and aft. (There are no detents on the rudder movement of the throttle stick.) Most pilots fly by the right-hand stick, simultaneously blending aileron and elevator movements, and use the throttle/rudder stick to guide takeoffs or for special aerial maneuvers, such as spins and wingovers. Additional special-purpose channels (on five-, six-, and seven-channel transmitters) are operated by switches and posi-

Magnetic actuator for Ace single-channel system swings rapidly from side to side according to the pulse rate transmitted. Movement of the transmitter control stick causes the actuator (hence the rudder) to shift its averaged neutral position for steering. (Preston photo)

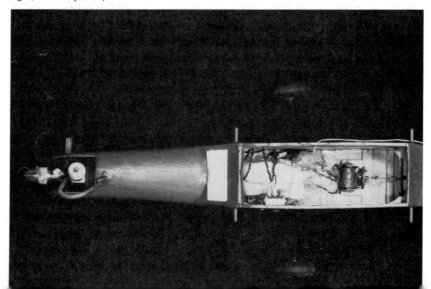

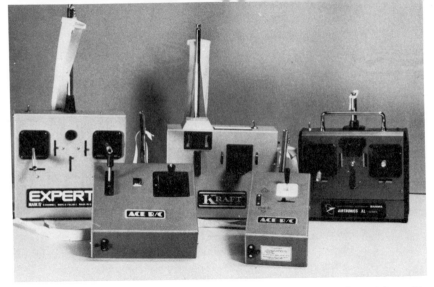

Typical transmitters (clockwise from right foreground): Ace single-channel for rudder only; Ace three-channel (throttle control on left); World Expert five-channel; Kraft single-stick five-channel; Airtronics six-channel with servo reversing and exponential for elevator and aileron. The Kraft single-stick transmitter combines elevator, aileron, and rudder on one stick; the knob on the top of the stick is turned for rudder response.

tionable small levers. These extra channels come into play for operation of retractable landing gear and wing flaps, etc. Usually, the landing-gear control is an on-off toggle switch on top of the transmitter at the left. Push it, and the gear retracts; return it to its original position, and the gear extends again. The sixth channel control is usually a small lever that projects from the top right of the transmitter case. This channel usually provides proportional operation because wing flaps can then be set in various degrees in between the full up or down position. (Note that some manufacturers of multi-channel radios may assign their channel functions in different sequences.)

All transmitters have a means of adjusting in flight the neutral position of any control, necessary to fine-trim the plane so that a compensating stick position does not have to be held constantly. Generally, there are small ratchetlike trim levers or wheels that project slightly from the transmitter face adjacent to each control stick. For example, the trim device located below the aileron/elevator stick can be moved as desired to the left or right to adjust aileron neutral. Alongside that stick in a vertical location, another trim device moves forward or backward to trim the elevator up or down. Similarly, there are other trim controls for throttle and rudder, adjacent to the left stick.

You may hear the terms Mode I or Mode II being used—this is "in" stuff. Occasionally experts prefer Mode I, which has elevator and rudder on the left-hand stick, throttle and ailerons on the right. However, virtually everyone else flies Mode II, with ailerons and elevator on the right, throttle and rudder on the left.

There are also single-stick transmitters that have from five to eight controls. In addition to controlling aileron and elevator movement, the stick has a rotatable knob on top which, when turned, actuates the rudder. Some skilled fliers like the single stick because it feels realistic, but it does require the coordination of three control movements simultaneously, as when taking off, and doing wingovers, stall turns, or even rolls.

Radio systems are evolving now with features that, a few years ago, would have cost close to $1,000, but now cost less than $300. At old five-channel prices, some systems now offer servo reversing and adjustable linear and exponential control responses on at least ailerons and elevators, all variable at the transmitter. Servo reversing means that all servos can be dropped into a plane without regard for direction of rotation. Small concealed switches in the transmitter allow rotation of any servo to be reversed. If airborne packs of matching frequency are used in two or more planes with just one transmitter, any surface that moves the wrong way on one plane can be reversed merely by pressing a switch at the transmitter.

"Linear control" means that the surface being controlled moves in an amount that agrees with the movement of the transmitter stick. "Exponential control" gives the skilled flier the ability to use less control surface movement close to the neutral position of the stick; as the stick moves so does the surface, at first in a smaller amount, and as the stick reaches full travel, so does the control surface. The plane can be flown more smoothly. The travel of both the linear and exponential movements is adjustable by potentiometers (called "pots") in the transmitter.

A step up is the addition of a rate control. When an extreme control movement is required for some maneuvers, a flip of the rate switch greatly increases or decreases the servo movement, hence the amount of displacement of the required surface. Exponential and rate controls do not coexist; the flier has a choice.

Some deluxe transmitters permit "coupling" of two or more controls, for example, aileron and rudder. Monster scale models in particular benefit from this useful feature. Ordinarily, for a smooth turn the pilot is required to apply ailerons with the right-hand stick, and a certain amount of rudder (with the left-hand stick) simultaneously (termed "coordination"). By throwing the coupling switch, the pilot can then, for example, apply ailerons with the correct, preset amount of rudder control (and/or aileron) automatically fed in. Sometimes a maneuver can be preprogrammed. For example, by pressing the roll button, the required controls respond to perform that maneuver.

Another feature of some transmitters is "mixing," which must be distinguished from coupling. In mixing, a single control surface is used for two functions. For example, a skilled flier, especially in Scale, may wish to use the ailerons as combination wing flaps and ailerons. Each of the two ailerons then is driven by its own servo, instead of the usual single servo. Mixing allows the ailerons to be dropped as flaps, simultaneously permitting their individual movements to control the aircraft; in the Vee-tailed (also known as the "butterfly-tailed") aircraft, a mixer permits using the elevators to lower or raise the nose, at the same time allowing independent use of each elevator as a rudder for steering. A mixer always requires two servos for the one dual-purpose control surface. The mixing device may be mechanical (fittings are provided for the servo drive arms) or electronic. The electronic mixer plugs into the receiver. In some super radio systems, an electronic mixer may instead be incorporated into the transmitter. For the flap/aileron combination, electronic mixing is used; for the Vee-tail, either mechanical or electrical mixing. You won't encounter these situations unless, as your experience grows, you become interested in such challenges. The beginner, and the majority of sport fliers, will never use such advanced control systems.

The ultimate transmitters have internal pot-adjustable control over the travel limits of a servo. For example, if a servo jams when you're trying to adjust throttle movement, turning a pot stops the servo arm travel where desired. Pots also allow adjusting servo neutral positions from the transmitter.

How many channels do you need? One channel is the cheapest buy, but it is limited to small, simple models. You will have to replace it with something more flexible as you progress to more advanced models, though one channel can always be considered a fun thing if you possess complex equipment as well. Although they are not quite as limited, two-channel systems also require replacement sooner or later if your flying improves. (However, two channels are suitable for many Soaring gliders that normally require only rudder and elevator controls.) Three channels, fine for the popular easy-to-fly planes that don't usually have ailerons, nevertheless may prove limited. The reason is that the differences in price between three-, four-, and five-channel systems are not great and, even if you don't use all channels immediately, such equipment allows for later expansion to ailerons, etc.

Check all possible catalogs, because systems range from less than $100 to nearly $1,000, and the money saved by comparison shopping is significant. You can sometimes find astounding bargains in up to seven channels.

HOW RADIO CONTROL WORKS

Engineers will be horrified by this description, but it serves our purpose well. Think of transmitted commands as telephone calls. You push numbers on the phone that single out an individual at a distance. The telephone exchange sorts out numerous simultaneous calls and routes each to its destination. The receiver is our "exchange." It decodes information encoded by the transmitter and directs the "message" to a servo, commanding it to move to a specified degree in either of two directions.

The servo has an initiative of its own, just as the person receiving a phone call can talk back to the caller, triggering new thoughts. Via the transmitter and receiver there is constant "conversation" between your hand on the stick and the servo at the other end.

The human ear can detect frequencies up to about 16,000 cycles per second (cps). Radio waves have frequencies much higher than sound. For example, a model transmitter operating on a frequency of 72.400 has 72,400,000 cps. Until the appearance of digital systems (what we use today), transmitters put out a steady RF signal upon which one or more audio tones were imposed. With rare exceptions the digital system does not in *the usual sense* transmit a steady RF or impose audio tones. Rather, a modulated RF is briefly cut off at precisely spaced intervals. The spacing of the off pulses controls the servo position. The accompanying diagram shows the pulse train by which this is accomplished. The upper line of pulses is roughly what you

The typical digital transmitter encodes intelligence (to receiver decoder) as a series of continuously recurring pulses within a frame rate of (in the example) 16 msec. The number of frames per second roughly equates with 60 cps. The diagram shows (top) all controls in neutral, the one at the bottom with aileron being applied.

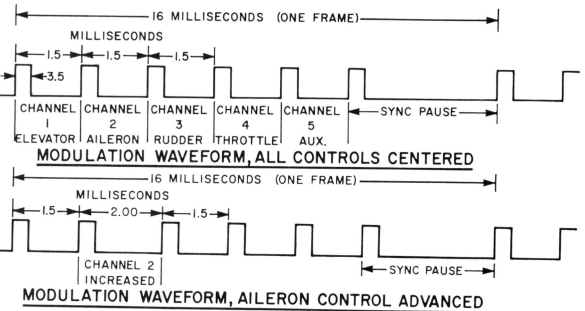

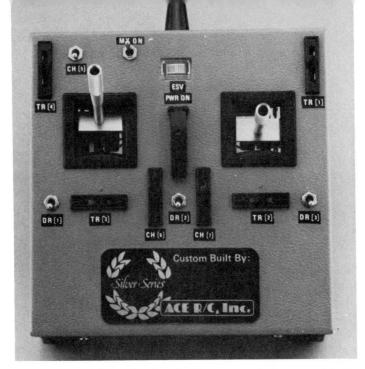

A deluxe transmitter, the Ace Silver 7, offered either custom-built or as a kit. The discriminating flier will note "cross trims." The normal trim control positions are relocated so they can be moved simultaneously by one hand while the other is working a control stick.

would see on an oscilloscope when all controls are in neutral—spacing between each pair of pulses is equal. In the lower line, one control—the aileron—has been activated. The width of that pulse has been broadened, and all pulses coming after it have been shifted to the right. Between each series of pulses, which follow constantly, note there is a sync pause and that the frame rate, which never changes, lasts (in this example) 16 milliseconds (msec.) If the pulses shift to the right as shown, the sync pause is reduced; if the pulses shift to the left, it is increased. The sync pause allows the receiver decoder to reset reliably.

Separation between frequencies of different transmitters is precisely governed by the use of crystals in both transmitters and receivers.

At the receiver, the transmitter pulses are detected, then fed to a decoder that synchronizes itself with the transmitted time frame and sorts out the channel control pulses. In the servo is an amplifier that uses the decoder output for the channel to which it is assigned, to command its electric motor to actuate the control surface. The output gear of the servo is connected to a wiper that rides on a pot. This action electrically provides the feedback intelligence from the servo to the receiver, so that the position of the servo is constantly matched to the pulses from the receiver decoder.

This explanation is oversimplified. If you want to understand exactly how

The reverse side of the Ace Silver 7. Switches (lower right) are for servo reversing. Seven pairs of pots allow adjusting the servo neutrals, and end movement limits. This transmitter offers additional advanced features, such as coupling of certain controls, mixing of others.

your system works electronically, obtain the book *Getting the Most from Radio Control Systems,* by Fred Marks (see page 284).

Power Supply

Although both transmitters and receivers (plus actuators or servos) are powered by either common dry-cell or nickel cadmium batteries, keen price competition in cheaper equipment causes some systems to call for dry batteries. Many ready-to-fly planes with radio systems, for example, use them. These batteries do not come with the equipment. The rechargeable nickel cadmium battery pack is far more reliable, and some manufacturers have conversion kits so that these packs can be substituted for dry batteries (which wipes out the "saving"). The dry battery transmitter usually has a meter that indicates relative battery voltage, a green-to-red dial; those for nickel cadmium indicate either voltage or signal strength output. The receiver's dry batteries, when fitted into a simple case with mechanical contacts, can be "intermittent" due to vibration. The user must have a voltmeter and regularly test such batteries under load—otherwise a crash is inevitable. Knowledgeable modelers use only nickel cadmium cells.

The better systems come with the appropriate nickel cadmium pack for the airborne installation, and with nickel cadmium transmitter batteries installed. Plus a charger. Usually, this charger plugs into a wall socket, and has two cable leads with appropriate connectors for both battery packs. Most chargers have a red-LED light for each lead, which indicates the equipment is charging (also a reminder that the charger is plugged in—batteries can be damaged by overcharging). The chargers are designed expressly for the capacity of the particular nickel cadmium packs. If different-sized packs are substituted—smaller or larger ones—the charge rate will be wrong. It can blow out the smaller pack, or take double the time to charge a large pack (you could go out to fly with a half-charged pack).

It is a simple matter for a technician to install a dropping resistor in the appropriate charger lead, if that charger is to be used with a lightweight pack of smaller capacity. Or he can make a "cheater" lead including the dropping resistor, so that the standard rate charger can be used for a smaller pack as well. Or you can just buy the correct charger. For a battery pack with a greater capacity, you can buy a matching charger if you want to charge in the normal amount of time. (See also mixed-rate chargers below.)

With nickel cadmium cells, most transmitters require 9.6 V, but some take 6 or 12. The airborne pack normally requires 4.8 V. These batteries come in various sizes, but the most common is the pencell size, with each cell having

A deluxe battery charger/cycler. Digital readout at the top gives the capacity in minutes when batteries are cycled. Periodic battery checks are made with the cycler, which drains cells to a safe minimum, then automatically switches to the charging mode. Readout reveals bad batteries or decreases in usable time with age. The transmitter charger (left) is switchable for three battery voltages; the receiver charger (right) has two rates to suit the capacity of airborne battery packs. (Preston photo)

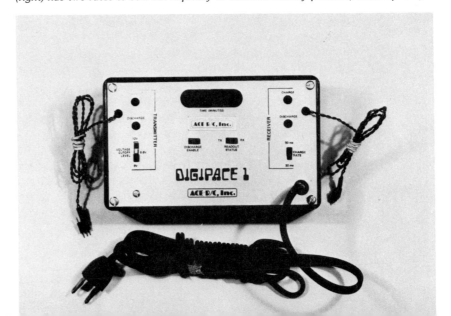

1.2 V. When freshly charged, each cell may show as high as 1.4 V, but they quickly fall back to a steady 1.2 V when used. Four such cells make up the typical airborne pack, wired in series to put out 4.8 V. The most common transmitters use eight cells in series.

Unlike a dry battery, which loses voltage as it is used, insidiously falling off to inevitable failure, the nickel cadmium battery maintains a steady voltage output (plateau) throughout a typical flying session. When it is foolishly overused, voltage drops abruptly and equipment fails (but it can be recharged overnight). For planes equipped with four servos for primary controls, at least five 10-min. aerobatic flights are safe in one session if the batteries are in good condition.

Very active fliers prefer to use deluxe charging equipment—such as the Ace Digipace or the Taylor Power Pacer—because such chargers allow detection of bad or weak cells, internal shorts, etc., and provide a final readout of the battery-pack capacity being checked. (Digipace also provides switch-controlled charge rates for three sizes of transmitter battery packs, and two sizes of receiver battery packs.) A test button "cycles" the batteries. It discharges them at a safe rate to a safe minimum, then automatically reverts to a charge mode. The next morning, the batteries are fully charged and there will be displayed either a digital readout in minutes of capacity, or a dial indication of the milliampere-hour capacity.

For example, the four-cell pack has a milliampere-hour (mAh) capacity of 450, the typical transmitter pack 500 mAh. If the charger readout displays 250 instead of the 450 or 500 new value, your safe flying time is only 50 percent of normal. Battery capacity does gradually decrease with age—say a year or so—and a battery cycler or charger/cycler is recommended to keep track. A readout of 450 mAh corresponds to about 90 min. of usable time. Another noteworthy charger is made by M.E.N. Not only does it have the ability to detect defective batteries, but after bringing the pack up to proper voltage it goes on a trickle charge rate, so that it can be left plugged in indefinitely. The flying equipment thus is always ready for use. With normal chargers, the practice is to charge overnight before the next day's flying. Overly long charging periods damage batteries.

Although most hobbyists fly without such checking equipment, batteries can be checked with an inexpensive voltmeter (on which 15 V is the maximum reading). If the 4.8-V airborne pack reads 5 or more volts, or the 9.8-V transmitter pack 10 or more, they are considered safe. (The overrun is due to the slight excess voltage of up to 0.2 V per cell immediately after charging.) If a freshly charged pack does not read properly, individual cells are checked with a voltmeter to match them against other cells in the pack. If the newly charged battery packs are not used within two days, they should be recharged the evening before you go out to fly.

When radio-system reliability problems appear, the system should be returned to the manufacturer for service (there is a warranty for a certain time) or to some designated service center. A service check is desirable

Simplified diagram of airborne installation in the Goldberg Eaglet—the battery pack behind the tank, receiver aft of the batteries. Both battery pack and receiver are wrapped in foam rubber to cushion and protect the equipment and to absorb engine vibration. The lower right drawing shows typical installation in a glider (a Goldberg Gentle Lady), which places batteries in the nose for balance.

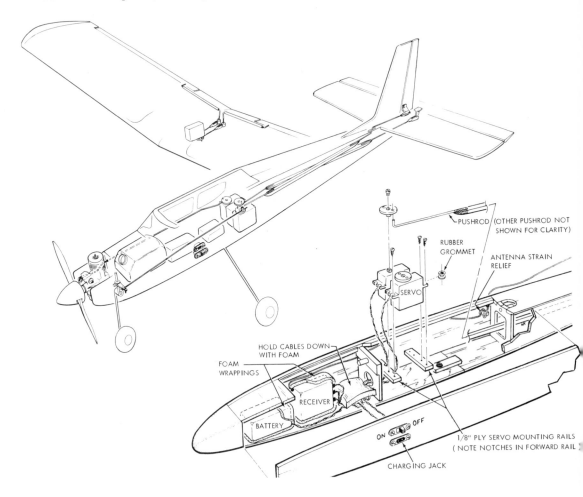

between seasons. An active flier should check the servos every year. The usual problem is a dirty potentiometer. A dirty pot or poor pot wiper contact pressure causes a servo to quiver steadily, which runs down batteries and possibly affects the operation of other servos. Most servos are easily cleaned; many modelers know how, so inquire at the field. Wiper contacts should be adjusted by an experienced fellow flyer, or by a service station technician. It is wiser to have the wiper replaced.

Location of Airborne Components

Several basic considerations govern the location in the plane of the battery pack, receiver, and servos. The most important are the correct center of gravity (C.G.) of the aircraft (balance point) and protection of the radio gear from vibration (assuming there is an engine) and/or crash damage. Easy accessibility for servicing and mechanical reliability are also important. Good kits show where components are located; some detail the entire installation.

If we visualize the side profile view of the fuselage, we may divide it into three zones: the nose area forward of the leading edge of the wing; the cabin area, normally the distance between the leading and trailing edges of the wing; and the aft area, from the trailing edge of the wing to the sternpost of the fuselage. And let's divide that cabin area into two portions so that we have numbered zones 1, 2, 3, and 4 running from nose to tail.

Experience has determined an almost standard installation, although variables in aircraft types and construction may dictate changes. For example, a Cabin or high-wing type of airplane has an open cabin top, whereas a low wing requires that the fuselage be open on the bottom (servos in that case are mounted inverted—which reverses control movement of elevator and rudder).

AREA 1 The nose normally contains both the fuel tank and the airborne battery pack. Most models have a nose hatch to provide access to the tank; in those that have no hatch, the tank is removed for servicing by withdrawing it through a large lightening hole in the forward cabin bulkhead. If there is a hatch, the battery pack can be dropped into position through the top of the nose; otherwise, it must be inserted from the cabin, through the hole in the front bulkhead. The battery pack is protected by wrapping it in foam rubber at least 1/2 in. thick, the foam held in place by two pieces of masking tape wrapped around it. When the foam-wrapped battery pack is located in the cabin, it should be, if possible, nested in foam pieces in front, on top and bottom, and both sides. If the battery pack is under the tank, it is placed in a small plastic bag with the neck wrapped around the battery cable and held by a rubber band. This protects the batteries from accidental fuel leakage.

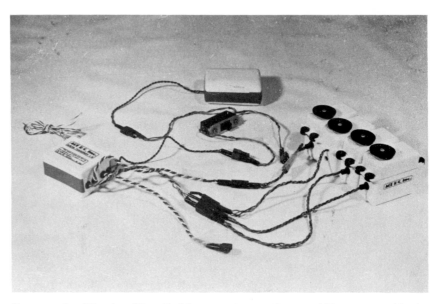

Components of the Ace Silver 7 airborne system as they would be connected in the plane. The unused connector off the right of the switch is used for charging the batteries. The other unused connector at bottom is for an optional auxiliary servo.

The battery cable is led rearward into the front cabin area. This cable plugs into the switch harness, with slack to prevent vibration fatigue of the wires.

AREA 2 The forward cabin is reserved for the receiver and the switch harness. The receiver is always wrapped in foam rubber—up to 1 in. thick if the plane size permits. If space allows, the receiver is placed in a horizontal position, running fore and aft. If space is limited, the receiver is sometimes located vertically. Receivers have connectors into which are plugged the power lead coming from the on-off switch, and the various servo cable plugs. Depending on the receiver's position in the plane, the sockets should be at the rear, or top, for accessibility. The switch mounts on the side of the fuselage that is away from the engine exhaust stack.

Since it is important to locate the receiver antenna away from servo cables or metal pushrods, the antenna wire exits the fuselage high on the side if the plane has a high-wing configuration, or through the side, top, or bottom in the case of a low-wing plane. Inside the fuselage the antenna must have some slack and a retainer that prevents its being pulled at the receiver if accidental tension is placed on its exterior portion. The antenna extends at an angle up to the top of the fin, attached by a light rubber band to a small hook to avoid excess tension or impact damage. Experienced modelers may install the antenna inside the fuselage; we suggest you don't do this.

With your radio set you receive a servo tray into which servos insert. This tray is attached with small screws to wood bearers extending across the cabin. Servos have rubber grommets to dampen vibration; the mounting screws insert through holes in the grommets, but not tightly enough to squash the grommets. Most trays provide a slot for mounting the switch, in which case a push-pull wire extension from the switch handle may be run out the side of the fuselage for easy operation (see the photo below). When plugging together the battery cable and its matching lead from the switch, wrap a small piece of Scotch tape around the joined connector pieces to prevent their becoming detached. Vibration, sudden stops, abrupt launching of sailplanes, and so forth can cause these connector pieces to separate.

AREA 3   The aft cabin is the servo compartment. There are two common tray arrangements for typical three-servo fuselages; three side-by-side, or two-plus-one. The latter means that the two rearward servos are side by side, but the third fits crosswise in front of the other two. The arrangement you use depends on the width of the cabin. There are two basic ways of mounting these two servo arrangements. One is on the servo tray provided with the system. The other is to attach the servos by small screws (also provided)

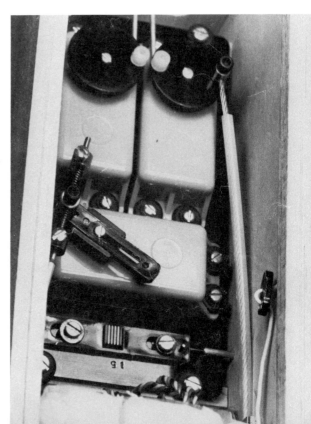

Two-plus-one installation of Kraft servos on a plastic servo tray. Nylon retainers (top) attach to elevator and rudder pushrods on the servo drive disks. At top right, a typical servo connector allows adjustment of the cable nosewheel steering pushrod. For this picture an adjustable-length Robart drive arm is shown on the throttle servo, plus a Du-Bro override throttle connector. Tiny springs absorb override to prevent servo jamming. (Deluxe transmitters allow setting this pushrod movement.) In the foreground is a slide switch with actuating wire passing to the outside through the fuselage side. Note the plastic stop on the antenna to prevent accidental pulls on the connection in the receiver. (Preston photo)

directly to two mounting rails (pine or other hardwood, never balsa), normally 3/8 in. sq. It is not sufficient to butt-glue the ends of the rails to the cabin walls. To the inside of the fuselage wall, glue 1/8 × 3/8 in. hard balsa strips extending from the fuselage bottom up to the servo rails (glue the joints between these strips and the servo rails). Small pieces of the same material are glued horizontally on the side walls with the aft ends snug against and glued to each of the rails. These strips will prevent the servo rails from breaking loose in a crash or from engine vibration. The servos must be accessible, not buried deep in a narrow fuselage where fingers can reach only with difficulty.

A servo tray is desirable for the two-plus-one arrangement. If you do not have a tray, make one from 3/32-in. plywood. Sometimes the two servos are mounted on wooden rails, and the third (for the throttle) attached flush to the fuselage side with servo tape, which is sticky on both sides. This is not advisable on powerful models because the servo is then subject to vibration damage. If a plane has only two servos, they are mounted side-by-side, or in tandem, if the fuselage is too narrow. Very small, low-powered planes, sometimes gliders, may safely use servo tape mounting, thus eliminating servo rails and/or trays entirely.

When a fourth servo is used for ailerons, it is mounted in the center of the wing, on the bottom of the wing if the plane is a high-wing model, on the top if it is a low wing.

When mounting servos directly to wooden bearers, the wood may block the entry of the cable projecting from the end of the servo body. Remove a small portion of wood in the immediate area with an X-Acto knife or rattail file until the servo can be inserted without squeezing its cable (this is shown in the drawing on page 230).

When three servos are side-by-side, the middle one normally is used for the elevator, the end ones for motor control and rudder (and nose-wheel steering if the plane has a tricycle landing gear). Which end servos you use for which

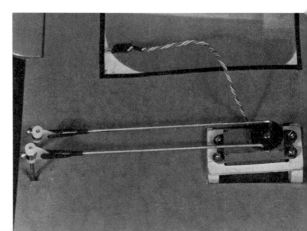

Installation of the aileron servo. Clevises are thread-adjustable for adjusting the aileron to neutral. Nylon fittings on the aileron drive arms (left) screw up and down on the arms to adjust the amount of control movement. On a high wing location the servo mounts on the bottom of the wing; on a low wing the servo mounts on top. (Randolph photo)

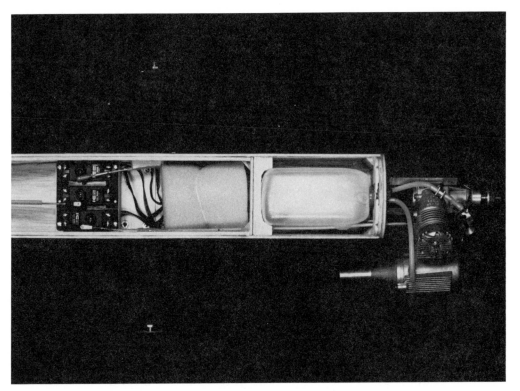

Installation in the Sig Kavalier. The servo at the bottom has a stiff pushrod running aft to the rudder and a flexible cable running forward for nose-wheel steering. The center servo operates the elevator, the one at the top operates the throttle via flexible cable in plastic conduit. (Preston photo)

purposes depends on what side of the plane you find the throttle and nose-wheel steering arm. Most radios (those without servo reversing in the transmitter) come with either one servo that turns in the opposite direction (if there is a total of three) or two (if there are four). This allows you to juggle servo location without obtaining a backward movement of the control. Each servo drive arm or disk has pushrod mounting holes on both ends, or both sides. Be sure to select the side that provides the correct control movement direction. In the case of the rudder and nose-wheel steering on one servo, the required movements of these two devices may sometimes be in opposite directions, necessitating the use of both ends or sides of the servo drive arm or disk.

It is recommended that you make a sketch of the servo system and pertinent controls to determine the desired movements of all servos before you make the installation. You may find there is a mechanical clash between two servo arms as both servos are simultaneously moved. Usually, the elevator (center) servo is turned around so that its drive arm is not in line with the drive arms of adjacent servos. This does not affect the direction of rotation of the servo.

When the two-plus-one arrangement is used, the forward servo is used for engine throttle; the other two operate rudder and elevator. The best arrangement is to run the paths of the rudder and elevator pushrods diagonally across ship to exit the rear fuselage on the opposite side (unless the elevator pushrod exists on the centerline). Naturally, the exit points at the rear of the fuselage are so located in elevation that the pushrods do not bind each other, or vibrate together when the engine runs.

AREA 4 The rear fuselage is just space to be bridged by the pushrods in order to connect the control horns on the rudder and elevator to the rear ends of the pushrods, which also attach in the cabin to the servo drive arms. Obviously, the pushrods must be located before the fuselage is completely finished. Leave the bottom open until the job is done. Unless you use square balsa (as for rudder and elevator pushrods—see below), pushrods require support by means of fairleads.

Several systems for pushrods are popular. First, let's consider the pushrod for the throttle. This rod may be either music wire (1/32 to 1/16 in., depending on the plane size and the length of the rod), plastic, or flexible cable. The stiff rod requires a virtually straight path to the throttle, so a flexible cable rod is preferred. The flexible cable follows necessary bends without the friction or drag that overloads or jams the servo. The throttle pushrod installation is the most difficult. Throttle arm movements frequently do not coincide with servo arm movements. The flexible cable will bend slightly at either end when the servo or throttle jams, diminishing the high electrical drain of the jammed servo. Servo jamming may increase battery drain 300 percent and thereby cause battery failure, which can then lead to a crash.

Adjustments to prevent this are possible, however. Some engine throttle arms have two or three holes for the pushrod attachment. The outermost hole yields the least movement of the throttle, and vice versa. The servo arm also may have two or three holes, the outermost yielding the maximum movement. In combination all these holes usually provide a means to operate the throttle freely. If a servo is jammed, it will hum. By moving the transmitter stick and throttle trim lever you can find the point where jamming disappears and then make corrections. (Deluxe transmitters permit adjusting this movement.) If the servo arm has only one hole, remove the arm and drill another hole nearer the servo shaft to reduce the travel of that pushrod if

This installation close-up shows useful accessories. Three steel clevises, attached to servo drive arms, are made safe by heat-shrink rubber tubing. The white object is a Du-Bro Ball Link, with a nylon socket pressed over a steel ball on the servo arm. The nylon socket is adjustable on the Du-Bro threaded connector. A Du-Bro soldering connector joins the Ball Link to flexible-cable pushrod at top.

necessary. Adjustable arms are found at hobby shops (made by Robart and other companies).

The nose-wheel steering arm normally is driven by a flexible cable pushrod, sheathed in a stiff outer casing. A stiff-wire pushrod would transmit severe strain to the servo gear train and the landing impact could break gear teeth. Nose-wheel steering must be minimal—perhaps not more than 1/8 in. to either side. Otherwise, steering is so sensitive that takeoff runs can zigzag erratically as directional adjustments are made with the rudder stick. (On the ground, both nose wheel and rudder move together; in the air the rudder alone is effective, since the nose wheel is not touching the ground.) To obtain the correct nose-wheel steering, the fitting of the pushrod is rather like that for the throttle pushrod, but not as difficult. Pushrod adjustments are made easier by servo connectors—see below.

Rudder and elevator pushrods are long, so rigidity and lightness are required for them. The simplest arrangement is the 1/4-in.-sq hard balsa pushrod (3/16- or 1/8-in.-sq. spruce on small 1/2A powered craft). On the

Thread-adjustable clevises attach to nylon control horns on the rudder and elevator. Note the trailing antenna, held to the fin top by a rubber band over a tiny hook. (Randolph photo)

1/4-in. sq. rod, a 1/16-in.-diameter stiff-wire extension attaches to both ends of the wood; usually, one end of the wire piece is bent at right angles and sunk into the wood, and the joint is wrapped with thread and glued (shown in the drawing on page 230). One wire end attaches to the servo drive arm; the other to the nylon control horn linked to the rudder or elevator.

Another popular arrangement is the stiff-wire pushrod (made by Du-Bro and other manufacturers) that runs through a plastic conduit. The wire extends beyond the ends of the conduit to reach the servo arm and control horn; one end of the wire is threaded to take a clevis fitting (see below), which attaches either to the control-surface horn or to the servo arm. (Clevises are not used on servo disks, as they cause jamming.) Length is optional to suit the plane, so both ends of the wire cannot be threaded. The unthreaded end is cut to the desired length. This rod requires near-straight runs to avoid binding.

When large bends in the pushrod path are necessary—for example, for operating elevators that are located on top of the fin, as on some sailplanes and Scale types—a heavy flexible cable running through a plastic conduit is required. Or use special plastic pushrods (such as Sullivan Gold-N-Rods) that snake around bends. In the plastic pushrod set, a snug-fitting rod with lengthwise edges rides against the inside wall of the outer plastic housing. A

threaded 1/16-in. stiff wire screws into the end of the inner rod for attachment by a clevis to a servo arm or control-surface horns.

Many manufacturers make clevis rods. This is a straight piece of stiff wire
(to be cut to length) threaded at one end for a clevis. The clevis is a tiny metal
or plastic yokelike device with an open end that passes over the control horn
or servo drive arm. On one jaw of the clevis is a tiny pin that penetrates the
hole in the arm or horn. When the jaws are squeezed together, the clevis is
securely locked in place. The clevis may be detached, screwed in or out for
adjustment of the pushrod length, then snapped in place again. Control horns
have two or more holes at varying distances from the base of the horn. The
outermost hole provides the least control-surface movement, the innermost
hole the most movement. Most fliers use a medium-positioned hole; extreme
movements are never used by the beginner because of the exaggerated plane
response. When a threaded device is used on both ends of a pushrod, one
end is secured by solder (which melts plastic) or epoxy, otherwise vibration
can rotate the rod, which can detach it.

Ideal for pushrod attachment is a "servo connector," a small cylindrical

*Typical power panel for field use mounts in the field box. It operates a power starter
for the engine, an electric fuel pump, and glow-plug booster, has an expanded scale
voltometer for checking the transmitter and airborne packs, and a fast-charge feature
to recharge batteries within 15 min. on the field.* (Preston photo)

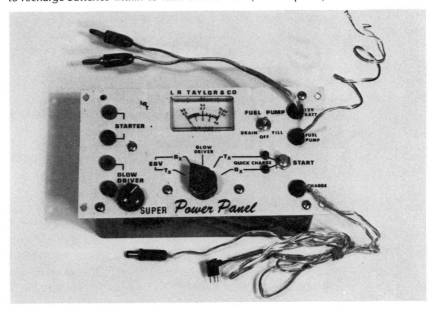

metal body that is free to rotate on a pin extending through the hole in the servo arm. A tiny plastic keeper is pressed over the pin under the arm, lock-ing the connector in place. An indent on the keeper pin allows removal of the keeper for repeated use. The cylindrical portion has a 1/16-in. crosswise hole, into which the stiff-wire extension of the pushrod inserts. The rod can be slid back and forth until the correct position is found (making for quick adjust-ments), and a lock screw on top of the body piece tightens down on the rod to lock it in place. Servo connectors can be used for the adjustable attach-ment of flexible pushrods to throttle arms and nose-wheel steering arms, as well as on servos that drive tail-surface pushrods.

Another device that is often used is the Du-Bro Ball Link. This consists of a steel ball with a mating nylon socket that press-fits over the ball, and is free to tilt moderately to compensate for any angularity in the pushrod attach-ment. The ball is made in one piece with a thin metal peg that attaches to a servo arm in the same manner as the servo connector. (Or it may have a threaded screw-in peg that is held by a nut.) The plastic socket is molded in one piece with a hollow extension tube into which a threaded pushrod end is screwed in place. Since the pushrod must be exactly the length that ensures control surfaces are precisely in neutral when the socket is snapped onto the steel ball, these threads permit adjusting the socket piece to the correct location.

Since wire pushrod ends are threaded on only one end, and because flexi-ble cable pushrods are not threaded, clevises and ball-links very often cannot be attached to such rods without using a threaded coupler (shown in the photo on page 235). The typical threaded coupler is approximately 1-1/4 in. long and 0.072 in. in diameter. About half of its length is threaded to take a ball-link or clevis; the other half is hollow. Pushrod ends fit into the hollow portion and the joint is soldered. The threaded coupler is often required to attach a ball-link to an engine throttle arm, since the throttle pushrod almost always is an unthreaded cable.

GIANT-SIZE MODELS Ultralarge machines require heavy-duty control sys-tems to avoid in-flight failures. Servos are larger and more powerful. The bat-tery pack has double the normal capacity. Since elevator and rudder push-rods are long and heavy, inducing vibration damage to servos, stranded cable controls similar to those used in full-size aircraft are preferred. Two cables, 20- to 30-lb. test, run to each surface, which have control horns on both sides. In fact, for really big planes with divided elevators (the rudder separates them) four cables are sometimes used, two running to the top and bottom horns on each elevator. Cables do not attach directly to servos. Rather, each servo utilizes a sturdy bellcrank mounted some inches behind it. A clevis rod is used for a short pushrod, extending from servo arm to bellcrank. The cables loop through selected holes (for desired surface travel) in the long arms of this bellcrank. Each cable doubles back on itself, and a short copper sleeve tube slides over the resulting parallel wires and is squeezed tight with a crimping tool. Cable attachment to control horns is similar. Because cables must remain taut, an adjustable turnbuckle is located in each wire. Firms that cater to builders of big models stock all these items, plus many exotic fittings in miniature that one encounters on full-size aircraft.

Most Scale aircraft have barn-door ailerons, as opposed to the otherwise popular strip ailerons that extend along the entire trailing edge of the wing of typical Sport and Pattern models. Many larger planes have a servo mounted in each wing rather than trust to two ailerons hooked up to the usual center servo. Sometimes the servo in each panel is mounted far out on the wing directly in front of the aileron horn, using a short, stiff pushrod from servo arm to control horn. However, this can cause radio interference problems due to the long electrical leads to the servo, unless you compensate electronically for them. The most reliable installation is a servo in each wing root between the first two ribs. (Almost all wings for monster-size models are made in two panels for easier transport.)

There are several ways to actuate the ailerons on giant models. One is by means of two cables to each aileron, attaching to the top and bottom control horns. The wires can run around special pulleys, or through a plastic conduit. Another method is to run a heavy flexible cable through a plastic conduit; this single cable is capable of both push and pull action without buckling. The Sullivan-type plastic pushrod sets are used in the same way (as described for tail-surface control). A simple method is to run a stiff-wire pushrod set, such as Du-Bro makes, in a straight line from the servo arm out to a bellcrank fixed in the wing forward of the aileron horn, and to connect the bellcrank to the horn by means of a clevis rod. Fairleads glued to each rib prevent buckling of the pushrod under load.

To detail everything that has been mentioned here would require thousands of words. While pertinent pictures and drawings help you visualize representative systems, anyone attempting a major project should study modeling magazines, plans and pictures, and seek advice from active modelers at some flying site.

chapter eleven

The Radio-Controlled Model

In Chapter 8, we saw that an airplane has three control axes: pitch, roll, and yaw. The radio-controlled craft (RC)—like a real plane—incorporates control surfaces that can be manipulated to cause the aircraft to rotate around these three axes in infinite combinations. Elevators depress or raise the nose. Ailerons, if present, tilt the wings. The rudder steers right or left. For smooth maneuvering, these various controls are used simultaneously.

Radio-controlled models are designed to a wide variety of options in the use of these controls, from rudimentary to sophisticated. For example, the rudder-only plane is controllable only around the yaw axis. If elevators and ailerons are added, we have control availability around all three axes, as with a full-size plane.

You might have noted seeming inconsistencies. If the plane has no ailerons, how can it be banked in a turn? If the rudder-only craft can only be steered, how is it able to climb and descend as well as bank smoothly? First, we need to understand that the elevator is not the altitude control as is generally assumed. Power is the altitude, or climb, control. The simple rudder-only plane will fly level at just one power setting when correctly balanced and trimmed. It therefore has reserve power available to create a sedate climb.

Suppose we add a throttle. If power is added, climb results. If power is reduced enough, or cut off, the plane descends. Adding an elevator control appears to affect the climb and descent, but these control inputs only temporarily increase or decrease the lifting force of the wing by changing its angle of attack, and it is the power setting alone that is the altitude control. It is difficult to accept this visual contradiction, but it is aerodynamic law that altitude and climb are related to power.

How the rudder-only plane (with or without throttle) can be turned and

John Preston making an overhead pass with a Falcon 56 radio model. Equipped with ailerons, this model is a popular Aerobatic trainer. (Doug Pratt photo)

Kids love radio control if given an opportunity. Here, a member of the San Francisco Vultures club shows a boy how to operate an Ace single-channel transmitter for a rudder-only plane.

banked without ailerons is determined by the dihedral angle of the wing (tips raised above the wing centerline like a shallow vee). An aerodynamic coupling effect results from a combination of dihedral with movement of the rudder. If the rudder is swung, lift is increased on the wing panel on the outside of the turn (it travels faster), and decreased on the panel inside the turn. The yawing effect of rudder, combined with the rolling effect of the dihedral, produces a smoothly banked turn.

What about a glider, which has no apparent power? All gliders have power! Gravity supplies power; it compels the glider to assume a nose-down attitude. Although the model can be steered, or banked, or nosed up and down in response to controls, it will not sustain climb to gain altitude unless "lift" or thermal conditions are present. So thermal lift and rising wind currents are a power source. The combination of these lift forces and gravity affects how long it takes the glider (or a plane with a dead engine) to descend to earth after it has been towed aloft. The angle of its descent is affected by the efficiency of the machine; it has a glide ratio (as do all planes) of, for example, 20-to-1, the 20 being the feet it will travel forward over the ground (asssuming no wind) for each foot of altitude lost.

Although a controllable engine throttle is found on almost all RC ships, we do see a fair number of rudder-only beginner models, as well as lightweight Schoolyard Scale types, flown without power control. The plane without a throttle climbs continuously at a shallow angle on maximum power. How do we control altitude in this case? By holding the rudder full right or left. As the plane turns and banks, the excessive rudder force puts the machine into a rapidly descending spiral. When the rudder is returned to neutral, automatic stability allows the machine to recover from the spiral. The stored energy from the dive is actualiy added power, and until excess speed is bled off, the plane is flying faster than is required for the normal slight climb for which the plane was designed and trimmed. It therefore has excessive lift and must climb (even zoom) until speed and lift become normal. When the rudder is

"Silent fliers" enjoy nothing but Soaring gliders. As the pilot (right) tenses to steer his sailplane during its swift near-vertical climb, his helper restrains the craft momentarily as pull builds up on its winched towline. (Pruss photo)

Warren Tiahart positions glider winches at the League of Silent Flight 1981 Tournament. Limited to a maximum length of 984 ft., the monofilament line doubles back around the pulley staked to the ground; the plane is attached to the line in the vicinity of the winch. Various classes of sailplanes perform such tasks as duration, speed, and distance in the tournament. (Pruss photo)

relaxed to neutral, the dihedral wings seek to rock the model back to an unbanked attitude.

Still another factor governs the choice of RC designs—something modelers call "pendulum effect." Simply put, this refers to the relative vertical location of the center of lift and the center of gravity (C.G.). The farther below the center of lift the C.G. is located, the greater the pendulum stability and the ease of flying. We can divide aircraft profiles roughly into three categories, with a descending order of pendulum effect: the high wing, the shoulder wing, and the low wing.

The high-wing model has its wing mounted in two ways: as a parasol on struts extending up from the fuselage (the Airtronics Q-Tee, for example) or on top of a cabin (the Sig Kadet). The shoulder-wing model has no center section struts or cabin, and the wing mounts on the fuselage top (as on the Goldberg Falcon). For cosmetic reasons we usually dress up shoulder-wing and low-wing planes with a plastic bubble canopy, or the like, atop the wing or fuselage. The low wing, of course, is mounted on the bottom of the fuselage (as on the Goldberg Skylark). The low-wing model is not recommended to the beginner because it has less stability.

Designers tailor wing locations to vary performance characteristics and to suit piloting skills. For example, the high wing results in a thrust line located well below the center of resistance or drag (C.D.) of the machine. All forces (lift, drag, thrust, weight) act through "moment arms" around the C.G. to exert leverage. With dihedral, the C.D. is higher relative to the profile view of the craft. Incidentally, there are three forms of drag: parasitic—caused by landing gear and other protuberances; skin drag—friction depending upon the amount of "wetted area" of the craft; and induced—caused by disturbance of the air by the wing. Induced drag is the major factor. It is greater with short, wide wings, less with long, narrow wings.

If the thrust line is low, it exerts more leverage around the C.G. (it pivots the aircraft) and the C.D. This leverage causes the plane (except for some low-wing models) to nose up with excess power. When the high-wing plane is slowed down on the landing, the pilot may add slight power to extend the approach. The beginner who abruptly adds too much power causes the plane to assume a nose-high attitude and perhaps stall. Both increased lift and thrust-line position contribute to the problem. The shoulder wing reduces nose-up leverage and provides generally steadier flight without excessive use of controls. The low wing probably has the thrust line running through, or close to, both the C.G. and C.D. so these disturbing "moments" are reduced or absent (although adding power still increases lift). This is why Pattern Aerobatic planes are almost always low wings.

Opposite: *Spanning a huge 6 ft. for its electric motor or 0.049 gas engine (you have a choice), Cox's ready-to-fly Sportavia has smooth-finish foam-and-plastic construction with single-wheel landing gear (and wing-tip skids). It has excellent gliding ability.* (Preston photo)

The airfoil section is another factor in the model's performance. The flat-bottom wing section (airfoil) has a maximum tendency to nose up with changes in the angle of attack, the semisymmetrical section much less, and the fully symmetrical section virtually none.

How much dihedral should a model have? A Cabin model will rock back to level flight after a moderate rudder or aileron application is neutralized, if each wing panel has approximately 7 degrees of dihedral. With 5 degrees of dihedral, this plane tends to continue the banked circle, but it still has sufficient stability not to steepen the turn into a spiral dive and eventually to return the wing to approximately level flight—provided the C.G. is where it should be. With less dihedral the plane will spiral more steeply, and if there is no dihedral, it may not recover without a corrective piloting command. Generous dihedral is a mark of the trainer and easy-to-fly Sport plane.

Designers vary dihedral in all three basic profile configurations to achieve various performance characteristics. For example, a Cabin model Bridi 40 has modest dihedral and a high degree of roll maneuverability, and tends more to remain where it is pointed, like a Pattern machine. But, being a high wing, it has sufficient stability to qualify as an *advanced* trainer. There is another reason for its minimal dihedral. Too much dihedral inhibits precision aerobatics with ailerons. The excess stability "fights" the pilot's aerobatic commands. A good example of the shoulder-wing model is the Sig Kavalier aileron trainer. For a low wing, the Goldberg Skylark has moderate dihedral. Most Pattern models have none. If more roll-axis stability is desired, a low wing requires a degree or two more dihedral than that used in a comparative high or shoulder wing. The C.G. in a low wing is quite close to the center of lift (minimum pendulum effect). Wings without dihedral are found in all configurations. The object is neutral stability to allow precision aerobatics by a skilled pilot.

Goldberg's smooth-foam ready-to-fly Ranger 42 for 0.049 power is a primary trainer capable of rudder-only operation, or it is available with elevators and possibly a throttle. On the market for more than twenty years, it has outstanding free-flight stability and makes an effective electric plane with an 05 motor. (Preston photo)

While easier-to-fly machines may have rudder-only control and a single-channel radio system (such as Ace R/C's Dick's Dream); or elevators and rudder (Airtronics' Q-Tee); or rudder, elevators, and throttle (the MRC Trainer Hawk), all require the "free flight" stability provided by at least 5 degrees of dihedral.

Designers evolve interesting compromises. The Sig Kadet Mark II has both generous dihedral and ailerons. Easier to fly than many aileron designs, it has a high degree of free-flight stability, but with certain aerobatic limitations. It's a basic Sport trainer. The Goldberg Falcon is another approach, since the kit plan provides a choice of two different amounts of dihedral. With more dihedral, it is an excellent three-channel rudder-elevator-throttle machine with surplus roll-axis stability. With less dihedral and ailerons, it permits improved aerobatics, but with reduced, though adequate, stability.

We don't mean to imply that machines with dihedral are not aerobatic. They perform basic maneuvers, such as loops and inverted flight, quite well. But for the skilled pilot, dihedral interferes with more specialized maneuvers, such as the stall turn and wingover. The required control inputs disturb the desired flight path because of the dihedral coupling effect when rudder control is applied. Both the stall turn and wingover depend on rudder, so the "flatter" the wing, the better.

Beginner and trainer models almost always have a flat-bottomed airfoil wing—these are also easier to build. The use of a semisymmetrical or symmetrical cross-section wing improves airplane tracking with less tendency to

TYPICAL RADIO CONTROL WING AIRFOILS

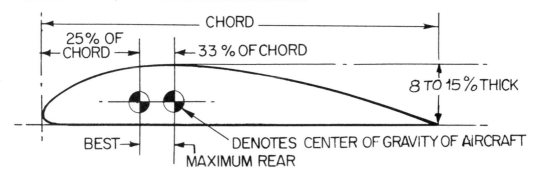

CHORD

25% OF CHORD

33 % OF CHORD

8 TO 15 % THICK

BEST

MAXIMUM REAR

DENOTES CENTER OF GRAVITY OF AIRCRAFT

■ FLAT BOTTOM – BEGINNER AND SPORT – BASIC AEROBATICS

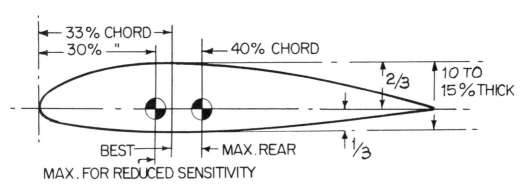

33 % CHORD

30 % "

40 % CHORD

10 TO 15 % THICK

2/3

1/3

BEST

MAX. REAR

MAX. FOR REDUCED SENSITIVITY

■ SEMI – SYMMETRICAL – SPORT, ADVANCE AEROBATICS, MORE STABLE

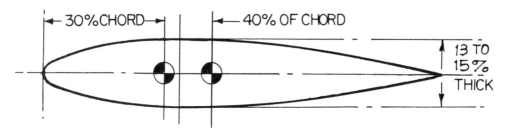

30 % CHORD

40 % OF CHORD

13 TO 15 % THICK

■ SYMMETRICAL – ADVANCED SPORT, MAXIMUM PRECISION
AEROBATICS , NEUTRALLY STABLE

Common airfoils used in radio-controlled machines.

Of all-balsa built-up construction, the Airtronics Q-Tee with 0.049 power is a delightful flier on two channels for rudder and elevator. Strong head and crosswinds cause steep climb and slight bank in this hand launch—note the frequency pennant on the transmitter indicating wind direction. (Pratt photo)

The popular MRC ready-to-fly all-foam Trainer Hawk has rudder, elevator, and throttle controls and a steerable nose wheel. The engine is 0.15 displacement. The MRC Guidance system radio is extra.

change fore and aft attitudes around the pitch axis. Here's why: the center of lift or pressure is exerted at a point well forward on the top surface of the wing and moves forward on the wing, toward the leading edge, as the angle of attack of the wing is increased. If this travel is great, the plane noses up more as the angle of attack increases and airspeed drops off. Such a wing requires more trim changes imparted by the elevators, and tends to "balloon" more when heading into a strong wind.

The semisymmetrical wing section (found on the Sig Kavalier and Goldberg Falcon) is more stable and less subject to trim-changed upsets. The symmetrical section found on Pattern machines is neutrally stable and requires only occasional, slight trim corrections.

Two- and Three-Wheel Landing Gear

The term "tail-dragger" means that the plane has a two-wheel main gear located forward of the C.G., and a tail skid or tail wheel, usually steerable in conjunction with the rudder. The "trike" gear, on the other hand, has the two main wheels located slightly behind the center of gravity, with a nose wheel steerable in conjunction with the rudder.

The trike is generally favored by modelers. For one thing, it does not require that up-elevator be held when the plane is taxied to prevent nose-overs. It also tends to track straight down the runway more readily on takeoff than the two-wheel gear. When the throttle is advanced abruptly on any aircraft, there is a tendency to swing left due to torque of the propeller. On the trike gear, only sight corrective inputs of right rudder may be required. If the nose-wheel steering is properly aligned, the three-wheeler usually takes off without rudder corrections until a slight input of up-elevator causes the plane to "rotate" and become airborne.

The tail-dragger requires full up-elevator while taxiing and very often for the first few feet of the takeoff run to prevent nosing over. If the tail rises abruptly and prematurely, the torque swing to the left is severe and requires heavy right-rudder correction. For the less experienced, this causes a series of overcorrections, the result being a zigzag takeoff path or ground loop. Unless the nose is held up on landing by elevator, the two-wheeler can nose over, resulting in a broken propeller or worse. A ground loop results in a dragged wing tip and, frequently, a tipover. The tail-dragger ground-loops more easily; the trike is almost immune. With practice, though, these things cease to be problems. The nose wheel does add drag, weight, and linkage complexity, but these things seldom compromise performance. However, competition Pattern models almost always feature a retractable tricycle landing gear, operated by a fifth-channel transmitter two-position switch.

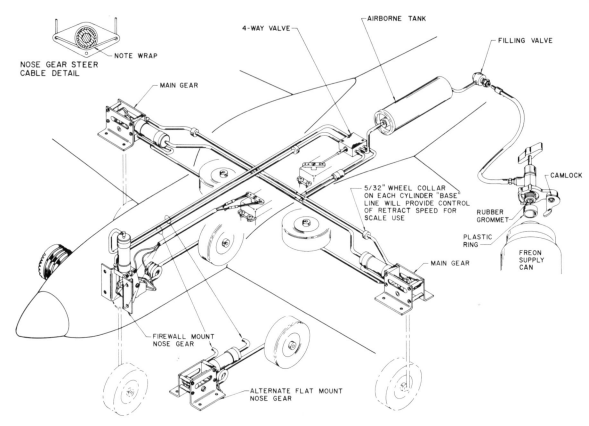

NOSE GEAR STEER
CABLE DETAIL

NOTE WRAP

4-WAY VALVE

AIRBORNE TANK

FILLING VALVE

MAIN GEAR

CAMLOCK

5/32" WHEEL COLLAR
ON EACH CYLINDER "BASE"
LINE WILL PROVIDE CONTROL
OF RETRACT SPEED FOR
SCALE USE

RUBBER
GROMMET

PLASTIC
RING

FREON
SUPPLY
CAN

MAIN GEAR

FIREWALL MOUNT
NOSE GEAR

ALTERNATE FLAT MOUNT
NOSE GEAR

The Rom-Air pneumatic retractable-landing-gear system used on Pattern and Scale aircraft. Various mechanical and pneumatic systems exist, including one with two wheels, as on the Corsair, where the wheels must be rotated as they fold rearward.

The Scale Model

Many people prefer the ultimate in realism. Although Scale models also divide into the basic configurations of high, shoulder, and low wing, the would-be Scale builder often chooses his or her subject for romantic reasons of one kind or another, without realizing the significance of the choice. Choosing a Scale subject may involve structural difficulties and heavy models that are distinctly erratic in any but experienced hands. The Piper Cub, a slow-flying high-wing plane with a lightweight, built-up framework, is a sensible choice for the novice. It is not erratic. The faster shoulder-wing Aerobatic or Racing machine is more of a challenge to the pilot, and is likely to have a fiberglass-shell fuselage and foam-core wings. It is lively. Scale planes such as the low-wing Corsair fighter or Curtiss P-40 have an even greater structural density—involving months of work, for which the so-so hobbyist is not truly qualified, and requiring expert piloting.

Racers, Aerobatic craft, and fighters are heavier and have less wing area than Sport machines, resulting in high-wing loadings that make them tricky to fly. Weight requires high power and higher flying speeds, allowing less reaction time to the pilot. If one must ponder about what to do at the controls, such machines will crash in the blink of an eye. A 9-to-12-lb., 60-in. fighter with a 0.60 size engine is a formidable challenge.

Depending on their size and desired performance, Scale craft may be flown, as can any RC model, by the rudder-only or by rudder and throttle, plus elevators, plus ailerons, and plus such extras as flaps and retractable landing gear.

Since most full-size aircraft have little or no dihedral, the builder does not have as much latitude in determining whether he or she wishes to include ailerons. Oldtimers, such as the SE-5 biplane, frequently have exaggerated dihedral, and could do without ailerons if a three-channel system is used. For true Scale it should have ailerons, requiring at least a four-channel radio system. A docile Piper Cub has modest dihedral, and could be flown without ailerons but does better with them. Many so-called Scale builders take liberties by increasing dihedral, tail-surface areas, etc., but the true Scale builder

For those who enjoy realistic construction of classic aircraft, planes such as this 0.049-powered Flyline Megowcoupe fly at near-Scale speeds. This 46-in.-span model weighs only 14 1/2 oz. and is equipped with a three-channel radio for operating just the rudder and elevators. A throttle can be added. (Preston photo)

The Top Flite Corsair fighter weighs 7 to 9 1/2 lb. on its 0.60 engine, and can be equipped with retractable landing gear and wing flaps. Such advanced Scale craft are popular with skilled fliers.

wants his or her craft to be as realistic as is feasible. With ailerons, a good flier can handle any configuration. Of course, ailerons are true to scale.

Small, lightweight open-frame Schoolyard Scale craft perform well with engines varying from 0.02 to 0.15 displacement. They are simple and slow because of their size. A 3-ft. Flyline Luton Minor with just a 0.02 displacement engine, having no throttle or elevators, climbs so slowly that it can be "free flighted" hands off with occasional steering by the rudder to keep it over the flying area. It has generous dihedral.

With a 0.09 to 0.15 displacement engine, a lightweight Waco biplane—it, too, has dihedral—does well on rudder, elevators, and throttle. If the model is much bigger, the builder would want ailerons for realism and improved aerobatics. A low-wing Mustang requires ailerons, so it is an unlikely School-yard subject, but fine at about a 5-ft. span with an engine of 0.40 to 0.60. A Top Flite J-3 Cub of about 7 ft. in span is nice on a 0.40 engine with ailerons. "Monster" Scale machines should be left to the experts. Even if their config-uration permits eliminating the ailerons, few people would do without them. Positive control is essential at high weights and speeds. More exotic Scale types, such as Byron Originals' Pitts, with aerobatic capability in the original, always have ailerons and are usually powered by chain-saw-derived engines turning propellers with a diameter of as much as 20 in. or more, or by belt-reduction 0.60 displacement engines that turn such big propellers at half the engine rpm.

RADIO CONTROL FLIGHT TECHNIQUES

Radio-controlled models normally take off from the ground. However, small, low-powered machines may be hand launched, an option that is especially helpful in windy conditions or when the surface is rough or grass too long. We will deal here with typical medium-size Sport machines, such as the Sig Kadet Mark II and the Goldberg Falcon, which are flown in overwhelming numbers.

The Preflight Check

Before taking the model to the field, be sure all control surfaces move freely in the proper directions when commanded, and that batteries are fully charged. At the field, make a range check before flying, both with the motor dead, and with it running. The latter ensures that vibration is not causing spurious control movements. (Model manufacturers provide directions for these tests.) As a rule, you should be able to walk away from the model to 150 ft. with the transmitter antenna retracted, and still operate all controls. When the control surfaces flutter, you are at your maximum ground range. Since control in the air is good for many times the distance on the ground, this check is relative. The air control range may exceed your ability to see the model clearly.

Range check being made with a Goldberg Falcon 56. With the transmitter antenna retracted, a good ground range is about 150 ft., corresponding to thousands of feet in the air. The 56 is a good Sport trainer capable of advanced aerobatics. (Preston photo)

In range testing with the engine running, you need a helper to hold the plane. The vibration test is made only before the first test flight. The range check with motor off should be made every time you go to fly.

If the radio range check reveals an appreciable loss of distance with the engine running, vibration from the engine is causing "interference" due to problems such as rattling metal pieces that touch. To find the source of this electrical "noise" you probably would need help from a more experienced flier. A typical cause of noise would be a metal clevis attached to a metal control horn or to a metal throttle arm. Examples of correct practice are a nylon clevis on a metal throttle arm and a metal clevis on a nylon control horn. You cannot fly safely if noise is present. Noise occurs across such a broad range of frequencies that it affects any radio frequency. Fliers of giant models encounter vague radio effects that have the same results as noise. These effects are caused by many metal flying wires supporting the wings, long cables extending to control surfaces, long electrical lead wires to servos located far from the receiver. However, such fliers are expected to be expert, and they know what to look for and how to eliminate the problems by electronic gadgetry.

The first distance checks done, restrain the model and run up the engine, adjusting the high-speed needle valve to ensure continuous running. Then hold the plane vertically, nose high, for at least 5 sec. (the helper does this if the plane is large—it's impossible to do with giant-size models). If the engine fades or stops immediately, open the needle valve until the engine maintains maximum rpm, then back off (open) the needle valve another couple of clicks because the engine will lean out slightly in flight. With the high-speed valve set, command the throttle from high to low, and vice versa. If the response from low to high instantly fails, the low-speed throttle adjustment is probably too lean; if the response occurs but is quite sluggish, the low-speed throttle control probably is rich. Follow the engine maker's instructions or ask for help from an experienced flier. To fly with an improperly performing engine risks a crash and/or a damaged engine. If the engine does not run properly in the air, immediately throttle down, bring in the craft, and make the necessary adjustments. Never take chances with any plane, full-size or model. You invariably lose!

For the flight, taxi the plane toward the runway, then throttle back to stop motion. Stand over the plane, facing forward, with feet planted in front of the stabilizer to prevent movement. Run the engine wide open and operate all controls. Be sure to look behind you at both elevator and rudder. Are all controls moving promptly (without quivering) in the proper directions? If so, you are ready for takeoff.

An electric-powered Spitfire is restrained by the author as pilot Don Srull prepares to switch on the motor for takeoff. Power is 15 Astro Flight with 2-to-1 reduction belt drive to turn a 12-in.-diameter, 8-in. pitch propeller. Flights last from 5 to 7 min. (Preston photo)

Byron Originals test pilot, Dean Copeland, with giant Pitts, powered by a 0.60 engine with 2-to-1 belt drive reduction to turn the huge propeller. Model comes in almost-ready-to-fly form. Fully Aerobatic like its real-life counterpart, this machine can climb straight up. (Byron Originals photo)

What comes after this requires a learning period, preferably with instruction from an experienced helper to make the first test flight and to show you how things are done. Therefore, we can tell you only how the plane is controlled. (If you cannot get help, start with a simple rudder-only plane.)

The Flight

For takeoff, open the throttle smoothly and, if the plane does not run straight, correct its direction with the rudder. If the takeoff run becomes too erratic, throttle back instantly, and try again. (Make necessary adjustments to the nose-wheel steering to obtain straight running, or to the rudder if the plane is a tail-dragger.) When good flying speed is attained, gently apply slight up-elevator. The plane should lift off smoothly. Hauling back on the stick may produce spectacular takeoffs, but the plane is vulnerable to stalls and snap-stalls. Such takeoffs require powerful engines to maintain flying speed.

After taking off, allow the plane to climb straight ahead until a safe altitude is attained. Maintain straight tracking with rudder, if there are no ailerons, or use the ailerons. If the climb is too shallow, hold slight up-elevator. More likely, the climb will be too steep. Hold the nose down with slight forward elevator stick; this is difficult for the beginner. (In either case, the elevator trim may need adjustment after landing.) Normally, at this point pilots reduce power modestly and/or crank in slight down-elevator trim with the trim lever so they don't have to continuously hold forward-stick. If, on the other hand, the plane then tended to nose down, they would crank in up-trim on the elevator.

When you have sufficient altitude to turn, bank modestly with the rudder (or ailerons, if present) into a wide half circle, or a series of turns adding up to 180 degrees, and come back over the field, still climbing, to the desired cruise altitude. While flying straight back, adjust the power setting (use less) and the elevator trim (more down or up) until the ship maintains straight and level flight. If it tends to wander off its heading, adjust the rudder trim (or ailerons) in the opposite direction. Beginning fliers usually fly back and forth in straight flight, making gentle turns at the end of each leg to reverse direction. When the plane comes toward you, right seems to become left and vice versa. Move the rudder or aileron stick (whichever) toward the down-tilted side of the wing as the plane comes toward you. That raises the low side of the wing. Try flying full circles (360 degrees), then perform gentle figure eights (a 360-degree circle followed immediately by a 360-degree circle in the opposite direction). This is good practice for maintaining circle size, banked attitude, and constant altitude, requiring coordinated use of both rudder (or ailerons) and elevator. Eventually, make rectangular patterns around the field, the downwind side of the rectangle being perhaps 200 ft. out, parallel to the runway.

If a turn is shallow, more aileron will steepen the bank, but may not tighten the diameter of the turn. Slight up-elevator when the plane is banked will force the turn to tighten. (In a steep turn, up-elevator does not necessarily make the plane climb.) Using opposite rudder, or ailerons (when present), slightly unbanks the turn to a level flight attitude if the nose appears to drop.

To descend, fly the plane downwind on a straight leg of the rectangle, perhaps 150 to 200 ft. away, parallel to the runway. When the plane is directly opposite the spot selected for landing, throttle back slowly to about 50 percent power, but continue briefly in straight flight, even if the altitude gradually decreases. While the model continues downwind for, say, 50 to 200 ft. depending on its size, speed, and the wind velocity, crank in up-elevator trim to hold the nose in slower flight, then make a shallow 90-degree turn toward the runway. After this turn, throttle back to about quarter power or less. During this approach the object is to "bleed off" air speed. As the plane begins to near the line of the runway, turn it shallowly 90 degrees toward you (corresponding with the runway direction). Aim it at yourself even if you are standing to one side of the runway. When the plane is straightened out, reduce throttle a bit, *but not quite to idle.* Don't allow the plane to free flight, but rather continuously "fly the stick." The nose will normally be slightly down.

If the approach is too high to hit the field, good fliers may increase the descent angle (if they have already throttled back) by holding slight down-elevator until the altitude seems correct. If the condition is extreme, experi-

Many transmitters have "buddy box" capability, which has no antenna—ideal for instruction. The instructor holds the transmitter with antenna connected by an electrical cord to the student's transmitter. The instructor can take over by flipping a switch. (Steucker photo)

At club flying sites frequency control is maintained by color-coded clips. When fliers have a clip on their antennas, they are assured no one is on that frequency. This stand incorporates a transmitter impound table for transmitters not in use, a further provision against them accidentally going on the air. (Pratt photo)

enced pilots add full power smoothly, and climb out again over the field, to set up another approach pattern. If the plane is high unskilled pilots should add throttle immediately and go around for another approach. If the plane is coming in short, a touch of power is added to increase the airspeed to reach the field. Never use elevator for this correction when power is available. The elevator upsets the final approach leg, and some planes can "balloon" into a nose-high attitude. The "galloping" approach is always abandoned in favor of another go-round. Don't fight the airplane, because erratic attitudes and desperate control inputs may result in a crash.

As the plane "comes over the fence," smoothly retard throttle to idle, allowing the plane to settle toward the ground, and keeping wings level. Close to the ground, slight up-elevator is used to "flare out." Properly done, this will make the plane touch down first on the main wheels, then on the nose wheel an instant later. If not flared out, it will at best land on all three wheels at once, though it will probably hit on the nose wheel first, causing a bounce, with an extremely rough landing as a result.

Aerobatics

How are aerobatics performed? In level flight a smooth application of up-elevator causes the loop. At the bottom of the completed loop, a slight jab of down-elevator ensures a level recovery. Good fliers throttle back some-what on the downside of the loop, then advance throttle at the bottom. If a loop does not occur from level flight (plane stalls or rolls out at the top of the loop), the entry is preceded by a slight dive to gain sufficient air speed.

Full aileron application rolls the plane. At the point where the craft is inverted (a half roll), a brief jab of down-elevator (visually it is now up) may be needed to keep the nose from dropping. In consecutive rolls, this jab of down is imparted each time the plane is inverted. However, if ailerons are sensitive, a plane may do axial rolls by aileron alone.

An Immelmann maneuver is performed by applying rudder (or ailerons if present) at the top of the loop, causing the plane to roll out to upright flight.

The stall is performed by climbing, steadily throttling back, and slowly applying more and more up-elevator. When stalled, the plane drops its nose abruptly, perhaps vertically to the ground. Allow airspeed to build up as power is smoothly applied, then pull out of the dive with gentle up-elevator. After the pullout occurs, slight down-elevator usually is momentarily neces-sary to maintain flight parallel to the ground.

For a wingover, the plane is pulled up as for the stall, but more steeply with more power. But before the stall occurs, rudder is used to turn the craft through a U-shaped (as you see it) maneuver that ends in a near vertical dive,

Opposite: *A field box makes a good operational center. This one has folding legs and rubber-padded supports to hold the model. The boxes are customized to contain elec-trical provisions for engine starters, fuel pumps, glow-plug boosters, and metered power panels. The plane is a Sig Kavalier aileron trainer.* (Preston photo)

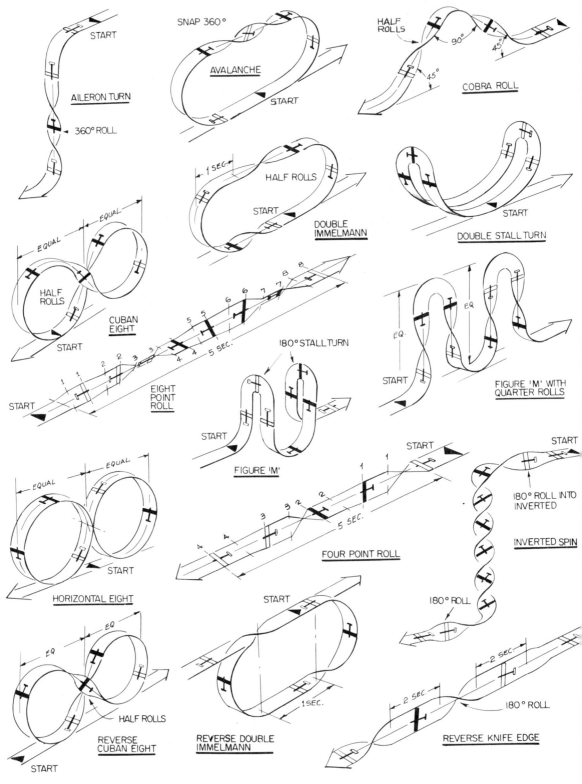

Typical A.M.A. Pattern maneuvers in alphabetical order as performed by Pattern pilots. In competition, maneuvers are flown in designated sequence within a tight time limit.

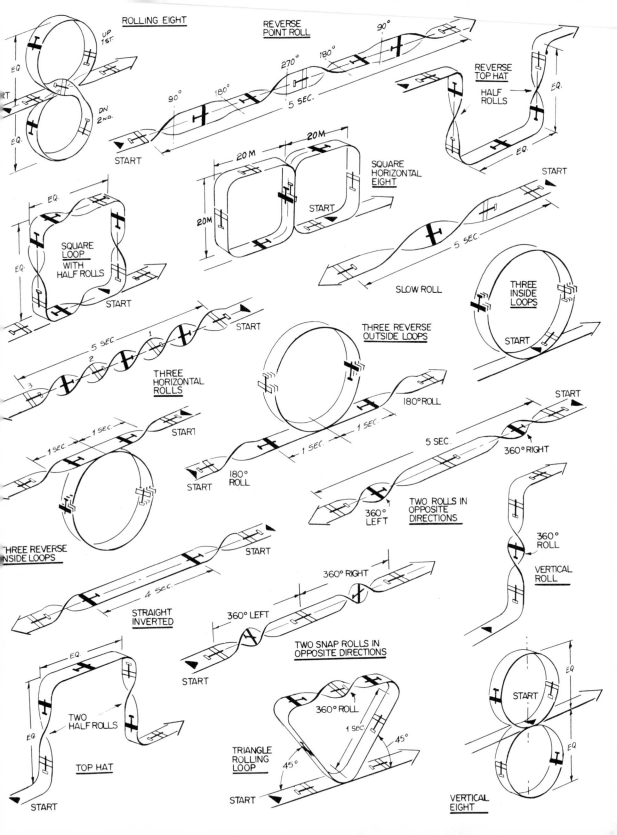

Helicopters are the most difficult to fly, although master pilots perform seemingly impossible stunts, such as inverted flight. Here, a model hovers motionless as its pilot guides it through prescribed maneuvers at a national contest.

the top of the plane facing you. Recover from the dive with smoothly applied up-elevator and add power. If the plane has a powerful engine, the power may have to be reduced sufficiently before the rudder is applied to execute the U portion of the maneuver. Some planes climb straight up at this point. Power usually is restored on the down leg, though this is a matter of preference and circumstance.

The stall turn requires a nearly straight-up entry, with throttle being retarded still more an instant before the stall. Simultaneously, rudder is applied to turn the craft on its yaw axis (the plane seems to pivot on a point), until the nose points straight down. In this maneuver, the diving path coincides with the straight-up entry path (that is, they are on the same line).

Inverted flight may be entered (with ailerons) by a half roll, then using *down*-elevator, if necessary, to hold the nose up (when the plane is upside down, down becomes up). A good pilot can steer complete circles while in inverted flight by using slight aileron, or rudder as required if there are no

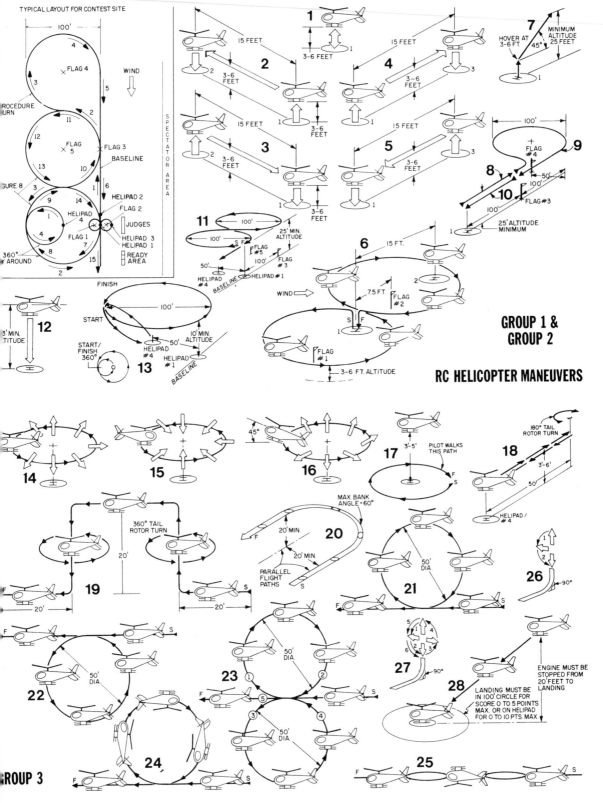

A.M.A. RC helicopter maneuvers used in competition (1983).

ailerons. Or the plane can be half-looped then, at the top of the loop, down-elevator held as required to hold inverted flight.

A spin is executed by gradually slowing up the plane by retarding the throttle and gently and continuously applying more and more up-elevator to produce a stall. At the instant of stall, before the nose drops, full rudder is held to whip the plane into the spin. A true spin rolls the plane at a high speed around a line vertical to the ground. If the plane flies around this line, it is in a spiral, not a spin. To recover, all controls are relaxed to neutral (after as many spin turns as desired) and, if necessary, opposite rudder and down-elevator are applied to stop rotation and to pick up flying speed. The exit from the dive should be on a selected heading, the plane pulled out with slight up-elevator power added, followed by a brief touch of down-elevator to recover in level flight.

You may require several months of practice, perhaps a year or two, to acquire this repertoire of maneuvers. The drawings on pages 262–63 illustrate a number of aerobatic tricks that you can try as you become more experienced.

Pilots of one-fifth-scale or larger models learn how to coordinate rudder and aileron sticks to make smooth turns, or to cross those sticks (opposite rudder to aileron) for forward slips and sideslips. Skilled Pattern pilots may use extras, such as rate switches (increases or decreases control throw) and roll buttons (to preprogram an automatic maneuver), and other tricky things that don't concern us here.

Helicopters are hard to fly, an art in itself that would require another chapter to describe. Basically, it means practice, practice, practice.

Although excellent trainers (like the Goldberg Eaglet) exist, we are impressed by the speed and ease with which people learn to fly such models as the Gentle Lady glider with a 0.049 engine on the nose, or the Wanderer glider with a Max 0.10 engine, especially when it is fitted with a two-wheel landing gear for takeoffs and landings. Flying RC is not a cinch; but with practice it can be enjoyed by modelers of all ages. One must be persistent and perhaps use up two or three planes (but not radio systems) before conquering aerobatics. The results, however, are worth it.

appendix a —————————

Glossary

Aerobatics Special flight maneuvers not associated with ordinary flying, such as loops, inverted flight, wingovers; performed for sport or exhibition and certain competitive events.

Aileron A hinged control surface at the rear of the wing used to bank the aircraft.

Airfoil Cross section (profile) of a wing, and sometimes a stabilizer in model planes, contoured for desired performance in terms of lift, efficiency, for aerobatics, etc.

Airscrew A propeller. An alternate term used in some parts of the world, notably Britain.

Airspeed Speed of an aircraft relative to the air—not over the ground.

Angle of Attack The angle at which an airfoil or flying surface meets the air.

Angle of Incidence The angle at which a flying surface is fixed to the fuselage.

Approach The final leg of a landing flight pattern, during which the plane descends on a straight path to land on the runway.

Area The product in square inches (on a model) of the span and chord of a flying surface, or by appropriate formula or measurements if that surface is not rectangular (such as elliptical or tapered).

Aspect Ratio The span of a flying surface divided by its average width (chord). Example: 36 in. divided by 6 equals an aspect ratio of 6-to-1.

Balloon　Informal term to describe action of a flying model that raises its nose, while losing altitude, as during the landing approach, but not necessarily attaining a stall angle.

Bank　The tilt of the wings during a turn, one tip high, the other low.

Bellcrank　A pivoted triangular or L- or T-shaped device made from aluminum, plywood, nylon, or steel, which transposes the direction of force by approximately 90° in a control system using pushrods.

Booster　Battery used to supply current to a glow plug of a model engine during the starting process.

Bore　The inner diameter of the cylinder barrel or liner.

Box　Slang for a fuselage with flat sides, top, and bottom, typical of simpler forms of model construction.

Bulkhead　A cross-sectional former used in fuselage construction.

Butyrate　The type of aircraft dope most commonly used to apply covering materials; also used to fill pores in covering and sometimes for finishing on structural surfaces.

Camber　Curvature of the surfaces of an airfoil. If the bottom is curved upward, it is "concave" ("undercamber"); if curved downward, it is "convex."

Canard　An airplane in which the stabilizer is located forward of the main wing, frequently seen in pusher-propeller arrangements.

Canopy　The transparent bubblelike shell that covers the cockpit to streamline the aircraft and to protect a pilot from the air blast—mimicked in models for realism or for scale.

Cantilever　A flying surface (wing typically) in which internal structure carries all loads, thus eliminating supporting struts. In real aircraft, distinguished by a wing that normally tapers toward the tip, both in width (chord) and thickness.

Cap Strip　Thin, flat strip of wood, usually balsa, glued to the top and bottom of a thin wing rib to add strength, providing better attachment for covering, while maintaining lightness.

Carburetor (also "carb")　An adjustable device exterior to the model-engine intake that converts air and fuel into a vaporized explosive mixture, the mixture being varied by an adjustable needle valve(s).

Cathedral The downward angling of both panels of a flying surface from the centerline to the top, occasionally seen on model stabilizers.

Cement Common model airplane glue.

Center of Drag (Resistance) (C.D.) The point as indicated on the front or side view of an aircraft at which the total resistance of the model to forward movement through the air is considered to be centered.

Center of Gravity (C.G.) The center of mass of an aircraft, precisely located in relation to the center of lift for balance and stability in flight.

Center of Lift (Pressure) A point on the top curvature of an airfoil or wing at which the lift forces are considered to be centered, a factor in design and aircraft balance and stability.

Center Section A short, flat portion of a wing, at the center, to which outer wing panels attach.

Charger An electrical device for restoring the voltage of discharged nickel cadmium, wet-cell, or gel-cell batteries. Converts household electrical current to required voltage and amperage to that required by a given battery(ies).

Chord The width of a wing or flying surface, taken as an average if the surface is not rectangular.

Compression The reduction in volume of fuel mixture within a cylinder by the upward travel of the piston, which compresses the air/fuel mixture for firing.

Connecting Rod The high-strength rod with a bearing at both ends that fits over the piston's wrist pin and the crankshaft throw pin to convert the up-and-down travel of a piston to the rotary action of the crankshaft in order to turn the propeller.

Cockpit Either open or enclosed, the place where the pilot(s), controls, and instrumentation are located.

Crankcase The bottom casting of an engine, which forms a chamber inside which the crankshaft is mounted.

Crankshaft The revolving shaft, driven by the piston/connecting rod, to which the propeller bolts.

Cyanoacrylate A thin glue that sets instantly, or within seconds, when surfaces to be glued are held together tightly.

Cycler An electrical accessory used to discharge, then charge nickel cadmium batteries so that capacity in terms of usable time may be checked.

Cyclic A model helicopter term to describe the mechanics and control ability to tilt the rotor-head assembly for selection of desired flight paths.

Decalage Defined by modelers as the difference in degrees between the angle of incidence of the wing and that of the horizontal tail.

Delta A vee-like or broad arrow-shaped wing (like the capital Greek alphabet character Delta). Usually a flying wing without a horizontal stabilizer, but occasional "double deltas" have similar shaped stabilizers located either at the rear or sometimes in a canard configuration.

Dethermalizer A timer-operated device to reduce the lift and increase the drag of a free-flight model, so that it sinks rapidly to terminate a flight.

Diameter The length of a model propeller measured tip to tip.

Differential Arrangement of mechanical controls within a radio-controlled model wing that results in more "up" travel of an aileron than "down." Purpose is to equalize drag (seen as yaw) of both ailerons. Ideal is 2-1/2 times up compared to down. ("Down" is more effective in response than "up.")

Dihedral The upward angling of the wing panels (or tail) from the centerline of the aircraft, or from the center section, upward to the wing tips.

Displacement The volume within the cylinder measured in cubic inches or fractions thereof, determined by the cylinder bore multiplied by the distance of piston travel from bottom dead center to top dead center. For example, 0.09 cubic inch displacement (abbreviated C.I.D.).

Dope A cream-consistency clear or colored liquid used to attach paper and cloth coverings, and to shrink those coverings when sprayed or brushed on. A form of "paint."

Doubler The lamination of a second layer of material (usually very thin plywood) to the forward inside portion of a fuselage.

Downthrust The downward sloped angle of the thrust line toward the aircraft nose, normally considered the angle made between the thrust line and a horizontal baseline of the fuselage, more effectively measured relative to the wing angle of incidence.

Elevator(s) The hinged control surfaces aft of the stabilizer spar which, when tilted up, cause the plane to elevate its nose, and vice versa.

Engine   The mechanical power plant, consisting of cylinder, piston, crankshaft, etc., to spin a propeller. To be distinguished from "motor," which defines an electric power plant.

Epoxy   A two-part glue that, when mixed, sets in a given time (5, 10, 30, 45 min., etc.) by the chemical reaction of the two parts, normally designated A and B.

Exponential   A feature of more costly radio control systems that produces less control-surface movement close to neutral stick positions, but maximum control with full control movements.

Filter   A cartidgelike device containing a fine-mesh screen placed in the fuel-feed line between tank and carburetor to block dirt particles that otherwise clog the fuel-feed orifice inside the carburetor. (Also an electronic term.)

Fin   The fixed portion of the vertical tail surface.

Fire Wall   In aviation terminology, the "bulkhead" forward of the crew (on a single-engined aircraft); it localizes an engine fire. It is also present in the nacelles of multiengine planes. In model terminology, a plywood bulkhead that serves as the base for mounting an engine or engines.

Flap(s)   Hinged surface at rear of wing inboard of aileron(s) that can be depressed to various positions to slow approach speeds, and to increase lift for slow flight.

Flareout   The portion of the flight path late in the landing approach where the plane is "rounded" out (if radio control or control line) to make a smooth landing.

Flying Tail   A one-piece stabilizer (without elevators) that is rotated up or down for control around an axis approximately 25 percent of its chord from its leading edge. (See jetliners at any big airport.) Sometimes used on the vertical tail.

Folder   A propeller used on rubber-powered models, sometimes with electric power plants, with hinged blades that fold back to improve streamlining after the propeller stops turning.

Former   Another name for bulkhead, but more normally smaller cross-sectional pieces added to a fuselage side, top, or bottom, to support stringers or sheet wood to produce contoured outlines.

Free Flight   A model flown without control from the ground by wires or radio. Also the art or category of flying free-flight models. Or a state of flight where the model flies temporarily without ground or radio inputs.

Freewheeler   A propeller used with rubber power that has a ratchetlike device on the hub's front face to allow the propeller to windmill after power is expended, thus improving glide angle and duration.

Frequency   Usually, designated specific radio frequencies in millions of cycles per second.

Fuselage   The body of an airplane.

Gel Cell   Typical sealed 12-V battery of 4- to 6-ampere-hour capacity used to power electric starters, glow plugs, and complete power panels for field service of radio models.

Glow Plug   Spark-pluglike device containing a coiled wire element, heated by a booster battery until an engine starts, after which the firing of the alcohol-base fuel provides heat to the element for continuous ignition without external electrical source.

Gusset   A structural joint reinforcement, triangular in shape, as at the intersection of a wing rib and trailing edge, or of a crosspiece and fuselage longeron in high-stress locations.

Hatch   A removable access panel, common on radio-controlled models for maintenance of fuel tanks, battery packs, etc.

Head   As in cylinder head, the bolt-on or screw-on contoured "top" that provides a sealed combustion chamber in which fuel mixture vapor is compressed, ignited, and expanded for power strokes.

Headlock   A trade name for a glow-plug booster line attachment that inserts over the plug, simultaneously locking in place and providing electrical contact when revolved a quarter turn to lock in position.

Headrest   The streamlined protuberance on a fuselage with an open cockpit, immediately behind the pilot's head.

High Wing   An airplane in which the wing is located on top of the fuselage, as in a Cabin model, or above it, as in a parasol configuration.

Horns   A metal, plywood, or nylon fitting that attaches to a control surface at its hinge line, providing a means of attaching the end of a pushrod.

Ignition   In modeling, refers to the system that provides a timed spark within the combustion chamber by means of a spark plug with electrodes, for a gasoline/oil mixture.

Iron-on (Film)   Covering materials that adhere to a framework when applied with a special iron, then shrunk tight by the iron or heat gun (similar, but not identical, to hair dryers).

Laminate/Lamination   The accumulation of two or more layers of material, with alternate cross grains in the case of wood, for antisplitting ability in high-stress locations.

Leading Edge   The front or entering edge of a flying surface, such as a wing, fin, stabilizer.

Lean   Descriptive word for the situation wherein the fuel/air mixture contains too much air and not enough raw fuel.

Lift   The upward force generated by the passage through the air of a flying surface, created by either or both the airfoil contour and the angle of attack of those surfaces.

Lift-Drag Ratio (L/D)   The mathematical relationship of the amount of lift developed versus the drag generated. Example: 20-to-1.

Liner   The hard metal sleeve inside the cylinder in which the piston rides up and down.

Loading   The amount of weight carried per square foot of flying-surface area. Also the amount of weight carried per cubic inch of engine displacement. (Wing loading—power loading.)

Longeron(s)   The principal load-carrying pieces of a fuselage which extend its full length.

Low Wing   An airplane configuration in which the wing is located at, or below, the fuselage bottom.

Megahertz (MHz)   Radio frequency. As in the radio control "72 band," upward of 70,000,000 cycles per second.

Meter   An electrical measuring device with a numbered scale and an indicator to read voltage, amperage, resistance, current flow.

Methanol   A type of alcohol used as the basic ingredient in "glow" fuel.

Microfilm A gossamerlike, superlight film for Indoor models, made by pouring a few drops of a special liquid onto a water surface.

Midwing An airplane configuration in which the wing location is roughly at the middle elevation of the fuselage, rather than on top, above, or below.

Milliampere (mA) The thousandth part of an ampere, a unit of measure of current (such as 500 mA).

Mixer A mechanical or electronic device that enables the use of a control surface for two purposes simultaneously—as for elevator and rudder on a vee-tail configuration.

Mixture The blending of air and fuel in precise variations by means of a needle valve in a carburetor. Also relates to various combinations of dopes and thinners, and fillers and sealers with thinning liquids for finishing and painting, etc.

Monocoque A shell fuselage structure in which principal loads are carried by the skin itself, as opposed to a built-up framework.

Monofilament A thin, high-strength plastic line (fishing leader) used for towline gliders, certain control actuation, etc.

Motor Propulsion or driving device other than a gas/piston engine, such as rocket motor, electric motor.

Mount The bearers or support for an engine or motor.

Muffler A chamber located on the exhaust port of an engine to reduce the annoying sound level.

Mush Slang to describe a condition of flight when a model slows down precariously, maintaining forward speed in a nose-high condition, causing a higher sink rate or a borderline stall.

Nitrate (dope) Like butyrate dope (and others), a cream-consistency liquid for applying and shrinking paper and cloth covering materials. Still used by some free-flighters, generally outdated because fuel will melt it and it catches fire quite easily.

Needle Valve Thin rod or screwlike device with tapered, threaded end that goes into needle-valve body (in carburetor) to control the fuel orifice to adjust fuel/air mixture.

Nitromethane A chemical ingredient added to alcohol/oil lubricated fuel mixture to improve starting, and idling, and to increase maximum rpm.

Original A model design created from scratch by an individual, as opposed to a kit.

Ohm (Ω) An electrical measuring unit for designating resistance—such as in a 20-ohm resistor.

Parasol Type of monoplane in which the wing is mounted on struts or a pylon above the fuselage.

Pattern A sequence of flight maneuvers or organized flight-path segments. A type of radio-controlled aircraft intended to perform sequenced aerobatics. Thin material cut to an outline shape to be transferred (as a template) to constructional material for cutting.

Pipe An especially shaped, extended "tuned" exhaust muffler to increase engine rpm and power.

Piston Cylindrically shaped object, sealed at its top end, which rides up and down within the cylinder to compress fuel mixture and transmit its explosive power to the crankshaft via a connecting rod.

Pitch The angle of a propeller blade as measured by the distance the propeller travels forward during a single revolution. The action of an aircraft in abruptly nosing up or down without a control input. (Pitch up.)

Pitch Axis An imaginary line drawn spanwise, around which the airplane noses up or down.

Plasticizer Chemical or agent (such as castor oil) added in minute quantities to modeling dopes to decrease the amount of shrinkage of a covering material to minimize warping.

Polarity The direction of electrical current flow indicated as plus or minus.

Port(s) Small openings in the cylinder barrel covered and uncovered in a timed manner by the moving piston, to control intake, compression, and exhaust of raw and burned fuel mixture. Also, the left side of plane when looking forward.

Polyhedral Multiple dihedral, as when a dihedral angle occurs on the wing centerline, and at a second station out on the wing panel such as at the semispan half point.

Potentiometer (pot) A variable resistor, as used for control sticks and in servos of radio control systems.

Pressure   Differential in air density flowing over and under a flying surface (as in lift.) Force (or "head") exerted on the fuel flow by a pump, gravity, or exhaust muffler that has a tap to which is connected a length of fuel tube line leading to the fuel tank.

Proportional   The prevailing type of radio control system in which primary control surfaces move in agreement with the amounts of control stick movement.

Pump   Device located in the fuel-feed line or engine backplate to feed fuel to the carburetor under pressure.

Pusher   An airplane having the propeller attached at the tail rather than nose, or any propeller located behind an engine or engine pod. On engine-powered models, pusher propellers have opposite pitch.

Pushrod   A rigid wood or wire, or flexible cable wire, or plastic rod connecting servo drive arms to horns on the control surfaces, throttles, etc.

Pylon   A type of parasol model with a finlike rigid support for the wing rather than struts.

Rate   A function of some radio control transmitters that permits a choice of increased or decreased control-surface movement by means of a rate switch—normally used for aerobatic maneuvers.

Receiver   The airborne "radio" that picks up and decodes transmitted instructions to activate and control servos that move control surfaces or perform mechanical actions, such as the throttle or retractable landing gear.

Reed Valve   A thin "flapper" metal valve that controls fuel flow to an engine by pressure variations within the crankcase.

Resistance   The air drag exerted against a plane's forward motion. Also an electrical term measured in ohms.

Rib   The airfoil-shaped cross-section member(s) of a flying surface, normally in the wing, sometimes in the horizontal stabilizer.

Rich   A descriptive word to describe the running condition of an engine when the fuel mixture contains more raw fuel and less air in the vaporized mixture, typified by a smoky exhaust and a lowering of engine rpm.

Rotor   The rotating blades of a helicopter that create lift; also the small, vertical propeller-type rotor at the tail of a helicopter to control yaw. The disk metal valve in some engines located at the rear end of the crankshaft to cover and uncover in timed fashion a fuel-intake port.

Rise-off-Ground (R.O.G.)   An early widely used term for takeoff, which today means a simple form of rubber-powered model.

Roll   The rotation of an aircraft around its longitudinal axis, commonly the maneuver executed by a 360-degree rotation by means of aileron application, starting and ending with the aircraft in upright flight.

Roll Axis   An imaginary line from nose to tail around which an airplane rolls. Also the "longitudinal axis."

Root (root rib)   The innermost cross section of a wing panel that butts against a fuselage or center section.

Rubber Lube   A lubricating mixture, such as green soap and glycerine, rubbed on a rubber motor to increase its turn capacity and to prolong its useful life.

Rubber Peg (rear)   A wooden dowel or aluminum tube extending across the fuselage of a rubber model aft of the wing to anchor the motor in place.

Rudder   The portion of the vertical tail behind the hinge line, normally fixed in free-flight and control-line models, but movable for yaw and steering control in radio control.

Schnuerle   A type of engine cylinder porting associated with high rpm. Hence, a type of engine.

Sealer   A liquid used to fill the pores of raw wood before covering and finishing. Example: Clear aircraft dope.

Servo   An electric-motor-driven device containing mechanical and electronic components that provides the "muscle" for moving a control surface or variable position part in a radio-controlled model.

Servo Reverser   A two-position switch control on a transmitter that reverses the direction of rotation of a servo motor to suit required control direction response.

Shaft Valve   The rectangular opening in the forward portion of a hollow crankshaft that provides vaporized fuel to the engine crankcase in timed fashion.

Shim   A thin piece of material (such as 1/32-in. plywood) placed between the leading or trailing edge of a flying surface and the fuselage in order to adjust the surface's angle of incidence.

Shoulder Wing   An aircraft in which the wing or wing panels attach to the fuselage approximately at the top fuselage longeron.

Side Thrust The slightly angled alignment of the thrust line, normally toward the right (airplane viewed from rear) to compensate for undesired turning of a plane due to prop torque and/or slipstream. Also used in free flight to produce desired climbing patterns.

Sink The vertical descent or rate of descent in relationship to the forward travel of a plane. Example: A sink rate of 10-to-1 equals 1 ft. loss of altitude for every 10 ft. traveled forward.

Snap Roll A violent rolling maneuver produced by application of up-elevator before full deflection of rudder.

Spar Rigid, load-carrying member(s) running spanwise in a flying surface.

Spark Plug The electrical device screwed into the cylinder head in such manner that two electrodes project into the combustion chamber to supply a timed spark for fuel vapor explosion in an ignition engine.

Spin A rapidly turning maneuver of a diving airplane while stalled, produced by slow speed, full up-elevator, and full rudder movement—or accidentally by allowing a plane to slow below safe airspeed.

Spinner The cone-shaped streamline part that fits over a propeller hub.

Spoiler A small hinged surface or fencelike device that fits flush with the top surface of a wing, but extends on command to reduce the total lift to increase sink rate (used on sailplanes).

Stabilizer The horizontal tail surface forward of the elevator hinge line; in free-flight models, the entire horizontal tail surface.

Stall The abrupt dropping of the nose with loss of adequate airspeed either accidentally or in a controlled aerobatic maneuver by raising the nose while slowing down.

Starter An electric-motor-driven device, normally hand-held and pressed against the prop spinner to induce propeller rotation. In large models an onboard starter operated by radio command via a gear or belt and clutch arrangement.

Stringer Thin, lengthwise external strips that extend along a fuselage surface to impart desired structural cross sections.

Strut Bracing member(s) that supports a wing panel, stabilizer, or fin, or for supporting a wheel axle in a landing gear, or to support a parasol wing at the fuselage, or to hold rigid in "interplane" fashion the wings of a biplane or other multiwinged craft.

Tail Stabilizing horizontal and vertical surfaces at the rear of the airplane.

Tail-Dragger Slang for plane having a two-wheel landing gear plus tail skid or tail wheel.

Tail Skid The fixed projection beneath the fuselage that prevents the rear of the fuselage from dragging on the ground.

Tail Wheel Similar to the skid, but equipped with a wheel to reduce the power required for taxiing, and to ease ground steering. In real craft only ancient machines had skids because paved runways destroy skids. The wheel is always steerable on radio-controlled and some other Scale types.

Tank The metal or nylon fuel reservoir, or any device—such as an eye-dropper or pen-bladder—used to hold fuel on some kinds of models.

Template A pattern for scribing bulkhead, former, rib, fire wall outlines, etc., on material.

Tensioner Projecting wire, screw, etc., on rear of rubber-model nose block to stop rotation of propeller (propeller-shaft hook engages stop) as coil spring on shaft, forward or in back of propeller, slides hook forward as rubber loses power. Prevents slack rubber disturbing balance; permits use of freewheeling or folding blade propellers.

Thermal Rising air current in which sailplanes and free-flight models circle to increase duration of flight.

Thinner Compatible liquid used to cut thickness or consistency of dopes and painting materials.

Throttle Controllable carburetor for increasing and decreasing vaporized fuel mixture to engine, allowing an rpm range from idle to full power.

Thrust Propulsive force provided by rotating propeller, or ducted fan "jet type" engine, or by rocket.

Thrust Line Line drawn as an extension of the propeller shaft relative to the fuselage and/or the wing cross section.

Touch-and-Go A landing under power followed by full throttle application before momentum is lost, thus resuming flight. A popular practice maneuver with radio-controlled models.

Transmitter Hand-held radio that "sends" instructions to the radio receiver in the airplane.

Tow Hook   Hook or accessory affixed to bottom of fuselage to which the glider towline attaches for launching purposes.

Trailing Edge   The rearmost edge of a wing or other flying surface.

Tread   The distance between wheel centerlines (main gear) when the plane is viewed from the front.

Tricycle Landing Gear   Three-wheel gear, with main wheels slightly aft of the center of gravity, and a nose wheel (often steerable) just aft of the model's engine.

Trike   Slang for tricycle landing gear.

Trim   The coordinated result on a plane's ability to fly "hands off," or in some desired attitude or pattern, by means of flying-surface settings and adjustments made by the modeler, or by means of small, movable surfaces known as trim tabs.

Twist   Slang for a warp, whether by accident or intentionally by the flier for flight-adjustment purposes.

Undercamber   The curvature of the bottom of an airfoil or rib. If the curvature is upward, undercamber is concave; if downward, it is convex.

Venturi   The shaped inner throat of the carburetor air intake.

Volt (V)   A unit of electrical measurement designating electrical "pressure."

Voltmeter   Meter with indicating needle to measure voltage when two clips or probes are touched to opposite polarity poles (plus and minus).

VOM   A more elaborate meter that reads voltage, resistance (ohms), and current consumption—in milliamperes for model radios, or amperes for household, etc., purposes. Also checks continuity of wires and circuits.

Washin   Variations in incidence angles from the root to tip of a flying surface, where the tip has the greater angle. Normally a warp, occasionally intended as a slight "twist" imparted to a free-flight wing for adjustment purposes. Undesirable on radio-controlled models because of its tendency to stall wing tips and induce accidental spins and undesirable variations in turn with various airspeeds.

Washout   The opposite of washin. Commonly used on radio-controlled models to guard against tip stalling and accidental spins (must be equal on both wing tips).

Yaw   Condition in which the nose swings to one side of the normal flight path, in a wing level attitude, or to an excessive degree not coordinated with proper turn and bank.

Yaw Axis   An imaginary line running vertically through the center of gravity. The axis around which the plane rotates in weathervane fashion, or is influenced by rudder action.

appendix b

Reference Works and Publications

BOOKS

In the last seventy-odd years, nearly one thousand aeromodeling books have been printed. Today there are perhaps two dozen excellent works available through libraries, hobby shops, mail order via the model magazines, and through special aviation book distributors who advertise occasionally in model magazines. The reader is advised to inquire at the public library—although many specialized books can be found only through the sources provided here.

Since more general model airplane books are easily identified at libraries, the following list mostly includes noteworthy special-interest books. These selections enable the reader to delve deeply into specialized modeling matters more generally treated in this work.

The Quiet Revolution, Robert J. Boucher (1979: Astro Flight Inc., 13311 Beach Ave., Venice, CA 90291). This 70-page, magazine-size paperback is a complete manual of electric propulsion systems. It describes manufactured power-plant systems, battery supply, appropriate free-flight and radio-controlled aircraft, boats, and a galaxy of technical aspects. Numerous charts and graphs, photos, and drawings. Boucher discusses man-carrying and pilot-less solar-powered machines (and models) whose epic flights he has been associated with.

Bill Dean's Book of Balsa Models (1970: Bill Dean's Books, 166-41 Powells Cove Blvd., Whitestone, N.Y. 11317. Also available from Arco Publishing Co., 219 Park Ave. South, New York, N.Y. 10003, and from Sig Manufacturing Co., Inc., Montezuma IA 50171). This 64-page, magazine-size paperback contains illustrated instructions for eighteen fast-building, simple models, complete with full-size plans. Six of the plans comprise a "training course," including hand-launched and towline gliders and rubber-powered models. Dean is an excellent draftsman, with over five hundred published designs to his credit, and his popular book is a highly recommended way for the non-modeler to get started.

Gateway to Aero-Science, Charles H. Grant. (1979: Charles H. Grant & Associates, Manchester Center, VT 05255. Also available through the Supply and Service Division of the Academy of Model Aeronautics, 1810 Samuel Morse Dr., Reston, VA 22090). A 302-page 6 × 9 paperback. Charlie Grant, the grand old man of model aviation—a famous pioneer in both full-scale and aeromodeling since before 1910, once a major manufacturer of ready-to-fly models, and the longtime editor of *Model Airplane News* in the glory days—wrote, illustrated, and published out-of-pocket this remarkable book summing up the fundamentals of design, relating models to full-scale craft. Plans depict model designs going back more than half a century. The first to fly a man-carrying machine in New Hampshire, a full-scale designer for the old Army Signal Corps at Wright Field, and an associate of Orville Wright in the Dayton-Wright company circa 1920, Grant used model planes in hundreds of experiments to solve full-scale problems. The book features firsthand descriptions and rare historical drawings and photos of such full-scale aircraft as the Wright 1906 biplane, the Santos Dumont Demoiselle, the Blériot Channel Crosser, the original Farman Voisin, and the Montgomery Glider of the nineteenth century, as well as a Tabular History of Flights with distances and times from the eleventh century up to Hubert Latham's 1909 8-mi. passenger-carrying flights in an Antoinette.

Peanut Power!, Bill Hannan (1980: Historical Aviation Album Publications, P.O. Box 33, Temple City, CA 91780). An 80-page, magazine-size, stiff-covered paperback by the outstanding authority on tiny rubber-powered scale models. Well illustrated by fascinating pictures, drawings, and plans. Instructive and fun to read, no matter what your model special interests are.

World Free Flight Review, Vol. 1, William R. Hartill (1975: World Free Press, 7513 Sausalito Ave., Canoga Park, CA 91304). This 416-page, coffee-table book is the only publication of its kind in the world. It is a superb presentation that captures the spirit of the competition free-flighter, with on-the-spot reports of world competitions and numerous plans of Indoor and Outdoor types, gliders, and powered models. Extensively illustrated by magnificent photos (many in four-color), sketches, and plans. An enjoyable and instructive book containing an overwhelming array of "secrets" otherwise unavailable to the general modeling public.

Harry's Handbook for Miniature Engines, Harry Higley (1980: Harry B. Higley & Sons, P.O. Box 532, Glenwood, IL 60425). A 92-page, magazine-size, stiff-covered paperback, this is a definitive work on "gas" engines for planes, boats, and cars. Higley's aims: Improved Performance, Longer Useful Life, Problem Diagnosis, Simple Repairs, Reduced Costs, Minimized Frustration. Relatively few hobbyists really know how to properly operate and care for an engine. Very few even realize the importance of maintenance, and only a handful know how to improve performance. Written at an advanced level, this profusely illustrated book with 233 photos, and extensive drawings, conveys a clear sense of hundreds of things that, until now, have seemed needlessly obscure to most hobbyists.

There Are No Secrets, Harry Higley (1981: Harry B. Higley & Sons, P.O. Box 532, Glenwood, IL 60425). An 84-page, magazine-size, stiff-covered paperback for the more experienced modeler interested in paints and finishes. Extensively illustrated with fine photos and sketches, this one-of-a-kind project is masterfully organized, with many step-by-step sequences, guaranteed to expand any hobbyist's proficiency. Sixteen chapters explain such things as paint contents, compatibility, and drying characteristics, adhesives, tools, sanding, plastic moldings, fillets and canopies, brushes and brushing, sprayers and spraying, compounding and buffing, and iron-on coverings. So many types of adhesives and paints exist that even proficient hobbyists—especially those interested in scale models—will benefit from a rare reference work by an expert such as Higley.

Fly It, John Kaufmann (1980: Doubleday & Company, Garden City, NY 11530). An 80-page hard-cover book, this volume has numerous sketches and a brief text covering a large number of kites, boomerangs, helicopters, hang gliders, and hand-launched gliders. An incisive how-to-do-it work enchantingly illustrated. Although primarily aimed at youngsters, one must add that it is suitable for "kids" of *all* ages. Kaufmann is a professional author and artist as well as an active modeler, and he has managed to distill a complex subject into a remarkably simple form.

Getting the Most from Radio Control Systems, Fred M. Marks (1980: Kalmbach Publishing Co., 1027 North Seventh St., Milwaukee, WI 53233). An 80-

page, magazine-size, stiff-covered paperback, written by an engineer who designs manufactured radio control systems, this book is aimed at the active RC flier who wishes to understand the working of systems and maintenance. An advanced book containing many detailed photos and drawings, as well as numerous schematics for older modelers who have an understanding of electronics. A definitive work for studious readers. (Kalmbach publishes many hobby books.)

Basics of Radio Control Modeling, Fred M. Marks and William Winter (1962, revised 1975 and 1979: Kalmbach Publishing Co., 1027 North Seventh St., Milwaukee, WI 53233). Originally written by Winter, this work was revised by Marks. It is an 84-page, magazine-size, stiff-covered paperback aimed at expanding the skills of RC modelers. For airplanes, boats, and cars, it covers tools, materials, radio equipment, engines, repairs, equipment installation, and flying. Of special interest is a chapter detailing five airplanes through the stages of building, installation, covering, and finishing, using a variety of paints and methods. Many pictures and drawings.

How to Fly U-Control, Dick Mathis (1973: Sig Manufacturing Co., Inc., Montezuma, IA 50171). Probably the best book on control-line models, this 48-page, magazine-size paperback is ideal for the new modeler who wishes to enjoy planes that don't require large flying sites. Typical chapter titles are: The First Solo, Learning Stunts the Easy Way, and Advanced Techniques for Stunt. Mathis, an internationally famous expert in the control-line field, has supplied excellent, comprehensive illustrations.

Building & Flying Indoor Model Airplanes, Ron Williams (1981: Simon and Schuster, 1230 Avenue of the Americas, New York, N.Y. 10020). A 272-page, magazine-size, stiff-covered paperback. Since Indoor models are a relatively small part of the activity, one is surprised that a major work of wide interest to all modelers could be published on this subject. But we have learned from *Scientific American's* Great International Paper Airplane contest in the late 1960s—followed by a large paperback book still on display—that such books, well done, can capture public attention. Williams's book surpasses the paper airplane work in that it is a project of love, dedication, and lasting value for the most demanding modeler as well as the general public. His work is that mother lode of the Indoor art. Williams is a professional artist, writer, and researcher, who spent three years preparing one of the finest model books ever done, with first-rate sketches and plans, and the only one that covers any one hobby category in complete detail. Erv Rodemsky, Interna-

tional Indoor Champion, describes it as "a classic textbook explaining everything from the basic fundamentals to the details of building the most intricate
structures." An Indoor modeler's bible, it also offers everything required for
the curious novice to get into advanced Indoor techniques.

ANNUALS

Model Aeronautic Yearbook, Frank Zaic (Available from Model Aeronautic
Publications, Box 135, Northridge CA 19324, or from the A.M.A.'s Supply
and Service Division, 1810 Samuel Morse Dr., Reston, VA 22090). In the early
1930s Frank Zaic began compiling, producing, and publishing the *Model Aeronautic Yearbook*—the last volume published in the late 1960s—all of which
are in demand, having been reprinted many times. These paperbacks are not
found in bookstores, or even at most hobby shops, and are seldom advertised. Yet they are world famous to longtime modelers. Some run to more
than 200 pages, and all contain hundreds of drawings and three-view plans
of outstanding models. Each is further distinguished by heavy, almost ran-
dom commentary on design, aerodynamics, and esoteric aspects of flight
that fascinate even the most erudite engineer. Interspersed with occasional
special books in the same format, the monumental Zaic works are a much
underpublicized wonder of the modeling world.

MAGAZINE BOOKS

Many books on special aspects of aeromodeling and Scale plans are published by several modeling magazines. *Flying Models* has an extensive list.
Model Airplane News has a number of unique works. *Radio Control Modeler*
has a library of books related to the design, construction, etc., of RC models.
(See below for the addresses of these magazines.) A.M.A.'s Supply and Service Division has a modestly discounted list of other publishers' books, some
also available at libraries, some staff created.

MAGAZINES

Flying Models (Carstens Publications, P.O. Box 700, Newton, NJ 07860).
Directly descended from the famous *Flying Aces* magazine (published 1930–
46, a mixture of popular aviation and model airplanes), *Flying Models* is a

general-interest publication covering radio control, control line, and free flight. Distinguishing features include outstanding reports on electronic systems of significance to the consumer, a substantial section on boats, and a beginner's department aimed at young hobbyists. Newsstand, hobby shops, and subscriptions.

Model Airplane News (837 Post Road, Darien, CT 06820). Founded in 1929 as *Universal Model Airplane News,* this was the first of the "modern" aeromodeling publications (others of the 1910 to 1935 era having vanished), and today leans heavily toward radio control. Includes boat and car features and excellent coverage of engines (including highly specific reviews by the world's outstanding authority, Peter Chinn of England). Newsstands, hobby shops, subscriptions.

Model Aviation (1810 Samuel Morse Dr., Reston, VA 22090). The official magazine of the Academy of Model Aeronautics, begun in the 1950s as an organizational news bulletin, *Model Aviation* became a full-fledged general-interest magazine in 1975. With a moderate leaning toward radio control, *Model Aviation* covers all forms of aeromodeling and, because of the varied competition interests of A.M.A. members, includes special-purpose models seldom seen in other magazines. Noteworthy for its large panel of special-interest columnists, and a 30-to-40-page section devoted to organizational affairs, rule making, contest reports, and a contest calendar, this magazine also interfaces government, notably the Federal Communications Commission, the Federal Aviation Administration, and the Smithsonian Institution (National Air and Space Museum). An optional membership benefit (at a modest extra cost), also at hobby shops and by subscription. No newsstand.

Model Builder (621 West 19th Street, Costa Mesa, CA 92627). Begun in the 1960s, this is a general-interest magazine, including cars and boats. Noteworthy for substantial support of various forms of free flight, especially small rubber-powered models that have attracted discriminating enthusiasts worldwide. Hobby shops and subscriptions. No newsstand.

Radio Control Modeler (120 West Sierra Madre Blvd., Sierra Madre, CA 91023). Begun in the early 1950s, this deluxe magazine is devoted exclusively to radio control (including cars and boats), with the most substantial coverage of that subject in the United States. Especially noted for excellent special columns and specific photo-illustrated step-by-step airplane-building projects. As the only exclusively RC magazine in this country, it has an advertising section that is a catalog reflecting the state of the art. Heavy hobby shop distribution, some newsstand, subscriptions.

Scale R/C Modeler (7950 Deering Ave., Canoga Park, CA 91304). A Challenge publication, first published in the early 1970s, this magazine is distinguished by strong illustrative treatment of premier remote-controlled Scale aircraft models only. Newsstand, hobby shops, subscriptions.

Foreign Publications

While dozens of excellent magazines are published in many countries, especially Britain, West Germany, France, Poland, Czechoslovakia, South Africa, Australia, Japan, etc., only British magazines are relatively easy to obtain in the United States, especially those published by MAP Publications, which advertises in some U.S. magazines.

Official Model Aircraft Regulations

Issued by the Contest Boards of the Academy of Model Aeronautics under the franchise of the National Aeronautic Association and the Fédération Aéronautique Internationale, this booklet of approximately one hundred twenty pages is issued in revised form every two years. It provides specifications of every form of competitive craft, how they must be flown, charts, tables, flight-pattern diagrams, and numerous related information. It is an encyclopedic guidebook and includes much that can never be published in magazines or books. To really understand all the ramifications of model aircraft, the rule book is a must. It is part of the annual membership package given to A.M.A. members, but may be purchased separately for $1 from the A.M.A., 1810 Samuel Morse Dr., Reston, VA 22090.

appendix c

Special Interest Groups

The following associations and societies, affiliated with the Academy of Model Aeronautics, exist because magazines are unable due to space limitations to publish the overwhelming amount of materials required by specializing modelers. The membership of these groups ranges from under one hundred to more than several thousand. Membership fees are charged. All of the groups publish newsletters, some quite substantial, almost magazine-type publications. The groups also help organize special meets and fly-ins, and many raise funds for international teams. Because officers and addresses change from time to time, the reader should send for information to the group of his or her choice in care of the A.M.A.

Control Line Racing Pilots & Mechanics (CL-RPM)

International Minature Aerobatics Club (IMAC)

International Miniature Aircraft Association (IMAA)   (very large RC models)

League of Silent Flight (LSF)   (RC gliding)

Miniature Aircraft Combat Association (MACA)   (CL models)

National Association of Scale Aeromodelers (NASA)

National Free Flight Society (NFFS)

National Indoor Model Airplane Society (NIMAS)

National Miniature Pylon Racing Association (NMPRA)   (RC models)

National Soaring Society (NSS)

National Society of Radio Controlled Aerobatics (NSRCA)

Navy Carrier Society (NCS)   (CL models)

Precision Aerobatics Model Pilots Association (PAMPA)   (CL models)

Index

Note: Numbers in italics refer to illustrations.